Contents

KU-203-002

THE COMPLETE **IDIOT'S** GUIDE® TO

Writing Nonfiction

by Christina Boufis

A

ALPHA

A member of Penguin Group (USA) Inc.

ALPHA BOOKS

Published by Penguin Group (USA) Inc.

Penguin Group (USA) Inc., 375 Hudson Street, New York, New York 10014, USA • Penguin Group (Canada), 90 Eglinton Avenue East, Suite 700, Toronto, Ontario M4P 2Y3, Canada (a division of Pearson Penguin Canada Inc.) • Penguin Books Ltd., 80 Strand, London WC2R 0RL, England • Penguin Ireland, 25 St. Stephen's Green, Dublin 2, Ireland (a division of Penguin Books Ltd.) • Penguin Group (Australia), 250 Camberwell Road, Camberwell, Victoria 3124, Australia (a division of Pearson Australia Group Pty. Ltd.) • Penguin Books India Pvt. Ltd., 11 Community Centre, Panchsheel Park, New Delhi—110 017, India • Penguin Group (NZ), 67 Apollo Drive, Rosedale, North Shore, Auckland 1311, New Zealand (a division of Pearson New Zealand Ltd.) • Penguin Books (South Africa) (Pty.) Ltd., 24 Sturdee Avenue, Rosebank, Johannesburg 2196, South Africa • Penguin Books Ltd., Registered Offices: 80 Strand, London WC2R 0RL, England

THE COMPLETE IDIOT'S GUIDE TO and Design are registered trademarks of Penguin Group (USA) Inc.

International Standard Book Number: 978-1-61564-229-8
Library of Congress Catalog Card Number: 2012939812

14   13   12   8   7   6   5   4   3   2   1

Interpretation of the printing code: The rightmost number of the first series of numbers is the year of the book's printing; the rightmost number of the second series of numbers is the number of the book's printing. For example, a printing code of 12-1 shows that the first printing occurred in 2012.

Printed in the United States of America

Note: This publication contains the opinions and ideas of its author. It is intended to provide helpful and informative material on the subject matter covered. It is sold with the understanding that the author and publisher are not engaged in rendering professional services in the book. If the reader requires personal assistance or advice, a competent professional should be consulted.

The author and publisher specifically disclaim any responsibility for any liability, loss, or risk, personal or otherwise, which is incurred as a consequence, directly or indirectly, of the use and application of any of the contents of this book.

Most Alpha books are available at special quantity discounts for bulk purchases for sales promotions, premiums, fund-raising, or educational use. Special books, or book excerpts, can also be created to fit specific needs. For details, write: Special Markets, Alpha Books, 375 Hudson Street, New York, NY 10014.

Publisher: *Mike Sanders*

Executive Managing Editor: *Billy Fields*

Executive Acquisitions Editor: *Lori Cates Hand*

Development Editor: *Lynn Northrup*

Senior Production Editor: *Janette Lynn*

Copy Editor: *Amy Lepore*

Cover Designer: *William Thomas*

Book Designers: *William Thomas, Rebecca Batchelor*

Indexer: *Celia McCoy*

Layout: *Ayanna Lacey*

Proofreader: *John Etchison*

Appendixes

Introduction

Take one true story. Add real-life characters. Stir in an interesting plot. Sprinkle in compelling dialogue. Leaven with vivid description and introspection. Add fascinating information and detail. And then leave the reader hungry for more. That's the recipe for narrative nonfiction: true tales told in a captivating way to move, inform, stir, entertain, or educate your reader. As a nonfiction writer, you combine reportorial skills with a personal voice and a literary love for language.

Do you love learning new things? Do you have a passion to communicate information? Have you lived through an extraordinary event or time and have a good story to tell? Are you curious and passionate about the world around you? Do you love reading and language? If you answered yes to many of these questions, you have the makings of a nonfiction writer.

The good news is that now is the time to be a nonfiction writer. The beginning of the twenty-first century has experienced an explosion of the form in books, magazines, blogs, and journals.

Like probably many of you, I've wanted to be a writer ever since I could spell. I always thought I'd write fiction, however, as that seemed to be what most writers did. When I began writing non fiction several decades ago, I didn't know much about the genre. I only knew it felt like I had found my form. I was teaching women prisoners at the county jail, and I didn't think fiction was the right way to tell their story and mine. The nonfiction form was there all along just waiting for me to discover it, or that's what it felt like. I've never looked back. But it took me several years to figure out just what nonfiction was as a genre and how to write it. I hope to save you that time in this book.

In *The Complete Idiot's Guide to Writing Nonfiction*, you'll find the tools you need to be a nonfiction writer, which I hope will motivate, inspire, and keep you writing your entire life. There's no shortage of raw material to write about in nonfiction; it's all around you. And it's never too late to be a writer in general and a nonfiction writer in particular. Indeed, one form, the personal essay, "frequently presents a middle-aged point of view," writes Phillip Lopate in his "Introduction" in *The Art of the Personal Essay, An Anthology from the Classical Era to the Present.* This is good news for those of us coming to writing later in life.

It's been said that you get to live twice as a writer: when you first have an experience and then again when you tell the tale. What greater gift could there be? This book will give you the tools to be a nonfiction writer. You'll be able to tell if you have a story, and you'll learn how to conduct research, interview sources, and turn your tale into something that reads like fiction—in that captivating, can't-wait-to-turn-the-pages way—except your story is real. It has real people for characters, real scenes, and factual descriptions and dialogue, and it is the truth as best you know it whether told from memory or reported. That's nonfiction writing.

Read on to get started in your nonfiction writing career. The time is now.

How This Book Is Organized

Part 1, An Overview of the Genre, begins with a brief history of nonfiction and an introduction to the different forms narrative nonfiction can take. Nonfiction is a malleable genre encompassing everything from travel and food writing to memoir and biography. But you need to have a story worth telling, and this first part will help you find a subject and structure your story.

Part 2, The Building Blocks of Nonfiction, explores the essential elements on which all nonfiction is built: action-packed scenes and summary, or exposition. You get to show and tell as a nonfiction writer. You'll also encounter some of the thornier issues in writing nonfiction, such as establishing your credibility as a reliable narrator, one who doesn't play fast and loose with the form and cross the fictional boundary.

Part 3, Drafting, shows you how to avoid procrastination, get a draft down, conduct research, and hone the reportorial skill of interviewing whether you're writing an essay or a book. All nonfiction requires research, even if you're writing about your own life, as you'll see in this section. We'll also explore the different short and long forms of nonfiction in this section.

Part 4, Crafting Memorable Nonfiction, teaches you that revision is the writer's best friend. This section includes a brief review of grammar, of what makes a sentence or a passage stand out and become memorable, and of how to revise for your focus or main point.

Part 5, After the Writing Is Done, shows you how to market your nonfiction, whether through consumer (paying) markets or in a literary journal that may not pay in anything but copies of the magazine. Both are valuable. Blogging and self-publishing are other options for getting your work out there. Finally, you'll learn how to maintain a nonfiction writing career for the long haul by building a community and setting writing goals.

You'll also find three helpful appendixes: a glossary of literary terms you'll encounter in the book; in-depth interviews with some of today's bestselling nonfiction writers, offering valuable tips for finding subjects, researching, writing, organizing your material, and how to keep going even when the going gets rough; and a list of books and online resources to help you launch or continue your writing career.

Extras

The Complete Idiot's Guide to Nonfiction Writing also includes the following sidebars to help guide you:

DEFINITION

Check these sidebars for explanations of key literary terms.

WRITERS' WORDS

In these sidebars you'll find inspirational quotes from famous writers on the craft and process of writing.

JUMPSTART

These sidebars provide brainstorming ideas and other writing exercises to propel your own nonfiction stories.

PITFALL AHEAD

These sidebars point out things to avoid in your writing and give advice on how to short-circuit writing difficulties.

Acknowledgments

I'd like to thank my agent, Marilyn Allen, for bringing this book project to me. To my husband, Scott Peterson, and our son, Gus, who make not only writing but also all things possible. To Jane Hammons, the best first reader and friend, without whose wise counsel I couldn't imagine writing a word. And to the many non-fiction writing students I've taught over the years, whose eager faces, moving stories, and provocative questions have stayed with me. This book is for you.

Trademarks

All terms mentioned in this book that are known to be or are suspected of being trademarks or service marks have been appropriately capitalized. Alpha Books and Penguin Group (USA) Inc. cannot attest to the accuracy of this information. Use of a term in this book should not be regarded as affecting the validity of any trademark or service mark.

An Overview of the Genre

It's a wonderful time to be a nonfiction writer. In fact, the end of the twentieth century and the beginning of the twenty-first may well become known as the golden era of nonfiction. From personal essays to food and travel writing, blogging, memoir, narrative journalism, and biography, readers are hungry for information about real events and real people.

In this first part, I introduce you to the explosion of nonfiction writing, discuss its origins, and show how it's a malleable genre roughly divided into shorter and longer forms. I'll give you guidance on getting started, such as finding your subject, figuring out whether you have a story to tell, and deciding how to tell it effectively. Along the way, there are writing exercises to help get you started and inspiration from current writers to keep you going.

What Is Narrative Nonfiction?

In This Chapter

- Defining narrative nonfiction
- The explosion of nonfiction in recent decades
- Why write narrative nonfiction?
- The difference between fiction and nonfiction
- Short forms: essays, profiles, and more
- Long forms: memoirs, biographies, and more

It's an exciting time to be a nonfiction writer. Memoirs, personal essays, travel writing, food writing, and long-form personal journalism seem to push novels and short stories off bookstore shelves. We want to read what's "real" and true.

What's more, nonfiction is a malleable form. As nonfiction writer and essayist Annie Dillard says about creative nonfiction in general and the essay in particular, "There's nothing you can't do with it. No subject matter is forbidden, no structure proscribed. You get to make up your own form every time."

While it used to be that only famous people could write their autobiography and memoirs, now anyone with an interesting story to tell can do so and find an audience. You can blog, self-publish using various platforms, or pen an e-book and bring your story to the world instantly. And because you are writing the literature of real life, you'll never run out of stories or material.

In this chapter, you'll learn that although narrative nonfiction may be *the* form of the late twentieth and twenty-first centuries, it actually has a much longer and venerable history. We'll explore reasons for writing nonfiction, and how it differs from fiction writing. Though many of the storytelling techniques are the same, there's one crucial difference: you absolutely cannot make anything up in nonfiction. Whether your goal is to write travel essays or long-form memoirs, nonfiction writing is your vehicle. Ready to discover what the buzz is all about?

Narrative Nonfiction: A New Literary Form

Narrative nonfiction has been called the new literary form of the twentieth century. You might have heard it called by its other names: creative nonfiction, the literature of fact, the literature of reality, literary journalism, or the fourth genre (after poetry, fiction, and drama). And chances are you've seen the explosion of nonfiction in bookstores over the last several decades. Perhaps you've picked up a memoir or read a magazine article and thought, "I could have written that. I've got a lot of stories to tell." Maybe you'd like to see your byline in a magazine rather than someone else's.

 DEFINITION

Narrative nonfiction is a true story told in a literary way where plot, character development, and dialogue are as important as the facts and research.

Early Developments of Narrative Nonfiction

It's not quite true that the twentieth century gave birth to narrative nonfiction. What *is* true is that we've seen an explosion of the form in the last few decades. No one knows who first coined the term "creative nonfiction," writes Lee Gutkind, who himself was called the "godfather" of the form in a 1997 *Vanity Fair* article deriding the new movement of "confessional writing." In 1993, Gutkind began the literary magazine *Creative Nonfiction*, the first journal devoted to publishing high-quality nonfiction.

But the form—which encompasses literary journalism, essay and nature writing, memoir, biography, even the nonfiction novel—has a much longer history. The sixteenth-century French writer Michel de Montaigne was the first to lay claim to what he called "essais," to write about himself introspectively in an experimental form of the personal essay. "It is as if the self were a new continent, and Montaigne its first explorer," writes Phillip Lopate in *The Art of the Personal Essay*.

 WRITERS' WORDS

"[Creative nonfiction] allows a writer to employ the diligence of a reporter, the shifting voices and viewpoints of a novelist, the refined wordplay of a poet, and the analytical modes of the essayist."

—Lee Gutkind, American writer sometimes referred to as the "Godfather behind creative nonfiction"

Lopate traces the forerunners of the essay as far back as the ancient Roman philosopher Seneca, who wrote moral lessons. Closer to home, fact-based narrative burst on the scene in 1946 with John Hersey's 31,000-word article "Hiroshima," published in its entirely in *The New Yorker*. Hersey's account of six people who survived the Hiroshima nuclear bomb stunned its readers, just as Rachel Carson's *Silent Spring*, her nonfiction account of the damaging effects of pesticides on the environment, did when it was serialized in *The New Yorker* in 1962.

There were also the new journalists of the 1960s and 1970s, such as Tom Wolfe, Hunter S. Thompson, Norman Mailer, Truman Capote, and Joan Didion, who "borrowed" fiction-writing techniques, used novelistic devices of scene setting, and immersed themselves in the material to tell true stories.

Since then you've no doubt seen how nonfiction crowds novels and short story collections off the bookstore shelves, and how magazines and newspapers are devoting more columns to personal histories. We seem to be hungry for nonfiction in whatever form it takes; we want true tales and we want them told well. This book is focused mostly on *narrative* nonfiction—telling true stories in a literary way.

WRITERS' WORDS

"Writing is magic, as much the water of life as any other creative art. The water is free. So drink. Drink and be filled up."

—Stephen King, bestselling American science fiction and mystery writer

Reasons for Writing Narrative Nonfiction

Even in elementary school, I wanted to be a writer. I clearly remember going to the library in third grade and seeing two big signs: Fiction and Nonfiction. It was fiction I was drawn to, and I secretly thought I'd be a fiction writer. It wasn't until I finished graduate school, got divorced, and moved to a new city (although not in that order) that I began writing narrative nonfiction as a way to make sense of all my life changes. I wasn't even sure what I was doing had a name; I just knew that I had to write what was truthful without the scrim of fiction. What are your reasons for writing nonfiction? Here are a few you may relate to:

- You want to write down your family history for future generations.
- You've lived through some exciting, painful, or extraordinary experiences, and you want to share them— you have great stories to tell.
- You have something to teach people or information to impart.
- You want to find out what you really think about a subject.
- You want to figure out the world and your place in it.

- You have survived a difficult childhood or adulthood.
- You want to give hope or inspiration to others.
- You want to explore the world and write about it.
- You love to try new things and have adventures.
- You are curious about people and the world around you.
- You're an expert in a field and want to share this knowledge with others.
- You love to do research and write about it.

JUMPSTART

Brainstorm a list of all the reasons you want to write nonfiction. Don't censor yourself; no reason is too grandiose or too small.

How Nonfiction Differs from Fiction

The techniques of nonfiction writing are similar to fiction: scene setting, characterization, dialogue, description, plot, and conflict. However, there is one crucial difference: you can't make anything up in nonfiction. While you can re-create dialogue (something I'll cover in Chapter 4), you can't create new dialogue. Narrative nonfiction writers tell dramatic stories from real life but do not make anything up; your credibility and reputation depend on you being as truthful and accurate as you can be.

Though the line between fiction and nonfiction today is sometimes not as straightforward as it was in my elementary school library (we'll discuss this more in Chapter 5), nonfiction differs from fiction in several important ways:

- Characters *are* real people, not based on real people.
- Characters cannot be combined. That is, if you're writing about your best friend, she cannot be an amalgam of qualities from all your friends; that's fiction.

- Dialogue is often re-created from memory to the best of your ability but is never made up.
- Events cannot be made up.
- Events cannot be compressed. You can't merge all the Saturdays of a few months into one spectacular Saturday unless you tell the reader you are doing this.
- You are as accurate and truthful as possible, which means doing research (something I'll cover in Chapter 7).

Short Forms of Nonfiction

Creative nonfiction is a flexible genre that can accommodate a variety of topics, but is most easily divided into shorter and longer forms. Short forms of nonfiction are those typically anywhere from 750 to 5,000 words and can include any of the following::

- Personal essay
- Lyrical essay
- Travel essay or article
- Food article
- Profile
- Literary journalism
- Science and nature writing
- Mosaic, vignette, or hybrid piece

Personal Essays

"The hallmark of the personal essay is its intimacy," writes Phillip Lopate in his introduction to *The Art of the Personal Essay*, a collection of essays from antiquity to the modern day and perhaps the definitive overview of the form. "The writer seems to be speaking directly into your ear, confiding everything from gossip to wisdom."

The writer of a personal essay is writing about him- or herself but with the purpose of seeing the universal in the particular, the "world in a grain of sand," to use poet William Blake's words. And though you may remember having to write essays in high school or college on large, abstract ideas, the personal essay, on the contrary, narrows the lens to what Lopate calls "the snail track," or the small and particular.

The movement of the essay is not necessarily linear, narrating an event chronologically. Rather, it's more like a spiral, delving deeper and attempting "to surround a something," writes Lopate, "a subject, a mood, a problematic irritation—by coming at it from all angles." The word *essay* comes from the French "essayer," meaning a trial or attempt, as the essayist attempts to get to the bottom of a subject, particularly when that subject is the essayist's self.

JUMPSTART

Write down 5 or 10 odd, quirky, or different things about yourself. It could be something as simple as you prefer to use your middle name rather than your first name or as major as you are a cancer survivor. Now choose one and write two pages of a personal essay, looking at this difference from all angles.

Lyrical Essays

No one quite agrees what exactly constitutes a lyrical essay, though this hybrid form incorporates both the lyricism of poetry and the prose of an essay. The word *lyric* is derived from "lyre," a stringed instrument used in ancient Greece to accompany poetry or song. Unlike a personal essay, a lyrical essay is more meditation than movement, focusing on artful and poetic language rather than narrative meaning. Or as *The Seneca Review* literary journal, which first began publishing lyrical essays in 1997, says, "The lyrical essay does not expound. It may merely mention." The lyrical essay is also a mosaic form, stitched together from different genres, part poetry, part prose. The logic is associative; that is, it moves by metaphor and by free associating and is not driven to convey information as in most narrative nonfiction, but rather to focus on the sound and imagery of words.

Travel Essays

It sounds like an ideal job: getting paid to travel around the world and write about it. But nonfiction travel essays are not guidebooks or top 10 lists; rather, just like the personal essay, they are literary meditations on travel and culture filtered through the writer's experience. Whereas we go to a Lonely Planet guidebook or to leading European travel writer Rick Steves to find the best travel bargains, we go to travel essays for something we can't get from these books: to learn about the world through another person's eyes. So "tell us something we wouldn't get in a travel guide" may well be the travel essayist's mantra.

Food Articles

From celebrity chef memoirs to food essays, there's no denying the renaissance of food writing in the last two decades. If you're passionate about food, you might consider nonfiction food writing, which is more than just a description of dinner or a list of ingredients in a recipe. Like travel writing, good food writing takes us places: it connects us to both the writer and the culture of food in a way that is informative, emotional, and soul satisfying.

Profiles

Nonfiction writing concerns itself with actual persons, places, and things, and all three can be the subject of a profile. You can profile a city, a celebrity, or a person who is doing something interesting in the world. The profile writer interviews the subject (and often people close to him or her) to bring to light what is interesting, different, and noteworthy about this particular person. Has she started an organization to help teenage runaways? Has he won a prestigious award? The point of a profile is to examine a person's education, history, and work background in order to capture what is noteworthy.

Literary Journalism

It used to be that journalists were forbidden to become part of the story; they were to be flies on the wall, observers and not partici-pants, and were supposed to stick to the five Ws—who, what, why, where, and when—and nothing more. But today we want more than the facts. We want to know what the facts mean, and we want to be entertained or transported by beautiful writing. That's where literary journalism comes in. Literary journalist John McPhee, who is often credited with pioneering the form and who has written about subjects as diverse as the geological history of North America to farmers markets and fishing, makes whatever he's writing about completely captivating.

Under the umbrella of literary journalism we can include almost any subject from food, travel, science, sports, medicine, nature, or even baseball. The attention to the craft of writing is just as important as the subject matter.

Science and Nature Writing

From explanations of why leaves turn colors to speculating on the origins of the universe, science and nature writing helps us better understand ourselves, the world, and our fellow creatures. Whether a call to arms (Rachel Carson's *Silent Spring*, which helped launch the environmental movement in the early 1960s), or a poetic treat-ment of our five senses (Diane Ackerman's *A Natural History of the Senses*), or essays on topics such as bacteria, medical statistics, or the fertility rates of chimpanzees (Mary Roach and Tim Folger's *The Best American Science and Nature Writing*), science writing inspires, delights, and informs its readers.

If you have a penchant for science and storytelling, you're in luck, because the market for good science writing that reads like a good mystery is in high demand these days. Just look at *The Immortal Life of Henrietta Lacks*, Rebecca Skloot's *The New York Times* bestseller, a fascinating account of a poor black woman whose cells, unbeknownst to her, fueled decades of medical research. The book, which took Skloot 10 years to write, is being made into an HBO movie.

Hybrid Forms: Vignettes and Mosaics

Not every piece of nonfiction writing fits neatly into one category or another. One of the great things about writing nonfiction is that it's so elastic. Perhaps you just want to capture that summer day when you were 12 and biked around Cape Cod, where your hair got so knotted from the salt water and lack of combing that you had to cut out the knots. Or maybe you want to record impressions from the first year of your baby's life. These *vignettes* are slices of life: short snippets, more like snapshots than a whole movie.

What do you do with these scenes? You can juxtapose them in a mosaic form. Just like a mosaic is made up of pieces of stone, a mosaic in nonfiction is assembled from little bits and pieces: a few scenes or vignettes, perhaps some prose poetry, even a recipe or two. The form is fluid enough to include whatever you like. Think of a mosaic form like a scrapbook of nonfiction and put in anything you'd like.

DEFINITION

A **vignette** is a short literary description or scene. From the French word "vigne," for *vine*, think of a vignette as something decorative or extra that is pleasing.

Longer Forms of Nonfiction

Long-form fiction may be book length—50,000 to 100,000 words—or anything in between. A hot new venue for publishing long-form narrative nonfiction—a cross between a long magazine article and a book (around 22,000 words)—is on e-readers. The tag line says they are "compelling ideas expressed at their natural length." Longer than a magazine article yet shorter than a book, these narrative nonfiction (and fiction) pieces attest to the appetite for work that is substantive yet can be read in one sitting. You can find a piece by journalist Joe Kloc about a NASA investigator and his mission to track down lost moon rocks in "The Case of the Missing Moon Rocks," or you could read "chick lit" author Anna David's funny tribute to her cats in "Animal Attraction." Long-form nonfiction can take any length from these singles to a book, depending on the subject matter and what you have to say.

Long-form nonfiction may be any of the following:

- Memoir
- Autobiography
- Dramatic book-length journalism on any topic
- Biography
- Nonfiction "novels"

Memoirs

"Memoir isn't the summary of a life; it's a window into a life," says master writing teacher and nonfiction writer William Zinsser in *On Writing Well: The Classic Guide to Writing Nonfiction*. "Think narrow, then, when you try the form," he advises. You can write many *memoirs* about your life and organize them by theme, by specific years, or by careers. Maybe you've struggled with weight your entire life, as Judith Moore discussed in her memoir, *Fat Girl: A True Story*, which traced this theme. Or take memoir master Mary Karr, who wrote three memoirs about her life: two that detailed her childhood and early womanhood, *The Liar's Club* and *Cherry*, and one that focused on her alcoholism and conversion to Catholicism in her later life, *Lit: A Memoir*.

DEFINITION

From the French word for "memory," a **memoir** is an autobiographical nonfiction form based on personal experience.

The best memoirs read like novels: a character overcomes an obstacle or several, whether it's surviving a horrific childhood, overcoming a disease like alcoholism, or recovering from a divorce and finding new love as Laura Fraser does in *An Italian Affair*. The memoir, constructed from the memory of the writer, shows in vivid detail what it was like to live through that time.

Autobiographies

While memoirs are "a window" into your life at a certain time, an autobiography is the whole life, soup to nuts. You don't leave much out in an autobiography. Perhaps you want to record your life for your grandchildren. Then you might consider a full-length autobiography of all that you've done in your life and all the people you know. Former president Bill Clinton recently published his autobiography, *My Life.* And that about sums up what an autobiography should do, which is to tell the entire life story.

Dramatic Book-Length Journalism

Ted Conover went undercover as a corrections officer to observe and write his firsthand account of the prison-industrial system in *Newjack: Guarding Sing Sing.* Jon Krakauer wrote about his expedition climbing Mount Everest in his 1999 bestselling book, *Into Thin Air: A Personal Account of the Mount Everest Disaster.* The climb ended in tragedy when a "murderous storm" took the lives of eight fellow hikers. These writers ask questions such as the following:

- Why does the United States imprison more people than any other country in the world?
- What's it like to live and work in a correctional facility?
- Why do people risk life and money to climb a mountain?
- What is the snow, ice, wind, air, and desperation like at over 8,000 feet?

WRITERS' WORDS

"Everyone is talented, original, and has something important to say."

—Brenda Ueland, American journalist, editor, and writer

Biographies

From Charles Dickens to Marie Antoinette, from dogs to cities like London and Venice, biographies are thorough investigations into a person, animal, or city. Writing a biography is not for the faint of heart: you'll spend years doing research, digging through archives (something we'll explore in Chapter 7), and conducting interviews. Your choice of subject is very important, for like a marriage partner, you will be spending a lot of time with this person, figuratively speaking. You might ask yourself: What is new to say about this person? What do you want the world to know that hasn't been said before? The best biographies not only bring a person to life, but his or her historical time period as well.

You may not know when you begin writing what form it will take. Short or long? Magazine article or book? Once you start writing, I believe there's an organic process at work, and the length will reveal itself to you.

But you won't know until you start. As Stephen King says, drink up, the water is free. If you don't tell your story or another's, who will? Perhaps you want to record your life for posterity, or maybe you have a tale that can help someone solve a problem similar to yours. You may have trunks full of photos or an innate curiosity about the world that leads you to ask questions and poke around. Perhaps like Rebecca Skloot, something your high school biology teacher said still resonates with you and you want to explore the topic, whether that is how human cells are used in research or how inspiration strikes, as bestselling author Jonah Lehrer does in his riveting book, *Imagine: How Creativity Works*. Whatever your topic, whatever you want to write, the time to be a nonfiction writer is now.

The Least You Need to Know

- In narrative nonfiction, you tell a true story in a literary way, paying attention to characterization, plot, and compelling language.
- Narrative nonfiction is perhaps the most popular form of writing in the late twentieth and early twenty-first centuries.
- Nonfiction writers write for a variety of reasons, from wanting to explore personal history to seeking to discover how the world works and sharing that information with readers.
- Narrative nonfiction shares many techniques with fiction writing, including dialogue and description, scene setting, characterization, plot, and conflict, but with one crucial exception: you cannot make anything up.
- Nonfiction can be divided into shorter forms that can be read in one sitting, such as personal essays, profiles, or magazine-length food, travel, or science writing.
- Nonfiction also encompasses book-length forms such as memoirs, biographies, autobiographies, and dramatic long-form journalism.

Story and Structure

In This Chapter

- Stories: the ties that bind us
- Provoking an emotional or intellectual response in the reader
- Taking the six-word story test
- The ingredients every story has
- Understanding story structure
- Telling true stories different ways

You're no doubt interested in writing nonfiction because you feel you have stories to tell. There may be things that shaped you as you were growing up, interesting people you've met, or places you've traveled along the way. No doubt you also adhere to the belief that truth really is stranger than fiction. Yet while life hands you the raw material that forms the basis of nonfiction, how do you shape it? How do you turn it into something that other people will want to read? The answer lies in the concept of story. Understanding what a story is and how to structure it will give you a framework on which to hang true events.

Perhaps another way to look at story is to think about the difference between merely reporting things—this happened, then this, finally this—and what the events mean. Why did they happen? What is the larger significance? This doesn't mean you'll be writing stories that have morals at the end, nor that you'll know the larger meaning from the outset when you start researching and writing, only that asking these questions will help transform event into story.

In this chapter, you'll learn how to scout out what makes a story worth sharing, the ingredients you must have to keep your reader turning the pages, and the different ways to tell stories. They don't always have to start chronologically or with "Once upon a time." In fact, once you understand what makes a good story you can break the rules, such as adding background material or starting at the end, and still keep the reader hooked. Ready to hear more?

What Is a Story?

We are a species hungry for stories. From our preliterate ancestors who passed down culture and history by telling oral tales to our current media-drenched world of blogs and e-books, narratives are the ties that bind us. It turns out that brains are hard-wired for language—and for stories. Recent psychological studies show that reading narratives satisfies a deeply human and evolutionary need— the need to belong. While reading, we psychologically become part of the characters and their community; because of this, our sense of well-being improves.

Storytelling is at the heart of all good narrative nonfiction. Fortunately for the nonfiction writer, real-life stories are all around us. The barista behind the counter where you get your morning coffee probably has a story to tell, or perhaps she would make an interesting profile. But how do you know when you have a story? And even more importantly, how do you know when you have a story worth telling?

WRITERS' WORDS

"Story is the umbilical cord that connects us to the past, present, and future … Story is an affirmation of our ties to one another."

—Terry Tempest Williams, American author, conservationist, and activist

In the simplest terms, a story is where something consequential happens. There must be something at stake for both the character (or characters) in the story and the reader of the story. This doesn't mean you should write only about dramatic, extraordinary true people and events. If you keep in mind the basic story elements, you can write about almost anything and still have your readers asking the central question that underlies all good stories: What happens next?

Provoking a Response in the Reader

A nonfiction story should provoke an emotional or intellectual response in the reader. If you read something and say, "So what?" chances are it's not a story. If what you're reading doesn't teach you anything new or cause you to feel differently about something, again, it's probably not a story. Not everyone will be moved by every nonfiction piece, but if no one is moved, you've probably written a mere reporting of events—this happened, then this, next this—but not a compelling story with drama and action that will keep the reader turning the pages.

Memoir writer Vivian Gornick puts it this way: "Every work of literature has both a situation and a story. The situation is the context or circumstance, sometimes the plot; the story is the emotional experience that preoccupies the writer: the insight, the wisdom, the thing one has come to say."

When you're writing your first, second, or even third draft of a nonfiction piece, it's entirely possible that you may not yet know what you are trying to say. Don't worry. I think it kills the writing of a piece to be too intentional when you start out. We'll talk about this more in Chapter 13.

Do You Have a Story?

How can you tell if you have a story? Take the story test. Legend has it that Ernest Hemingway was once challenged to come up with a six-word short story. His response? The shortest short story in the English language: "For sale: baby shoes, never used."

Why is this a story? If you think about it, there are characters, though we don't know their names. There's at least a mother and a father. There's a baby, who may or may not be alive or who may or may not have even have been born. The conflict? It's written in the fact that someone bought baby shoes, indicating a desire for a child. But that there is no baby? That's the conflict. There's also a resolution, albeit a sad, poignant one: someone is selling the shoes because, for whatever reason, they are no longer needed.

Believe it or not, there are also actions in this story, condensed as they may be. We can see this in the phrases "For sale" and "never worn." Our mind fills in the rest, and indeed, it is the reader who really creates the story in this story, a clever ploy by Hemingway. Was the baby aborted? Kidnapped? Given up for adoption? Did it die in a stillbirth? Did the couple go their separate ways because of this? Is it the mother or father who is selling the shoes? Both?

A nonfiction writer wouldn't necessarily leave you hanging this way. The nonfiction writer has an obligation to tell the truth and to ferret out as much information about the subject as possible. But the bones of storytelling are the same: find an interesting character or set of characters, give them a problem to solve, set them in motion by showing the actions resulting from this problem, and provide a fitting resolution—one that provokes a response by the reader.

In 2006, in the spirit of Hemingway's brief yet evocative short story, Larry Smith and Rachel Fershleiser, editors of the online storytelling magazine *Smith*, challenged readers to write their own life stories in six-word memoirs. The results, by well known, unknown, and anonymous writers, were published online and later in a series of six-word memoir books. Here are a few:

> "I still make coffee for two." —Zak Nelson

> "Fifteen years since last professional haircut." —Dave Eggers

> "Barrister, barista, what's the diff, Mom?" —Abigail Moorhouse

> "I asked. They answered. I wrote." —Sebastian Junger

JUMPSTART

Write your own six-word memoir, answering this question: what have you most learned in life?

What Are the Ingredients of a Story?

At its core, a story has a protagonist who faces some kind of problem or obstacle, whether internal (such as struggling with depression or expectations, or low self-esteem) or external, and who comes to some new resolution or understanding of the conflict. Now, that doesn't necessarily mean solving the problem. Life is messy, and you can't make things up to have a happily-ever-after ending. But there has to be movement so that the protagonist (and the reader) lands in a different place from where he or she started.

The ingredients of a story include the following:

- **Character:** Usually a sympathetic or likeable person to whom the reader can relate. Also called the protagonist. **Conflict or complication:** A problem or obstacle (whether external or internal) that the main character must face.
- **Setting.** Where the story takes place.
- **Plot:** A careful selection and arrangement of events to reveal cause and effect or a larger purpose.
- **Resolution:** Overcoming the obstacle or conflict. In nonfiction writing, this does not necessarily mean "solving" the problem, but rather having the protagonist come to some understanding of it.

Characters

"Characters are the soul of creative nonfiction, whether it's memoirs, new journalism, or personal essays you're making," writes nonfiction writer and professor Bill Roorbach in *Writing Life Stories: How to Make Memories into Memoirs, Ideas into Essays, and Life into Literature.* You can't tell a story without a character or characters.

I learned this the hard way. My first teaching position after graduate school was working with women prisoners in the county jail. I came home every night exhausted and sad and overwhelmed, and for the first time in my life, I started keeping a regular journal, more as survival than anything else. But I was put in touch with an editor at *Glamour*, as I'd pitched another story (about my divorce) to an editor at another woman's magazine, who told me to send it to her friend at *Glamour*. The articles editor passed on the divorce story but asked me what else I was working on. I blurted out that I was teaching at the jail and was writing about that. She suggested I send her a story. I didn't know where to begin, but luckily she told me what to do next. "Pick three or four of the women and use them to structure the piece," she said. I did. And something clicked for me then: without characters, you don't have a story.

Conflict

You also don't really have a story without conflict. Now students hear the word *conflict* and often say to me, "But I had a happy childhood. What if I don't have any conflicts in my life?" And I tell them we're all very happy for them, but if they don't find some kind of tension—the discrepancy between the way things are and the way they would like them to be—they won't keep the reader interested.

Conflict doesn't have to be a bad word. Perhaps you love your spouse so deeply that you can't bear to be apart from her or him for the entire day. Perhaps you're so fond of rescuing animals that you have 17 cats, 1 turtle, 2 guinea pigs, and 4 rabbits, and you don't have room to adopt more. That's tension.

JUMPSTART

In full disclosure, I stole this exercise from a workshop I took with novelist Lynn Freed, and I've never forgotten it. Finish the following sentence and write two pages without lifting your pen off the page or your fingers from the keyboard: My mother (or father) never _____.

Setting

Setting is where the story takes place. It could be the town where you grew up, your grandparent's house, your bedroom, or even your mind as you wrestle with a problem. The setting does more than just anchor the piece in time and place; the right setting can establish a mood for your piece—gloomy, sunny, foreboding, promising—and even become a character in its own right.

Bestselling *The New Yorker* writer Susan Orlean does a brilliant job of using the setting as a character in *The Orchid Thief: A True Story of Beauty and Obsession* when she describes the state of Florida as "less like a state than a sponge." We'll discuss how to write about time and place in Chapter 6.

Plot

Not just the events that happened but why those events took place—the causality or consequences of the events—that's the plot. At the risk of sounding contradictory, not all nonfiction pieces have a plot. Profiles of people, for example, often don't have traditional story plots, but probably somewhere in the profile itself there will be a mini story with a plot. Your subject may have overcome some demon or obstacle, and you'll give the bare bones of this plotted story to reveal her character, for instance.

You can't make up a plot in nonfiction: if something didn't turn out the way you expected or would have liked, you're not allowed to write otherwise. Though, of course, you can say that you wish it had turned out otherwise, that's allowable. But as a nonfiction writer, ordering the events into some kind of cause and effect or order of importance is what makes the plot.

Resolution

In nonfiction writing, real life doesn't necessarily present you with nice, tidy endings in which all problems are solved. And you certainly can't invent a happy ending—or any ending that didn't happen at all. That's okay. But your story should still arrive somewhere different from where you started out.

For instance, in his brilliant personal essay "Under the Influence," which recounts his attempt to understand the effects of his father's alcoholism on his life, Scott Russell Sanders does not so much "solve" the problem and get over these devastating effects as bring them out into the open. "I am moved to write these pages now because my own son, at the age of ten, is taking on himself the griefs of the world, and in particular the griefs of his father," writes Sanders. "And that crushing sense of responsibility is exactly what I felt at the age of ten in the face of my father's drinking … I write, therefore, to drag into the light what eats at me—the fear, the guilt, the shame—so that my own children may be spared," he states in the conclusion of the essay. The essay is "unresolved" in the sense that the narrator still suffers from the effects of alcoholism—the grief, shame, guilt, and unhappiness that stems from his father's drinking—but he is open and honest about it, and discovers the connection to his own addiction to work.

By the end of your story or essay, your character should have changed or grown or learned something new. Without this movement, you don't have a story.

WRITERS' WORDS

"If nothing happens, it's not a story."

—Flannery O'Connor, American novelist, short-story writer, and essayist

Story Structure

The novelist E. M. Forster once wrote that if you write, "The king died, and then the queen died," you have a narrative, which is merely a chronology of events. But if you write, "The king died, and then the queen died of grief," you have a plot. Plot is what structures your nonfiction story. It's not everything that happens to your character, just the relevant events that show your character wrestling with a conflict.

The late Gary Provost, often called "the writer's writer" for his essential how-to books on writing, wrote that 90 percent of the stories we read have some form of the following plot. Here's what his co-writer Peter Rubie calls the "Gary Provost Paragraph" in *How to Tell a Story: The Secrets of Writing Captivating Tales.* Can you spot the ingredients of the story and see how they give shape to the plot?

> Once upon a time, *something happened*, to someone, and he decided that he would pursue a *goal*. So he devised a *plan of action*, and even though there were *forces trying to stop him*, he moved forward because there was a *lot at stake*. And just as things seemed as *bad as they could get*, he learned an *important lesson*, and when *offered the prize* he had sought so strenuously, he had to *decide whether or not to take it*, and in making that decision he *satisfied a need* that had been created by *something in his past*.

PITFALL AHEAD

One problem that befalls beginning nonfiction writers is writing episodically. That is, writing a series of true-life episodes, one after the other, with no larger purpose tying them together. To avoid this problem, include only those events that have an important causal relationship: one event happens because of the next. You'll find it easier to make a plot this way—and to structure these events into a story.

The Narrative Arc

Even if you've never read Aristotle, you've probably heard of his famous line in *Poetics* about how a dramatic plot must be "whole" and have a beginning, middle, and end. In nonfiction writing, the beginning, middle, and end can be plotted along what's called a "narrative arc," basically a fancy way of saying that there must be some sort of rising tension that reaches a climax or resolution and then falls off in what the French call "denoeument," or the winding down of events.

I can still remember my elementary school English teacher drawing this arc on the board. Graphically, it looks like a small mountain: a rising line until the tension reaches a climax, and then it falls off in the denouement or falling action. But it wasn't until I started writing some decades later that I realized its importance.

Here are the plot points along the narrative arc:

- **Inciting event:** The event that catapults your character into action.
- **Rising action:** Where the tension is building. Things are getting complicated for your protagonist.
- **Climax:** This is the showdown, the turning point for your character where something changes.
- **Denouement:** The falling action where things wind down for your protagonist.
- **Resolution:** The final outcome of the plot.

Not every piece of nonfiction writing will have such a neatly plotted narrative arc. But if your writing is flat on the page, ask yourself: Where's the narrative arc? Where's the tension that propels the story forward? Without some kind of rising tension or forward motion, you may have a vignette or a slice of life but not a story in the true sense of the word.

JUMPSTART

Think of something that happened to you last week. Something not as trivial as forgetting your keys but not as monumental as someone dying. Write down exactly what happened in chronological order. Then try another version where you start in the middle. Finally, tell the story but break the flow of the narrative to provide background information.

Different Ways to Begin a Story

Despite what Aristotle wrote about beginnings, middles, and ends, there's no rule that says your nonfiction piece must start at the very beginning. Unless it's a very good place to start. In fact, good nonfiction writers, while they understand story structure, know how to play with it.

While you can't make up events or facts, you do get to decide in what order to tell them. Following are some ways to begin a story.

In Medias Res: Into the Midst of Things

Starting *in medias res* plunges the reader into the middle of the narrative or plot. For example, think about the opening scenes of the last action-adventure movie you saw. Or any James Bond thriller. Could you tell the good guys from the bad guys at first? Maybe not. But chances are you didn't care. The action was fast paced, the adrenalin flowed, and you just wanted to see what happened next. You were plunged into the middle of things and trusted that, in due time, you'd figure out who was shooting at whom from a speedboat. In the meantime, you were happy to be along for the ride.

> **DEFINITION**
>
> **In medias res** is a literary technique in which the story begins at the midpoint or conclusion rather than at the beginning. This technique uses flashback to establish the characters, setting, and conflict of the story.

You won't lose the reader by starting in medias res if you start with something exciting—arresting dialogue or an exciting scene—and if you begin as close to the conflict as possible.

Here's an example from the essayist Katha Pollitt's "Learning to Drive," which first appeared in *The New Yorker*:

> "Over there, the red Jeep, park!" Ben, my gentle Filipino driving instructor, has suddenly become severe, abrupt, commanding. A slight man, he now looms bulkily in his seat; his usually soft voice has acquired a threatening edge. In a scenario that we have repeated dozens of times, and that has kinky overtones I don't even want to think about, he is pretending to be the test examiner, barking out orders as we tool along the streets above Columbia University in the early morning. I am impersonating the would-be licensee, obediently carrying out the instructions.

Pollitt first plunges us into the action and then weaves back and forth in time in the rest of the essay, alternating between scenes in the car with her driving instructor and showing how her "weakness for observation" led her to overlook the signs of cheating by her live-in "soul mate."

Chronological Order

There's nothing wrong with starting at the beginning and telling a story straight through. It's a tried-and-true method that works perfectly well for much nonfiction, and as the old adage goes, "If it ain't broke, don't fix it."

When novelist Stephen King tells his nonfiction account of getting hit by a car that nearly killed him, he does so chronologically. King begins this tale in the "Postscript" chapter of his memoir, *On Writing: A Memoir of the Craft*, with this sentence:

> When we're at our summer house in western Maine—a house very much like the one Mike Noonan comes back to in *Bag of Bones*—I walk four miles every day, unless it's pouring down rain.

Each opening line of the next few paragraphs narrows the chronology further:

> The third week in June 1999 was an extraordinarily happy one for my wife and me; our kids, now grown and scattered across the country, were all home.

The following paragraph starts:

> On the nineteenth of June, I drove our younger son to the Portland Jetport, where he caught a flight back to New York City. I drove home, had a brief nap, and then set out on my usual walk.

And then in the fourth paragraph King writes:

> I set out on that walk around four o'clock in the afternoon, as well as I can remember. Just before reaching the main road ... I stepped into the woods and urinated. It was two months before I was able to take another leak standing up.

That chronology works for me. How about you? Does it make you want to read on?

Reverse Chronology

Reverse chronology is starting at the end and moving through time backwards, perhaps with flashbacks thrown in.

Judith Moore begins her memoir, *Fat Girl: A True Story*, in the present: "I am fat. I am not so fat that I can't fasten the seat belt on the plane. But, fat I am."

We know from the start—Moore tells us so—that the memoir will not end happily ever after. The narrator will not get thin. "I am a short, squat, toad of a woman," she writes. "My shoulders are wide. My upper arms as big as those maroon-skinned bolognas that hang from butchers' ceilings." And though we know how this story ends, we want to read to see how it began.

My writing students often want to tease the reader and think they should not reveal the ending right up front, for if they do who will want to read on? I always tell them that nonfiction writing isn't poker. If you're holding aces—as I think Moore is here—then it's fine to show your hand.

Breaking the Narrative

Breaking the narrative is interrupting the flow of events to provide exposition or background. For example, in Sebastian Junger's *The Perfect Storm: A True Story of Men Against the Sea*, his nonfiction account of the 1991 "storm of the century" that brought down the swordfishing boat the Andrea Gail, Junger interrupts the tale to talk about the history of swordfishing from the 1800s until the present day. These digressions break the narrative, but we don't mind. Even though we know the story will end with all six men killed in the storm, we keep reading. Junger has us on his hook with good storytelling, so we happily follow him on any digression. Give your readers a good hook, reel them in with a good story, and they'll follow you anywhere.

The Least You Need to Know

- Storytelling is at the heart of narrative nonfiction, and we are a species hungry for stories. They are the ties that bind us together and help us make sense of the world.
- In a good nonfiction story, something must happen; the character must change or grow, and the reader is moved emotionally or intellectually.
- All stories have these ingredients: a main character (or protagonist), a sympathetic character, conflict, setting, plot, and resolution.
- The spine of a story is the plot, and plotting out events on a narrative arc can help you maximize the tension in a story.
- You don't always have to tell stories chronologically; you can begin in the middle of the action, tell the events in reverse order, or even break the forward motion of the narrative and intersperse it with background material or history.

Finding Your Subject

In This Chapter

- Where to find original ideas
- Who's your audience?
- Developing your voice as a nonfiction writer
- Understanding first person, second person, and third person point of view
- Multiple narrators and an omniscient narrator

The good news for the nonfiction writer is that there's no shortage of material. Ideas from life are all around you. Harnessing your curiosity, following your passion, and mining your expertise are all avenues to finding great ideas. But how do you know which topics are worth pursuing and which are better left in the dustbin? We'll cover that and more in this chapter.

And then there's finding and honing your writer's voice—the place where you sound most like yourself in writing and no one else. Perhaps you've been told never to write in the first person or to always use the pronoun "one." You can certainly forget those "rules" now. The best nonfiction writers have distinctive, personal voices. It's not something you can imitate, but you can develop your own authentic voice, and this chapter will give you tips on how to do just that.

Once you have an interesting topic, how do you tell the tale? First person, third person? You'll find out what this means in this chapter and which viewpoint suits your material.

Finding Story Ideas

Perhaps the most frequent question a nonfiction writer gets asked is, "Where do you come up with your ideas?" Finding a good story from your own life or from someone else's is the result of curiosity, research, intuition, luck, and just plain hard work. Often it means chasing down blind alleys that may lead nowhere. Other times, ideas for stories come when you least expect them—while walking the dog, taking a shower, reading a magazine, or striking up a conversation with a stranger in line.

When asked about the inspiration for her fiction, short-story writer Flannery O'Connor purportedly said, "Every morning between 9 A.M. and 12 P.M., I go to my room and sit in front of a piece of paper. Many times, I just sit there with no ideas coming to me. But I know one thing. If an idea comes between 9 and 12, I am ready for it."

What Are You Passionate About?

For the nonfiction writer, the more curious and passionate you are, the more ideas will come to you. One of the best ways to come up with ideas is to start with yourself and your interests. What are you passionate about? What are your pet peeves, the things that drive you crazy? Your hobbies? How do you prefer to spend your free time? What beliefs do you hold dear? If you're passionate about recycling, for instance, you might wonder where your yogurt container goes when it leaves the curbside recycling bin. Does that plastic truly get turned into other objects? And does it matter if you didn't rinse out every last bit of yogurt? Are you curious enough to find out? If so, you might have the topic for a story—"From Trash to Toothbrush"—born from your curiosity about recycling.

"Find your passion, find the subject—because the subject begins with the writer," writes nonfiction writing guru Philip Gerard in his book *Creative Nonfiction: Researching and Crafting Stories of Real Life*.

That's why, he says, "the Delphic oracle's admonition 'Know thyself' is not just of lofty concern to the soul; it's of urgent, practical value to the craft."

Look Around You

Another way to find story topics is to look in your own backyard, both physically and metaphorically speaking. What do you see around you? What do you notice throughout your day? For instance, you buy a cup of coffee and see that you now not only have the option of small, medium, and large, but also of fair trade, organic, and shade grown. What do these terms mean? Is one more environmentally friendly than the others? Is one better for coffee producers? You start to ask questions and do research and see where it leads you. It could lead back to a profile of coffee farmers or to a personal essay on the ethics of choice in general and coffee in particular. But if you're curious about coffee, chances are there's a story in this material somewhere.

Think Like a Writer

The novelist Henry James once admonished an aspiring fiction writer to "try to be one of the people on whom nothing is lost!" That goes double for the nonfiction writer, who has an endless stream of material in real life. One way to make sure that what you see around you won't be lost is to write it down. Get in the habit of carrying around a notebook, a few index cards, your smartphone, or whatever works to record ideas for stories.

"'That woman Estelle,' the note reads, 'is partly the reason why George Sharp and I are separated today,'" writes the essayist and memoir writer Joan Didion in her famous essay, "On Keeping a Notebook." Didion's piece is a meditation on why she records things in her notebook: bits of overheard conversation, impressions of people, what was served at dinner. Not for their factual quality but to bring back the past, her past, and how things *felt* to her. "But our notebooks give us away," writes Didion, "for however dutifully we record what we see around us, the common denominator of all we see is always, transparently, shamelessly, the implacable 'I.'" That's why your notebook would be no good to someone else: it is the record of your filtered experience, which can be mined into meaning.

Keeping a notebook is one way to think like a writer. Try going about your day recording what you see and hear. What do you notice that may be the start of a good story?

JUMPSTART

Brainstorm a list of 10 things you are passionate about. Don't think about their significance yet or of turning them into stories, just write down everything that moves you. Now circle one of those things that seems to have the most charge or spark. Let yourself write for two pages without stopping on that topic.

Mine Your Expertise

Everyone is an expert in something. When you're just starting out as a nonfiction writer, mining your own expertise not only can give you material to write about but also can convince editors that you and only you are the person who to write a particular story.

Don't feel you need to have an advanced degree in a subject to be an expert. You've no doubt heard the old adage to "write what you know." Mining your experience is a version of that. As a nonfiction writer, you'll also write about things you don't know, which is one of its pleasures because you get to learn new things, but for now, let's start with the things that make you an expert.

Have you undergone a divorce? Well, your experience qualifies you to write about it. Are you a parent? Then you know that childrearing has a steep learning curve. What will you do with that knowledge? Write about it. Do you have pets? Play a sport? What about your day job? What do you do for a living? You are an expert in your profession whether you're a dog walker, accountant, or special education teacher.

Here's an example of something unexpected that I became an expert in. I've yet to pitch the story idea, but someday I will. For several months I'd noticed that my cat seemed to have a hairball, and though he coughed he never expelled anything. It wasn't until I came home and found him struggling for breath that I rushed him to the animal hospital and found out he had feline asthma. "Asthma, are you kidding me?" I asked the vet, several thousand dollars later. "I didn't know cats could get asthma." Most people don't know that, I realized. And as the signs of an asthma attack mirror that of a hairball, the disease often goes undiagnosed in cats. Of course, I read everything I could on the subject and for a while even joined a listserv devoted to feline asthma, so though I've yet to pitch the story (probably to cat or animal magazines), I'm certainly an expert on it. (By the way, cats with asthma can live long, happy lives with the proper medication.)

JUMPSTART

What are you an expert in? Brainstorm a list of subjects you feel qualified to write about, including your hobbies, your pets, and your other interests.

Check Your Local Newspaper

Another great source for story ideas is your local newspaper. In my paper, there is a section for hometown heroes, those people who are honored for doing something notable in the community. Perhaps one of these people has national appeal? Or maybe you can find other women or men making a difference in their communities that you can turn into a nonfiction magazine article profiling several of them? Because national magazines are in big cities—usually New York City—they miss much of what is going on in smaller cities across the country. Oftentimes if you're casting about for ideas that you can pitch to national magazines, your local newspaper can be a goldmine of resources.

For years, I wanted to write for *O, The Oprah Magazine.* It was my dream as a freelancer to appear in this magazine I respected for its smart coverage of women's issues. In fact, I owned every copy of the magazine since it first premiered in 2002. One day, I read about a young woman in my local paper who had received not only an award for community service but also a MacArthur genius grant for her work with at-risk young women. I quickly pitched the story to *O, The Oprah Magazine*, where I'd had some success reaching an editor, and within 24 hours they asked me to do the piece as part of a longer series of profiles called "Women with Chutzpah."

Another time, I found a story in my local newspaper about two Catholic nuns who against all odds had opened a daytime homeless shelter for drug-addicted women. I knew one of the nuns by reputation because she wrote mystery novels on the side, something I'm passionate about. So I pitched the profile to a local magazine, beginning the pitch with one of the plots of the nun's mystery novels, and received the green light from the editor to write a longer profile. All because I read mysteries—and the local paper.

I know many writers who clip newspaper stories the way savvy shoppers clip coupons: they have files and files of story ideas, some topical and timely, some not, and whenever they're in need of a fresh idea, they pull out a folder and get to work.

JUMPSTART

Skim your local newspaper looking for interesting people to profile. Whose life would make a good story? What has the person done that other people might find interesting? Start your own file of newspaper clippings that you think may have national appeal.

Mine Your Memories

In addition to keeping your eyes and ears open for story ideas in the present, mining your past experience is essential for finding ideas for personal essays, memoirs, and nonfiction pieces. Did you keep a journal or diary at some point in your life? Perhaps you've saved every email you ever wrote in your sent mailbox. Even if you've never kept any kind of written record in the past, you probably have old photographs, scrapbooks, or yearbooks. These sources are invaluable for giving you story ideas and insight to your past. We'll talk more about using these sources as research in Chapter 7.

For now, just start by looking through what you have. Try to find patterns, recurrent themes, or anything that jumps out at you. Perhaps you sent emails to your best friend every day during the first year of your son's life. What did you learn about being a new mother that could be pitched to a parenting magazine? Perhaps it's something about how your relationship changed not only with your spouse, but also unexpectedly with your non-mom friends, something that may be fodder for an essay. Or perhaps you recall your struggle to get your body back in shape after a C-section, which is what's called an "evergreen" subject, meaning that these topics are run frequently in magazines, often with a hook – some new research that might make the topic worth exploring again. Just keep a running list of ideas as you pore through the archives of your past.

Who's Your Audience?

This is a fundamental question, says nonfiction writer and teacher William Zinsser in *On Writing Well: The Classic Guide to Writing Nonfiction*, an essential book on the craft that has undergone more than 30 editions since it was first published in 1976. "[A]nd it has a fundamental answer: You are writing for yourself," says Zinsser.

What Zinsser means is that to succeed as a nonfiction writer, you must be true to yourself. You can't write thinking about what might sell, or to please the editor at *Vanity Fair*, or to appeal to the widest possible audience, but you may do all of these things if you write for yourself. "If you write for yourself, you'll reach the people you want to write *for*," says Zinsser.

Although I agree with Zinsser that you write for yourself—to find out what you think, to make sense of the world, to discover new things—I do think it's easier to write if you have some sense of an audience in mind. I write thinking of one of my closest friends. How would I explain something to her? What can I reveal to her? Picturing a friendly face reading my writing makes the process, for me at least, less intimidating and isolating.

Finding Your Voice

It's rumored that Flannery O'Connor once said, "If you want style, buy a hat." Nothing can kill a nonfiction piece quicker than trying too hard, perhaps by adopting a literary "style" or mannerism that is not your own. What is style? It's the product of your voice in writing, that place where your writing sounds most like you and no one else. Just as no two people have the same fingerprints, no two writers have exactly the same voice.

You may not know yet that you have a voice in writing, but you do. Think about the last time you wrote a letter or a long email to a friend. Did you have trouble getting your thoughts down? Were you stuck grasping for words? Probably not. When you're writing a letter, especially to someone you know, you are writing closest to your own voice. You're probably not writing for the marketplace or to flaunt your literary prowess. You're writing to reveal what you authentically think and feel: this is where you're writing in your voice.

Like a gardener clearing away the weeds from a rose bush, I often feel my job as a writing instructor is to clear away the detritus that prevents students from finding their voices. Perhaps they think they should consult a thesaurus to find a polysyllabic word so they sound "smarter." Or perhaps they've been told to never use the first person but instead to always write "one thinks" and "one sees," so that their writing sounds disembodied or like a critic from the 1950s. Not true. One of the delicious freedoms of nonfiction writing is that you get to speak from your own personal point of view.

Here are several tips for developing your voice:

- Read everything you write out loud. You'll develop your ear for language and be able to hear your voice.
- Write truthfully from your heart. You will write with passion and clarity this way.
- Pretend that you're writing a letter to a friend or loved one. Even start your piece as a letter with a salutation.
- Write as you speak—conversationally.

- Write without censoring yourself.
- Write as if no one will ever read it and be as emotional as you like.
- Don't compare yourself to another writer or copy another writer's style.

WRITERS' WORDS

"Write as if you were dying. At the same time, assume you write for an audience consisting solely of terminal patients. That is, after all, the case. What would you begin writing if you knew you would die soon? What could you say to a dying person that would not enrage by its triviality?"

—Annie Dillard, American poet, critic, and nonfiction writer

Choosing a Point of View

Now that you have some ideas for nonfiction stories and a sense of your voice, the next thing to ask yourself is: who is telling the story? Answering that question will determine the point of view. Personal essays and memoirs almost always demand that you write in the first person: I. Profiles and biographies, on the other hand, almost always require the third person point of view: he, she, or it. Sometimes you can use the second person ("you") such as in travel or food writing, or whenever you want the reader to feel that she is there narrating the experience. The point of view is the lens through which the story is told, so choosing a point of view determines how much your narrator knows and what your readers see.

First Person

If you are writing about yourself in a memoir or personal essay, it would be strange to write in anything but the *first person* ("I," "we," "us"). Though we may think of using the first person as an act of egoism or as indicative of a twenty-first–century preoccupation with one's self, the first person point of view has a long history. "I went to the woods because I wished to live deliberately, to front only the essential facts of life, and see if I could not learn what it had to teach, and not, when I came to die, discover that I had not lived," wrote Henry David Thoreau in his 1854 meditation on solitude and self-reliance, *Walden*. The language is simple and unadorned, which matches the subject, and though there are five uses of the word "I" in that sentence, it doesn't feel self-absorbed or solipsistic, but rather universal in its appeal for what it means to live.

> **DEFINITION**
>
> The **first person** point of view tells the story using "I," "we," or "us." When you write in the first person, the reader won't know any more than the narrator, usually "I," knows.

Second Person

You might use the *second person* point of view ("you") in how-to pieces or travel writing in which you address the reader directly. Using the second person has the benefit of putting the reader right into the story, but it can quickly become annoying if done too frequently. "You walk down the streets of Paris and notice that even the babies are impeccably dressed, from their unscuffed expensive leather booties to their adorable lime-green pea coats. And you wonder if the Parisians were born with a fashion gene." If the piece were to continue addressing the reader with "you" for another 2,000 words, it would get not only tiring but also irritating. A little second person goes a long way.

> **DEFINITION**
>
> The **second person** point of view uses "you" to narrate the story, as if you're giving directions, or telling the reader what he is thinking, feeling, or doing.

Third Person

For a masterful example of using the *third person* point of view, look no further than novelist Truman Capote's *In Cold Blood: A True*

Account of a Multiple Murder and Its Consequences, which was hailed as the first nonfiction novel and caused a literary sensation when it first appeared in serial form in *The New Yorker* in 1965. The book, which Capote spent six years researching, details the savage and senseless murder of four members of the Clutter family in Holcomb, Kansas; its aftermath; and the execution of the two killers. The story moves effortlessly between all the characters' points of view, including the murderers' and the investigators'. And though the veracity of Capote's assertion that every word and scene is true has come under attack, there is no denying that Capote effectively and skillfully uses the third person point of view to get his readers inside the head of each character. "He thought of himself as balanced, as sane as anyone—maybe a bit smarter than the average fellow, that's all," writes Capote from the viewpoint of one of the killers, Richard (Dick) Eugene Hickock. "But Perry—there *was,* in Dick's opinion, 'something wrong' with Little Perry," referring to his partner in crime."

> **DEFINITION**
>
> The **third person** point of view uses "he," "she," or "it" when narrating the story. This can sometimes be limiting as you are looking through one person's point of view and can only reveal what this person sees and knows.

Multiple Narrators

It's possible to alternate first person points of view, even in a memoir, through the use of multiple narrators. James McBride does this beautifully in *The Color of Water: A Black Man's Tribute to His White Mother,* a memoir exploring his confusion about race. Each chapter is told in the first person, alternating between his story and his mother's, which, incidentally, took him 14 years to get her to reveal. "As a boy, I never knew where my mother was from—where she was born, who her parents were," writes McBride. "When I asked she'd say, 'God made me.' When I asked if she was white, she'd say, 'I'm light-skinned,' and change the subject."

McBride's mother, the daughter of a Jewish rabbi, raised 12 black children, mostly on her own, sent them to college and graduate school, yet never talked about race and was evasive about her past. The memoir format alternates between two first person voices, and in so doing both mother and son come alive on the page.

"I'm dead," states Ruth McBride Jordan, in the first chapter told from her point of view. "You want to talk about my family and here I been dead to them for fifty years. Leave me alone. Don't bother me. They want no parts of me and I don't want no parts of them. Hurry up and get this interview over with," she tells her son. "I want to watch *Dallas*. See, my family, if you had a been part of them, you wouldn't have time for this foolishness, your roots, so to speak. You'd be better off watching *The Three Stooges* than to interview them, like to go interview my father, forget it. He'd have a heart attack if he saw you."

An Omniscient Narrator

An omniscient, or all-knowing, narrator is like the wizard of Oz behind the curtain. This narrator sees all and knows all but doesn't necessarily reveal everything all at once. *The New Yorker* writer Malcolm Gladwell does this his nonfiction book *Blink: The Power of Thinking Without Thinking*. He interviewed psychologists, art curators, a tennis coach, policemen, and a musician, among others, to show how our "adaptive unconscious," our gut instincts, works, and how sometimes it is more trustworthy than empirical evidence.

Gladwell begins with an account of an ancient Greek statue, a kouros, bought by the Getty Museum in Los Angeles but later proved to be a fake. Despite empirical evidence of the statue's authenticity, "The kouros, however, had a problem," Gladwell writes. "It didn't look right." Though Gladwell has all the evidence, all the interviews, he lays out his material in such a way as to make it a mystery. Why is it that the statue didn't look right? Why did one curator feel "intuitive repulsion" when looking at it? Why did another think it "was fresh" and not ancient? Gladwell unspools the information in such a way that we are on a journey with him to see how powerful intuition can be.

The Least You Need to Know

- Promising ideas for nonfiction topics are all around you; you can draw not only on your personal history but also on your expertise, passion, curiosity, hobbies, even your local newspaper to come up with interesting stories to write about.

- Think about your audience as a trusted friend. Write for yourself and what you feel passionately about, not for what you think might sell.

- Your voice in writing is as individual as you are. Developing that voice means writing in an authentic, truthful way, being as honest and open as you can.

- You can choose how to tell the story by deciding on first person, second person, or third person point of view.

- Alternating first person points of view or using an "all-knowing" omniscient narrator are techniques you can use to make your story interesting.

The Building Blocks of Nonfiction

Part

2

Characters in nonfiction are not based on real people; they *are* real people. One of the building blocks of all good nonfiction writing is bringing these real-life people to the page respectfully and honestly. In this part, I introduce you to the other building block of nonfiction writing—summary or exposition. As a nonfiction writer, you get to both show and tell, and knowing when to dramatize and when to summarize will help you build a compelling nonfiction narrative.

This part also covers the slippery slope (for some writers, anyway) between nonfiction and fiction writing, so you can see what's allowed and what's forbidden. While nonfiction "borrows" many of the techniques of fiction writing—scene-setting, dialogue, description, and summary—there is one crucial difference between the two: you can't make anything up in nonfiction. I introduce you to writers who bend the form and stretch the genre of nonfiction and those who break it.

Building Characters from Real People

In This Chapter

- Understanding characters in nonfiction
- How you can use physical description to capture characters
- Using specific descriptive words to "show" rather than "tell"
- Using dialogue effectively
- Guidelines for writing about real people

When you write nonfiction, you're writing about real people, your-self included. What could be easier? asks the fiction writer. You don't have to make anything up, just copy from real life. What could be harder, asks the aspiring nonfiction writer, than writing about people you know and love without betraying or offending them? What do you owe the real people, living and dead, whom you write about? And just how do you bring them to life on the page?

This chapter will help you write about real people so that they pop off the page in three dimensions, not lie flat in two dimensions. We'll also explore the thornier issue of how to be fair to the real people you write about.

Characters in Nonfiction

We use the word "character" to refer to the people who appear in the pages of nonfiction, but they aren't characters in the fictional sense: they are real people, some still living, others who have passed on, but none of them made up. Characters are probably the most important element of your narrative nonfiction. What happens to the characters is the plot, but without characters there is no plot. And without likeable, memorable, interesting, or fascinating characters, your reader won't stick around for long.

But you don't have to go looking for people who've engaged in extreme sports or scaled mountains or risen to the top of their profession to write about. What makes a character interesting or engaging? Conflict. The two together can make a character pop into life on the page. Think about your favorite characters from movies or TV shows. Do they have problems? Even minor ones? Isn't that what makes them memorable?

When you write autobiographical nonfiction, whether it's a personal essay or memoir, you are a character as well. Yet it's not your entire self you're putting onto the page—everything you've ever thought or done—but only what is relevant to the particular story you're trying to tell. How do you turn yourself into a character? You'll find tips in this chapter, but the most important one is to be honest, open, and vulnerable in your writing.

Flat vs. Round Characters

You may have heard the English novelist E. M. Forster's famous distinction between round and flat *characters* in literature. Flat characters are two-dimensional; they don't develop or change during the course of the novel or story. Round characters, on the other hand, do change; they're lifelike. "The test of a round character is whether it is capable of surprising in a convincing way," writes Forster. "If it never surprises, it is flat. If it does not convince, it is flat pretending to be round."

JUMPSTART

"Personal writing works best when it has a rueful aspect—illusions shed, wrong turns taken," writes memoirist Adair Lara in *Naked, Drunk, and Writing: Writing Essays and Memoirs for Love and for Money*. Write about a time when you took a wrong turn. Don't beat yourself up, but don't be afraid to write about what really happened.

Yourself as a Character

When you write personal essays, memoirs, first person travel pieces, or personal narrative nonfiction, you must also portray yourself as a character. But though you are writing in the first person and using "I," it's not your entire self that you're revealing on the page; rather, "The 'I' is a narrow gate," says essayist Scott Russell Sanders. It's a snapshot of yourself at a certain time and place, no more representative of your entire person than one single photograph can sum up your life.

How do you write about yourself as a character? First, it helps to have some perspective or distance rather than writing in the heat of the moment. One kind of distance is that of time. If what you're writing about is still very emotionally charged, you may not be able to see all sides of an issue, which is paramount if you're writing a personal essay. I tell my students to wait at least six months after a major event to write about it in an essay; in the meantime, I tell them to keep notes.

Let's say you'd like to write about your divorce. How do you think your account would differ after the papers are signed and the assets divided as compared to during the weeks following your discovery your spouse was cheating on you? You could, of course, use the diary you kept during this time as part of your research, but if you let the dust settle you might be able to write a more honest assessment of what happened and your role in it rather than writing in the heat of the moment.

The second way to both get distance and turn yourself into a character is to not be afraid to inventory yourself—both your strengths and your shortcomings. We all have our flaws and our strong points. Deciding which of these you will focus on for a specific piece will help you narrow down your "I" to a coherent character.

Think about yourself as a character this way: we all wear many hats in life. In a single morning you may be mother, wife, carpool driver, dog walker, short-order cook, sister, writer, neighbor, and bake sale maven organizer. Write down every single role you play during the day. Then write two paragraphs on each one.

Now step back from what you've written and reread it. In which of these descriptions is there conflict? That is, which has some tension in it, perhaps the difference between the way things are and the way you'd like them to be? Perhaps you and your sister had a falling out recently and now you talk infrequently on the phone, which troubles you. This could be a topic for a good personal essay. How you write about the self who's on the outs with her sister is probably very different from how you'd write about yourself as the efficient bake sale organizer. You'd focus on different sides of yourself. This is what it means to be a character in nonfiction.

Wants, Needs, and Desires

I once attended a talk by the novelist Michael Cunningham, who spoke on writing *The Hours*, his Pulitzer-prize winning novel, and how to write about characters. Cunningham mentioned that he thought one of the characters, Laura Brown, a 1950s housewife, would be the easiest to write because she was based in part on his own mother. Instead, Laura Brown proved the most difficult; she just wasn't coming alive on the page. It wasn't until Cunningham decided to give her a creative vocation and a goal—baking the perfect birthday cake for her husband—that the character came alive.

Needs, wants, desires, motivations … these are the things that can help translate real people, including yourself, to the page. Think about what you desire. Or what the people you write about in nonfiction desire. What are their needs and wants?

"There is no object of desire quite like a house," writes Meghan Daum in her memoir, *Life Would Be Perfect if I Lived in That House*. "Few things in this world are capable of eliciting such urgent, even painful, yearning." The book chronicles Daum's lifelong quest for what she labels "an ineffable state of being I can only describe as domestic integrity," symbolized by the perfect house. This desire is the driving force of the narrative and of Daum's character in the memoir.

Desire is also at the heart of Susan Orlean's *The Orchid Thief: A True Story of Beauty and Obsession*. "To desire orchids is to have a desire that will never be, can never be, fully requited," writes Orlean. From the Victorian orchid hunters who risked life and limb in their pursuit of these complex plants to the main character, John Laroche, whose passion for obsessively collecting nonhuman things in general and orchids in particular causes him to break laws, desire drives the book and the real characters in it.

JUMPSTART

Write about the time you desired something or someone just out of reach. What or whom did you want? Show us the yearning on paper by writing at least two pages without censoring yourself or stopping.

Physical Description: It's in the Details

Mr. Clutter "cut a man's man figure," writes Truman Capote in his nonfictional novel *In Cold Blood: A True Account of a Multiple Murder and Its Consequences.* "His shoulders were broad, his hair had held its dark color, his square-jawed, confident face retained a healthy-hued youthfulness, and his teeth, unstained and strong enough to shatter walnuts, were still intact." It doesn't surprise us that this man weighs the same as he did when he graduated from college decades before. Nor that Clutter doesn't smoke and eschews coffee, tea, alcohol, and stimulants of all kinds. Capote's description highlights Clutter's integrity; he's a Methodist, a temperate man, a successful farmer, and a community leader. Who would want to slit his throat and then shoot him, his wife, and two of their children in cold blood?

When you write about characters, you will include physical description but always in the service of a particular point of view. For example, Orlean writes in *The Orchid Thief,* "John Laroche is a tall guy, skinny as a stick, pale-eyed, slouch-shouldered, and sharply handsome, in spite of the fact that he is missing all his front teeth." The description captures the essence of Laroche: he's attractive, yet there's something off about him.

In addition, clothing can really help make the man or woman you're describing. If you're writing about an art teacher who always wears long, flowing skirts and is a colorful dresser, combining apple-green tights with a purple plaid jacket, such details (assuming, of course, they are true) can help capture her colorful, bohemian character. Similarly, a person who wears a black wool coat, black pants, and long sleeves, no matter the weather, may suggest a person who is uncomfortable revealing herself.

WRITERS' WORDS

"The difference between the almost right word and the right word is really a large matter—it's the difference between the lightning bug and the lightning."

—Mark Twain, American author and humorist

Using Specific Descriptive Words

If you're writing about a first date with someone who brought you flowers, you'd want to mention the kind of flowers. Were they deep red roses, indicating his passionate intentions? Were they wildflowers he picked for you on a motorcycle ride when he was thinking of you? When you have the opportunity to use a specific noun, such as "roses" as opposed to "flowers," you should always seize it.

Your goal is always to "show" rather than "tell" in description, but this description should be in service of a central idea. For instance, does the man you are describing wear Lee or Wrangler jeans? This can make a difference if he's a rodeo king, where Wranglers are considered *de riguer.*

With all physical detail, you use it on a need-to-know basis. Ask yourself: does your reader need to know that the person you are describing prefers to dress in pastel colors rather than earth tones? If so, include this detail. If not, leave it out.

Here are some questions to ask yourself when portraying real people:

- What physical traits help define them?
- What do you notice about their posture? The way they walk, eat, or carry themselves?
- What kind of clothing do they typically wear?
- Do they have a characteristic habit, such as laughing when nervous, biting their nails, or chewing on a shirt collar?
- Do they have other revealing actions, such as always being late or never offering to pay for dinner?
- What do other people think of them?

WRITERS' WORDS

"What is character but the determination of incident? What is incident but the illustration of character?"

—Henry James, American novelist

Using Dialogue to Capture Character

Another way to capture real people is to let them speak in their own words. You do this by including dialogue. Although you can't create dialogue out of thin air, and you probably haven't carried a tape recorder around your entire life, you can re-create dialogue— remembering what a person said—to the best of your ability.

Using dialogue not only reveals character but also moves the narrative along quicker and tells the reader, "Hey, pay attention to this. This stuff in quotation marks is important." So when you use dialogue, ask yourself if it's absolutely crucial to conveying character or if it's better to say it another way, by indirectly reporting what the person said.

Conversation's Greatest Hits

You want your characters to speak just like real people do in your nonfiction, but that doesn't mean you transcribe everything they say word for word and use it. "Dialogue is not conversation," says short-story writer Amy Bloom; rather, "it is conversation's greatest hits." Not every spoken word will make it into your nonfiction; the trick is separating the best hits from the unmemorable and thus forgettable.

So how do you write dialogue's greatest hits? One way is to practice. Writing is like exercising; the more you do it, the better you get. And learning to pay attention to how people speak also requires exercising your muscles: the listening muscles.

Here's one exercise I always give my students to help them capture the rhythms of ordinary speech: Go somewhere, whether it's a café, restaurant, or shopping mall, where you can eavesdrop unobtrusively. Write down word for word what you overhear. Don't worry if you don't get it all down; you probably won't. Just write as fast and as much as you can. Monologues are fine, too. If someone is talking loudly and openly enough on her cell phone in a public place, then I think it's fair game to practice writing down what she's saying. Do this exercise at least three times in three different locations. See if you get better at both writing down what you hear and listening for the juiciest, most telling parts—conversation's greatest hits.

Now take a look at your eavesdropping. What did you capture? What do you notice about the way people talk? Is it in complete sentences? Are there a lot of verbal tics, like "ums" or "likes"? Lots of profanities? Or maybe shorthand like "OMG" or "LOL!"? As you're looking critically at your eavesdropping, what do you think must be omitted to make the dialogue readable? What part is memorable and revealing of character? What parts are not? Is there anything else you have to add—body language, for instance, or the setting of the conversation—that would help add to the characterization?

There are certainly much less labor-intensive ways to record conversation. And, as a nonfiction writer working in the twenty-first century, you can make use of tools other than pen and paper: smartphones, tape recorders, iPhone apps, all of which we'll cover in Chapter 8 on interviewing.

But I still suggest you keep pen and paper handy so you can keep your ears open at parties, work meetings, or the PTA. You never know when someone will reveal something telling through speech. And don't be surprised, too, if you find that writing dialogue makes you a better listener.

Re-creating Dialogue

But what if you're writing a memoir or a personal essay, and you're trying to recall a conversation that took place years ago before smartphones? Or maybe when you were 10 and didn't have that tape recorder handy? It's possible to put yourself back in time, to practice hearing others in your life, almost as if you were eavesdropping on them today.

Fiction writer Alice Hoffman beautifully channels her grandmother in her short essay "Advice from My Grandmother." The piece is a moving tribute that captures her grandmother's character solely through one long monologue of the things Hoffman's grandmother must have habitually said. Hoffman begins, "When crossing the street, never trust the judgment of drivers. They may not stop for you. They may roll over you and keep going. In fact, never trust anyone. They're not your family, their blood is not half as thick as water, why would you take their advice?"

Try this for yourself. Think of people you know well. Channel their voices by thinking of the kinds of things they frequently say. What advice do they give? What are their complaints or favorite expressions or topics of conversation? Write down everything you can think of, and don't worry if it doesn't make sense. Try your mother first. Then your father or sister.

JUMPSTART

Pick someone you know well: your mother, your mother-in-law, your spouse, or your boss. Write a dialogue of the two of you talking about something significant, perhaps an argument or disagreement. Write down everything you can remember that was said during the actual conversation. How much can you recall?

Here are some tips for writing dialogue:

- Always use "said" or "says" for tag lines. Don't worry about overusing the word; it is unobtrusive and most readers' brains will gloss over it. They will get hung up on words like "exclaimed," "sputtered," "laughed, or "sighed," so unless you are writing children's books or romance novels, avoid those tag lines. You can also use other unobtrusive words like "explains," "states," or "adds," but for the most part, "says" works just fine.

- Avoid quoting information for information's sake. That is, don't quote dialogue that has too many names, dates, logistics, or other information that you could just as easily provide as exposition.

- Don't quote small talk or simple "yes/no" questions such as, "I asked her if she'd like a cup of coffee. 'Yes,' she said. 'With milk and sugar.'"

- Prune the verbal tics. Too many "ums," "uhs," and "likes" can get annoying. While you want to capture the way someone habitually speaks, a few "likes" go a long way.

- Ask yourself: Is this necessary dialogue? Does it reveal something about the person? If not, paraphrase by putting it in your own words or leave it out.

- Smooth the language to make it read grammatically. We speak mostly in fragments. Often we say introductory clauses at the end of the sentence or don't always get a verb tense right. You are allowed to alter the language a bit to make sense grammatically.

- Add your own words of explanation in brackets if necessary. "I can't fix [her statement] if I don't understand what she says," is made clearer if you specify what "it" is.

- Don't overdo the dialect. Yes, you must be truthful to the way another person speaks, but just as with verbal tics, if you include too much dialect you run the risk of caricaturizing your character rather than capturing him.

How to Write Respectfully About Real People

The thorny issue of how to write about real people as characters without offending them comes up over and over again in nonfiction writing seminars. What are the rules? How do you write about someone who is living without risking your relationship? Is it better to wait until that person is dead before you turn him or her into a character in nonfiction?

I don't think it gets easier to write truthfully after someone has died; memories of loved ones can be just as inhibiting as the thought of what flesh-and-blood people will say. And you never know how someone will react to what you write. I've heard from fiction writers who wrote that people were offended when they *couldn't* recognize themselves as characters, and some nonfiction writers say that some of their most flattering portrayals of loved ones yielded unexpected acrimony.

 PITFALL AHEAD

Every writer must weigh what to reveal about friends and family and what to keep private. The issue can get even thornier when writing about children. Ask yourself: How will you feel in five years when the information is still out there? How would you react if you were the person being portrayed?

Memoirist and writing teacher Adair Lara stated that if she could go back in time, she wouldn't have written her memoir, *Hold Me Close, Let Me Go: A Mother, a Daughter and an Adolescence Survived*. Though her daughter gave her permission for the book, "it wasn't my story to tell," writes Lara, particularly as the book centered on her daughter's rocky adolescence.

Doing Unto Others

Memoirist and writing instructor Bill Roorbach abides by a simple motto when using real people as characters. "DO UNTO OTHERS AS YOU WOULD HAVE OTHERS DO UNTO YOU

[Roorbach's emphasis]," he states in *Writing Life Stories: How to Make Memories into Memoirs, Ideas into Essays, and Life into Literature.*

Nothing smacks of self-righteousness more than having an axe to grind in nonfiction. Your reader will pick up on this and have little patience if you are writing to settle a score or enacting a form of vengeance through character assassination. But if you are fair and respectful, if you let people speak for themselves in a way that captures them accurately but not meanly, then you are abiding by a golden rule.

Changing Names to Protect the Innocent

But what about changing the names of your characters so they can't recognize themselves? Or writing under a pseudonym so that you can write without fear of retribution by a friend or family member?

I see nothing wrong with changing the name of real people to protect them. It happens frequently, even in journalism. Let's say you are writing an article for a woman's magazine about women who have cheated on their husbands, and, as true for most magazines, you need to find "real women" sources willing to tell their stories. Granting these women anonymity by changing their names is fine (if your editor approves and if you let the reader know in the article) and often is the only way you'll get the story.

In writing my article about the women in jail, though I had media releases from the women and permission to use their real names, I decided to use pseudonyms. I just felt that at some point in time they might regret this decision, and as I could see no benefit to revealing their true identities, I changed the names. In my blog for womansday.com, I chose to use pseudonyms for my husband and son (though hardly creative ones), as I felt it gave me some distance to write about them and gave them some sense of anonymity. Especially my son, who at age 8 did not ask to be in a blog.

While Ted Conover uses real names for some of the people in his book *Newjack: Guarding Sing Sing*, he also states at the outset that "to protect the privacy of certain officers and inmates, I have made up the following names for real people," and he lists 48 made-up names.

Conover also states he did not make up scenes, but he did have to re-create dialogue.

PITFALL AHEAD

Be wary of using a pseudonym for yourself in nonfiction. Since the reader trusts you are telling the truth, using a pseudonym implies you have something to hide.

Conflating Characters

Let's say you are writing about your favorite aunt, but you decide to take the characteristics of your father's twin sisters and combine them into one ideal aunt, making a composite character. Is this allowed in nonfiction? It's certainly done. I've read books where the author says that to disguise the characters she has created composite figures, conflating the characteristics of several people into one person. Or that he's changed certain distinguishing details to make the person unrecognizable.

"[D]on't round corners—or compress situations or characters—*unnecessarily*," writes the "godfather" of creative nonfiction, Lee Gutkind, in an article titled "The Creative Nonfiction Police?" "Rounding the corners" is also the expression John Berendt used to describe making up transitions to ensure the narrative read more smoothly in his novel, *Midnight in the Garden of Good and Evil*.

Ultimately, it's up to you and your conscience whether or not you want to write composite characters or "round the corners" in this way. I personally don't like it. It seems dishonest. When I read nonfiction, my pact with the writer is that she is telling the truth, the whole truth, and nothing but the truth. If I find that the character is a composite of several people, I ask, why didn't he write fiction? For me as a reader, you've lost me at the word "composite."

The Least You Need to Know

- Characters in nonfiction are not based on real people; they are real people and are the soul of nonfiction writing.

- In autobiographical nonfiction writing, you are the main character, but it's not your entire self you're putting on the page; rather, depending on the story you're telling, it is you at a certain time and place.

- You can capture real people outwardly by using specific descriptive words to illustrate physical traits, and inwardly by showing them wrestling with a conflict or desiring something.

- Use only unobtrusive words—primarily "said" or "says"—for tag lines when writing dialogue. Anything else can sound melodramatic.

- You are allowed to re-create dialogue from memory to the best of your ability, but you should never create new dialogue.

- Be fair and respectful when writing about real people. It's a good policy to write about others as you would have them write about you.

Truth, Lies, and Nonfiction

In This Chapter

- Can you make things up in nonfiction?
- Stretching the boundaries of nonfiction
- Establishing your credibility as a narrator
- What you owe your readers

When you write nonfiction, no one makes you swear that what you're writing is the truth, the whole truth, and nothing but the truth. But I believe you should keep that pledge in mind. Your credibility as a narrator is on the line when you write nonfiction. But truth—particularly the "truth" of a situation that's recollected from memory—can be somewhat slippery. We all know that memory is a fallible faculty and it's not like accessing a computer file. Just ask any siblings how they remember an event from childhood and you're bound to get different answers. That's fine. As long as you're writing your experience as best you know it, as truthfully as you can, and admitting what you don't know, your reader will believe you.

Of course, you've probably heard of those writers—particularly in the memoir category—who play fast and loose with the fiction/nonfiction categories. Sometimes it's for comedic effect, sometimes it's at the risk of public shaming. Why do they do it? Perhaps because memoirs seem to be the preferred choice of readers these days. Memoirs pay more. But some publishers have been duped, and readers and talk show hosts outraged. What, if anything, is fair to fudge in nonfiction? What's not? Will the nonfiction police come after you? The answers to these questions are in this chapter.

Did It Really Happen?

I still remember the workshop where one of my students brought in a short memoir he'd written about his childhood in England. This was a student who was an excellent writer, whose work we were all eager to read every week for his use of telling details to capture a vivid picture of life in a small British town 65 years ago, as well as for his realistic dialogue, captivating real characters, and poignant musings. As he was reading the piece aloud and describing a scene on a bus where as a young boy he was trying to conceal a puppy in a paper bag, I noticed the other students shifting in their seats. The puppy on the bus didn't seem right. It didn't feel right. We could all sense it. And it wasn't right. The student confessed to making up this detail. He'd wanted to "lighten the mood" of a dark story, he said, and thought the puppy would do the trick. It didn't.

When you write nonfiction, your credibility and reputation are on the line. You're absolutely not allowed to make things up. Though there is no "creative nonfiction police," in Lee Gutkind's words, there are ethical considerations. You've made a pact with the reader that what you've written is the whole truth as you know it. Of course, there are writers who take liberties with the form, but they usually get caught.

Taking Liberties with the Truth

Take the public shaming of James Frey on *The Oprah Winfrey Show* in 2006, when she found out that his bestselling memoir *A Million Little Pieces*, which detailed Frey's addiction to drugs and alcohol and his subsequent recovery, was part fiction. Frey admitted to fabricating information about his characters and the amount of time he'd spent in jail—a few hours rather than a few months. Oprah said that she and her millions of readers felt betrayed.

The New York Times journalist Jason Blair resigned in 2003 when it was discovered that he had plagiarized from other journalists' work and made up quotations for the parts he hadn't plagiarized. Stephen Glass, of *The New Republic* magazine, was similarly exposed for fabricating events and quotations in 27 of the 41 articles he wrote for the magazine.

WRITERS' WORDS

"[M]emory has its own story to tell. But I have done my best to make it tell a truthful story."

—Tobias Wolff, American author known for his memoirs and short stories

Then there are the memoirs that are completely false. Margaret B. Jones' *Love and Consequences* (2008) was pulled from the shelves (and readers offered a refund) when it was found out that the author, Margaret Seltzer, was neither part American Indian nor raised in foster homes in gang-ridden South Central Los Angeles, but instead was Caucasian and raised by her biological family in a prosperous Los Angeles suburb. In Misha Defonseca's *Misha: A Mémoire of the Holocaust Years* (1997), the main character turned out not to have traveled 1,900 miles across Europe as a young girl, ending up in a Warsaw ghetto where she lived with wolves and killed a Nazi soldier. Rather, she was Catholic, not Jewish, and attended school rather than trekking alone through Europe.

The Media Fallout

"It's publishing's version of *Groundhog Day*," writes reporter Malcolm Jones in *The Daily Beast* of the proliferation of phony memoirs. "Must publishers fall for the same scam again and again?" he asks. Part of the reason is that memoirs sell.

As recently as 2011, nonfiction writer Jon Krakauer exposed the financial and literary crimes of bestselling author Greg Mortenson, whose *Three Cups of Tea*, an account of building schools in Afghanistan and Pakistan, Krakauer renamed "Three Cups of Deceit: How Greg Mortenson, Humanitarian Hero, Lost His Way." In his expose (available on byliner.com), Krakauer shows the falsehoods behind the man and the book. Mortenson was not captured by the Taliban as he claims, and he plays fast and loose with the funds he raised for his charity, the Central Asia Institute, spending them on promoting the book rather than building schools, according to Krakauer.

Yet at least one critic, Laura Miller of Salon.com, does not find Mortenson guilty of nonfiction writing crimes. "*Three Cups of Tea* belongs to that category of inspirational nonfiction in which feel-good parables take precedence over strict truthfulness," she writes. "Its object is to present a reassuring picture of the world as a place where all people are fundamentally the same underneath their cultural differences, where Americans can 'make a difference' in the lives of poor Central Asians and fend off terrorism at the same time. Heartwarming anecdotes come with the territory, and as with the happily-ever-after endings of romantic comedies, everyone tacitly agrees not to examine them too closely."

I believe that examining these anecdotes closely for the truth *is* the job of the nonfiction writer—and of the fact-checker before the book goes to publication. So while Miller thinks it's an overreaction to put Mortenson in the same camp as James Frey and claims the ends of his actions justify the means, Krakauer and others, like myself, believe firmly that the line between fiction and nonfiction should not be crossed. Or if it is, why not say that the events are "based on a true story" rather than *are* a true story?

Stretching the Forms of Nonfiction

At the risk of sounding contradictory, there are writers who stretch the boundaries of nonfiction in ways that I don't mind. Author David Sedaris is one. Though not everyone thinks his work should be labeled nonfiction, almost everyone agrees it's very, very funny.

Comedy and Exaggeration

In 2007, *The New Republic* magazine called David Sedaris on the carpet for stretching the truth. In his review titled "This American Lie," a riff on "This American Life," the NPR radio show where

Sedaris got his first big break reading his SantaLand Diaries, a hilarious account of working as a Macy's elf, Alex Heard sets about fact-checking Sedaris's collection of essays *Naked*, particularly his stint as an adolescent working in Dix Hills, a North Carolina mental hospital. Heard finds one nurse who claims that Sedaris is "lying through his teeth" about his duties there. Heard even checks in with Sedaris, who tells him something different than what he wrote in the piece. "That cleared it up," writes Heard. "Everything in *Naked* is true, except for the parts that weren't." And despite the fact that Heard thinks "Sedaris exaggerates too much for a writer using the nonfiction label," he's still mostly a fan of his work.

When asked whether he exaggerates by a reporter for *Mother Jones* magazine, Sedaris replied, "Boy, do I. And if it weren't for *The New Yorker* fact-checkers, I'd do it more."

WRITERS' WORDS

"When I set out to write a memoir, I decided to fact-check my life using the prosaic tools of journalism .... I decided to go back and ask the people who were there ..."

—David Carr, American journalist, on fact-checking his memoir as a drug addict in *The Night of the Gun: A Reporter Investigates the Darkest Story of His Life: His Own*

So why call it nonfiction? Nonfiction sells more than fiction, says former *San Francisco Chronicle* book editor Oscar Villalon. Also, if you label your work nonfiction, you don't have to work quite so hard to convince your reader to have a "willing suspension of disbelief" as you would in fiction. "It's one thing to make mistakes of memory or reporting," writes Villalon, "but it's entirely another to knowingly bend the truth or create composite characters or make up events and facts in any nonfiction. No excuse, none."

In his story about his Greek grandmother, "Get Your Ya-Ya's Out," Sedaris writes this portrait of Ya Ya: "She wasn't senile or vindictive, she just had her own way of doing things and couldn't understand what all the fuss was about. What was wrong with kneading bread dough on the kitchen floor? Who says a newborn baby shouldn't sleep with a colossal wooden cross wedged inside the crib? Why not treat your waist-length hair with olive oil? Why stains on the sofa? I don't know what you're talking about."

Even Sedaris's father, according to Heard, thought the portrayal stretched the truth and was not all that pleased with it, though he was later convinced by his other children that the story was "funny" and let it go at that.

From picking dandelions from the neighbor's yard to talking about her goldfish "having a suicide," Sedaris's Ya Ya is a funny, if not altogether believable, character. Yet in full disclosure, I had a Greek grandmother who did indeed pick dandelions from the neighbors' yards to boil and eat. And honestly, I don't find his portrayal all that distant from reality.

But when I am reading Sedaris, whose prose and humor are idiosyncratic, I understand that while he may sacrifice the "literal truth" for comic effect, underneath there is an emotional layer of truth that he doesn't fabricate. Sound contradictory? It is. But I'm not the only reader willing to grant Sedaris such nonfiction latitude: he has his defenders among editors and writers who find that nonfictional humor should be judged by a different standard.

Imagining Things When You Weren't There

Jo Ann Beard brilliantly re-creates the last two years of a real person's life, Cheri Tremble, as well as the moments before her Dr. Kevorkian–assisted suicide, in an essay *The New Yorker* pulled because it didn't fit the magazine's nonfiction criteria. Beard, whose interview you can read in Appendix B, blends fiction and nonfiction in many of her nonfictional essays, and yet I believe she's doing something so unique with the nonfiction form that, rather than violating its rules, she's pushing its limits.

Beard's poignant and one-of-kind essay, "Undertaker, Please Drive Slow," published in the literary magazine *Tin House*, comes with an editor's warning to the reader that once you read it "you may never be the same." In the piece, written from the third person point of view, Beard imagines what goes through Tremble's head in the moments before she dies. As the IV drugs that will kill her begin to take effect, Tremble imagines "a Mexican lizard on an adobe wall, panting like a dog; a pair of dusty ankles; her father in a sport coat nuzzling a kitten; her brother Sean with a sparkler, framed against a night sky, spelling out her name with big cursive flourishes, the letters disappearing even as they are written."

I agree with the *Tin House* editor's assessment about not being the same after reading the essay. I wasn't. And while Beard does not adhere to all the criteria of nonfiction writing, she does something with the form that is neither fiction nor quite nonfiction, but that I'd put in the ballpark of the latter. Again, I contradict myself, but in certain cases, I find that this deliberate pushing of the boundaries of nonfiction—and letting the reader know you're doing it—is not dishonest but fascinating and gets at a truth more than fiction.

Deconstructing the Memoir

"This is a work of fiction," writes Dave Eggers on the copyright page of his 2000 bestselling memoir, *A Heartbreaking Work of Staggering Genius*, "only in that in many cases, the author could not remember the exact words said by certain people, and exact descriptions of certain things, so had to fill in the gaps as best he could. Otherwise, all characters and incidents and dialogue are real ...." He later says that "All events described herein actually happened," though he's taken certain small liberties with the chronology of events "because that is his right as an American."

So is it fiction? Or nonfiction? Sometimes when reading Eggers, I think of the old commercial for margarine, "I can't believe it's not butter." For Eggers calls attention to the way he plays with truth and fiction in this memoir, often commenting on the form itself and the readers' expectations. He writes that the dialogue has "been almost entirely reconstructed" but that it's all "essentially true." He admits to changing the name of a character and making him an "amalgam" and to compressing time.

Does calling attention to these liberties make you believe the "truth" of Eggers' memoir more or less? Are you content to put the book in the nonfiction camp when you know that these liberties have been taken? If not, Eggers invites the reader to "PRETEND IT'S FICTION [Eggers' emphasis].

The playful tone, the breaking of traditional narrative by including long introductory material, including "Rules and Suggestions for Enjoyment of this Book" and a list of themes and omitted passages make the book certainly one of "jest," according to reviewers, but also brilliant, funny, and "raw and real." While there's no denying the basic truth of the events of his memoir—both parents dying of cancer within a few weeks of each other and Eggers raising his 7-year-old brother as a result—the fact that it doesn't strictly follow nonfiction writing "rules" makes it less easy to classify.

Yet again, I give this book a nonfiction pass, not only because Eggers calls attention to what he's doing, but also because it is so well done and still packs an emotional truth. If Eggers were less up front about his blurring of fiction and nonfiction, if he deliberately tried to hoodwink the reader, then I would be far less inclined to do so.

JUMPSTART

Memory begets memory. The more you write, the more you'll remember. Try this exercise from Anne Lamott. Pick a year in your life—the year you turned 10, the first year of your marriage, the year you got your driver's license. Put "I remember" at the top of the page, and brainstorm everything you can think of about that year. What songs were playing on the radio? Who was your best friend? What clothing was fashionable?

Establishing Your Credibility

The persona you establish on the page is that of the narrator. It's not you but rather you at a certain time, place, and age. With these exceptions, you may be wondering, just how do you establish your credibility as a narrator so that the reader trusts you're telling the truth? With honesty about yourself and your feelings, by admitting ignorance, and by probing not just what you think but why and what it means.

Best-selling writer Mary Roach states in her book *Spook: Science Tackles the Afterlife* that she "begins a project from a state of near absolute ignorance." And it is this narrator, one who is unafraid to admit what she doesn't know, who charms the reader.

What lies at the heart of all good nonfiction writing, says nonfiction guru William Zinsser, is "the personal transaction" in which the writer reveals him- or herself with honesty and warmth. "Ultimately the product that any writer has to sell is not the subject being written about, but who he or she is," writes Zinsser. And that saleable product depends on you being a credible, truthful writer.

Admitting What You Don't Know

Be honest about what you know and don't know. There's nothing wrong with not remembering something and admitting this to the reader. In memoirist Meghan Daum's book *Life Would Be Perfect if I Lived in That House*, about the crazy real estate market before the housing crisis, she states that both she and another house-hunting friend felt ill after seeing ridiculous prices for modest and rundown houses. "[O]ne of us said she felt like throwing up, and the other said she felt like crying," Daum writes. "I can't remember which of us said what, but I do remember that this trip was the beginning of the end of our house-hunting phase." A few paragraphs later, Daum "invents" dialogue from this friend about why they feel like they always come to things too late. "'Because we're Gen X,' she said. 'We were born both too late and too early. The economic forces conspired against us ....' Daum then admits, "She didn't exactly say that, but she came close and might as well have."

What is wrong with admitting what you don't know? Nothing. That will often make you a more, not less, reliable and believable narrator. You're also allowed to "invent" things that might have occurred if you alert the reader and if the things are in keeping with what you think probably happened.

For instance, when Scott Russell Sanders, in his essay "Under the Influence," writes about when his alcoholic father resumed drinking after being sober for 15 years, he imagines the scene. His father had just retired from his factory job. He and Sanders' mother were moving to a new house in a new state. The van was loaded when "the sweaty movers broke open a six-pack and offered him a beer," writes Sanders. "'Let's drink to retirement!' they crowed. 'Let's drink to freedom! to fishing! hunting! loafing! Let's drink to a guy who's going home!'"

"At least I imagine some such words," states Sanders, "for that is all I can do, imagine, and I see Father's hand trembling in midair as he thinks about the fifteen sober years and the doctors' warning, and he tells himself, *Goddamnit, I am a free man*, and *Why can't a free man drink one beer after a lifetime of hard work?* and I see his arm reaching, his fingers closing, the can tilting to his lips."

Did the scene happen? Perhaps not. But the essay describes similar scenes in which his father is drinking or has broken promises, so it rings true. In addition, Sanders uses phrases like "at least I imagine" to let you know he's not making it up and passing it off as if he were there. "I even supply a label for the beer," he states, and you know you are in the hands of not only a reliable narrator but also one who feels, observes, thinks, and agonizes deeply.

Using Conditional Words to Signal the Reader

It's fine to "make things up" in the way that Sanders does, as long as you signal this to the reader and as long as it's in keeping with probability, so much so that if you were a betting person, you'd win the bet that the words were spoken or the event actually occurred.

Perhaps you want to put words in a character's mouth that you didn't hear but is probably something she'd say. Or reconstruct a scene when you weren't there. This is "allowed" if it rings true and you alert your reader. I'd be wary of using these words too frequently, however, as you won't look like a narrator who has a very good memory. And too many conditionals will make your prose read in a wishy-washy fashion.

Here are some conditional phrases to use when you want to write about an event when you weren't there:

- I imagine
- It could be

- Perhaps
- It's likely
- It might have happened like
- It may be
- I suppose

JUMPSTART

Pick an event from your past for which you don't know all the details. Write at the top, "I don't remember …" and just keep writing for two pages. You may be surprised that you remember more than you thought. How could you "re-create" what you don't know so that it is believable?

Re-creating from Memory

No one says you must have an infallible memory to be a nonfiction writer. It's assumed that you are re-creating dialogue from memory if you're writing autobiographical nonfiction. But you must try to the best of your ability to remember dialogue and events.

Sometimes your memories will not jibe with others'. That's okay. It's your story to tell. For example, I remember that it was me who backed into a tree while trying to parallel park on one of my driving tests. My sister remembers that it was she who lightly tapped the tree and received her third automatic failure. If I ever use this story, I may include both versions because I know them.

WRITERS' WORDS

"Still, memory is not, fundamentally, a repository. If it were, no question would arise about its accuracy, no argument would be fought over its notorious imprecision."

—Patricia Hampl, American author and memoirist

What Do You Owe Your Readers?

If you're writing autobiographical nonfiction, you owe your readers the truth as best you can remember it. But what if you're writing about an event when you weren't there? What can you do? Are you always bound to write about things that you yourself experienced? No. My advice is to think like a journalist: research and interview (skills I'll cover in Chapters 7 and 8) to find out all the information you can, and admit what you don't know.

To that end, you can look at Sebastian Junger's "Foreword" to his book *The Perfect Storm: A True Story of Men Against the Sea* as a model for how to solve the problem many nonfiction writers face: how to write scenes when you aren't there. "*Recreating* the last days of six men who disappeared at sea presented some obvious problems for me," Junger states. "On the one hand, I wanted to write a completely factual book that would stand on its own as a piece of journalism. On the other hand, I didn't want the narrative to asphyxiate under a mass of technical detail and conjecture." Though Junger states that he "toyed with the idea of fictionalizing minor parts of the story—conversations, personal thoughts, day-to-day routines—to make it more readable," he decided that this would undercut the facts he did find.

Ultimately, Junger decided to use his journalistic skills to come as close as he could to the actual scene. "If I didn't know exactly what happened aboard the doomed boat, for example, I would interview people who had been through similar situations and survived. Their experiences, I felt, would provide a fairly good description of what the six men on the *Andrea Gail* had gone through, and said, and perhaps even felt." In this way, Junger respects not only the form of nonfiction, but also, and perhaps most importantly, the memories of the real people he characterizes.

Compressing Time

There is another compression, that of time, which means rearranging the order of events for the sake of the narrative or packing events closer together when in reality they didn't occur that way. Say, for example, you are writing about a terrible Tuesday, and you condense several mishaps that occurred over a span of several days into one horrendous day. That's compressing time.

Or perhaps you're writing a memoir that takes place over several years, and you decide to move one event that happened in March into January, where it "fits" the narrative better. This, again, is compressing time.

John Berendt admitted to setting some events before others in his 1994 bestselling "nonfiction" novel, *Midnight in the Garden of Good and Evil*, which was based on a true murder in Savannah, Georgia. Compressing time can keep the tension of your narrative, but again, unless you tell your reader what you're doing, you run the risk of not being a credible nonfiction writer.

Principles for Writing Nonfiction

Though he claims not to be "the nonfiction police," Gutkind does establish a checklist for nonfiction writers that is handy for when you're dealing with the thornier issues of where the boundaries lay.

Here are four principles to keep in mind, according to Gutkind:

- Strive for the truth. Tell your story as accurately as you can remember.
- Don't make up dialogue or things your characters may be thinking, unless you ask them.
- Don't round corners or compress situations or characters *unnecessarily*. Or at all, really.
- Show your work to those you write about before you publish.

This last one is tricky. Some writers do and some don't. Annie Dillard, in *To Fashion a Text*, writes that she "tried to leave out anything that might trouble [her] family." She states, "Everybody I'm writing about is alive and well, and in full possession of their faculties, and possibly willing to sue." So what does she do? Dillard shows her family her books before publication and takes out anything anyone objects to. Writing is not the place to "air grievances," states Dillard, who says she cautions young writers that "while literature is an art, it's not a martial art."

> **PITFALL AHEAD**
>
> American memoirist Patricia Hampl writes in her essay, "Other People's Secrets," how she betrayed her mother by writing about her mother's illness in an autobiographical poem. Though her mother ultimately gave Hampl permission to publish the poem, she did so reluctantly and out of love for her daughter, not because she approved. When you ask friends or loved ones for permission before you publish, you gamble on them saying no, but also on them saying yes for the wrong reasons. If you choose to get permission, make sure your motives are clear.

I was once asked by an editor of a major magazine, whom I'd met at a conference, to send her an essay on doing couples therapy with my sister, something I'd mentioned to her in a pitch session. She was quite enthusiastic about the topic and even tracked me down after she left one publication and moved to another. While it's true that I had mentioned the subject, I was less sanguine about writing about this particularly painful chapter in my personal history. But I knew that even before I could consider writing the essay, I needed to get my sister's permission, which she gladly gave. I even promised to send my sister the rough draft and have her approve every word before it went into publication. She declined, saying that she didn't want to revisit that unhappy time in our lives. I wrote the essay and sent it to the editor, and thankfully, it got killed by a new senior editor. I was hesitant writing it, and that probably showed in the prose. But in any case, my conscience told me that the right thing was to get permission first.

What is the right thing for you? Only you can decide. I tell my students to write everything—especially in the first draft—and not worry as they're writing who will see it (easier said than done, I know). I had one student who wrote about her conflicted feelings for someone else during her husband's cancer treatment. I advised her to write everything, to get it all down, which she did. She later not only deleted the files, but also reformatted her hard drive. She did not want to take any chances, no matter how slim, that her husband could read what she'd written.

The Least You Need to Know

- Unlike with fiction, when writing nonfiction you cannot make up events or details that aren't true.

- Though there have been journalists and memoirists who have plagiarized, invented quotations, and even written entire phony memoirs, they usually get caught and lose all credibility.

- Some writers, particularly memoirists, take liberties with the form of nonfiction, stretching the boundaries through humor, imagination, or playfulness.

- Your credibility is on the line when you write nonfiction. Doing research and interviewing to fill in the blanks when you were not there, and admitting when you don't know something, makes you a believable, reliable, truthful narrator.

- Some nonfiction writers show their family and friends what they write before publication and give them veto power over the narrative.

Scene Setting and Summary

Chapter

6

In This Chapter

- Understanding how to write a scene
- Thinking through your senses
- Capturing place
- When to show and when to tell in nonfiction writing

The best writers do it all the time: they write in scenes, making things real for the reader. "Scenes are the building blocks of creative nonfiction," writes Lee Gutkind, "the primary factor that separates and defines literary and/or creative nonfiction from traditional journalism and ordinary lifeless prose." Think of a scene as the ultimate place where you show and not tell, where you make something so real that the reader cannot help but feel as if she or he is there.

As a reader, you know when you've gotten to a scene in a book or article. You find the pace of the narrative picking up. Your heart beats a little faster because you're experiencing the action. Scenes usually include dialogue; they use active verbs, and generally dramatize a conflict. And they move the narrative forward.

So how do you write a scene that is three dimensional? This chapter will show you. We'll also explore how to capture a physical place by thinking through your senses. And you'll learn when to show and when to tell in your nonfiction—and when to do both. Ready to think like a cinematographer? Read on.

Lights! Camera! Action!

What is a scene? Think of yourself as a film director instructing the cameraperson to zoom in and capture the action in real time. That's a scene. Now think about how you might convey background information. Maybe in a voiceover where there isn't any action? That would be a summary or exposition. All nonfiction moves by alternating scene and summary.

We think in scenes all the time, so there's nothing to fear in writing scenes. Think back to the most memorable times in your life. You probably recall them in scenes. The moment you held your baby for the first time. The night your husband proposed. The time you dove off the 30-foot-high diving board and how your knees shook as you looked down fearing you were plunging to your death.

In a scene the events you're writing about always occurs in real time and place. Without these anchors, you could be writing a summary or giving background material, but you're not dramatizing something in real time.

Orienting Your Reader in Time

If you begin by indicating a specific time and day, you're almost guaranteed to plunge the reader into a scene. Can you picture the following from the late essay writer Caroline Knapp's essay, "Solitude in the Culture of 'We'"?

> Nine forty-five P.M. I am standing in my kitchen preparing my very favorite meal, a zesty blend of wheat flakes, Muslix, and raisins that comforts me deeply. It is a Thursday, which means that *ER* is on in 15 minutes, and it is mid-May—sweeps month—which means that I am filled with anticipation: yes, a new episode. I feel serene. I am wearing torn leggings, a T-shirt, a bathrobe. The dog is in the living room, curled contently (and wordlessly) on the sofa; the phone machine is blinking with several messages, which I've dutifully screened and have no intention of answering until tomorrow. And a thought comes to me,

a simple statement of fact that arrives in a fully formed sentence. I hear the words:

I am the Merry Recluse.

Are you in the kitchen with Knapp? I am. What makes this scene so vivid? Part of it has to do with Knapp's use of the present tense: "I am standing," "It is a Thursday," "I am wearing," "a thought comes." You don't always have to use the present tense when writing a scene (some scenes described in past tense have the feel of happening in the present), but using the present tense can help plunge the reader right into the action.

Notice how Knapp orients the reader in time: it's 9:45 P.M. on a Thursday in May, just before *ER* comes on the air. If Knapp were to write about several Thursdays in this passage, she would probably have summarized rather than dramatized. See the difference?

The other crucial aspect of writing a scene is that it must have a goal or purpose, such as leading your protagonist to a realization or showing her engaging in a conflict. The ending of the scene has to propel the narrative forward.

What does Knapp realize in this brief scene? That she is happy in her solitude. That she is "the Merry Recluse," something the rest of the essay explores. If you dramatize something in a scene without having a purpose or goal for doing so, the reader will quickly lose patience. It's like the person who cries wolf too often. You're calling attention to something important in a scene, but if nothing major happens—if there's no forward motion at the end of it—you are, in a sense, crying wolf.

Using Descriptive Words in Your Scene

What else makes this passage from Knapp come alive? For me, it's the use of specific details: Knapp is eating not just cereal but "a zesty blend of wheat flakes, Muslix, and raisins." I can picture this. She's wearing not just something like "her favorite lounging outfit" but "torn leggings, a T-shirt, a bathrobe." These kinds of intimate details help put a picture in my mind. Do they do the same for you?

When you write a scene, you want to use the most specific details you can. Think of painting a portrait in words so that your reader can "see" the action.

See if you can spot the specific descriptive details in this scene from screenwriter and essayist Nora Ephron's "A Few Words About Breasts: Shaping Up Absurd," her frank essay about her wanting to develop breasts. And notice how she anchors the reader in time and place:

> It is September, just before school begins. I am eleven years old, about to enter the seventh grade, and Diana and I have not seen each other all summer … I am walking down Walden Drive in my jeans and father's shirt hanging out and my old red loafers with the socks falling into them and coming toward me is … I take a deep breath … a young woman. Diana. Her hair is curled and she has a waist and hips and a bust and she is wearing a straight skirt, an article of clothing I have been repeatedly told I will be unable to wear until I have the hips to hold it up. My jaw drops, and suddenly I am crying, crying hysterically, can't catch my breath sobbing. My best friend has betrayed me. She has gone ahead without me and done it. She has shaped up.

What is the point of Ephron's scene? How does it move the narrative forward? It shows her anxiety about developing breasts and her feeling of being less than a woman, something explored in the rest of the essay.

JUMPSTART

Try writing your own scene. Start with a time and a day. "It is 6:30 on Sunday night. I am …" and just keep writing for two pages. You can substitute another day or time. But just jump in, use the present tense, and try to capture the scene.

Orienting Your Reader in Place

Just as it helps to give the reader specific anchors of time, you also want to anchor your scene in a specific place. You wouldn't dream of shooting a scene for a film unless you knew where you wanted that scene to take place, right? The same holds true in writing nonfiction.

When you write a memoir, or autobiographical nonfiction, you're creating scenes from memory. How do you remember what happened in a scene from your past? Sometimes just visualizing the location can help trigger your memory. For instance, the novelist Russell Banks once wrote that when he wanted to re-create a scene for his memoir, he'd think about where the furniture was placed in a specific room. How were the chairs arranged? The sofa? Helping him visualize the furniture led him to visualizing the people who were sitting on those chairs.

Thinking Through Your Senses

A cold, dispiriting winter day. The unnamed narrator in Marcel Proust's novel *Remembrance of Things Past* is given a cup of tea by his mother, something he ordinarily doesn't drink, and a madeleine, a fluted cookie to dunk into his cup. You might know what happens next. It's often referred to as "the episode of the madeleine." "An exquisite pleasure had invaded my senses," the narrator states, "something isolated, detached, with no suggestion of its origin …. Whence could it have come to me, this all-powerful joy?" Dunking the cookie into the tea has involuntarily unlocked the narrator's past.

"And suddenly the memory revealed itself," writes Proust. "The taste was that of the little piece of madeleine which on Sunday mornings at Combray (because on those mornings I did not go out before mass), when I went to say good morning to her in her bedroom, my aunt Léonie used to give me, dipping it first in her own cup of tea or tisane." This memory triggers other memories: "the Square where I used to be sent before lunch, the streets along which I used to run errands, the country roads we took when it was fine," writes Proust. "[A]nd the good folk of the village and their little dwellings and the parish church and the whole of Combray and its surroundings, taking shape and solidity, sprang into being, town and gardens alike, from my cup of tea." The memory is captured in one of the longest novels in the world, Proust's 7-volume *Remembrance of Things Past or (In Search of Lost Time)*. All this from dunking a cookie into a cup of tea.

While researchers are learning more about the brain and where memories are stored (over several geographic locations, it seems), there's no denying that our senses play a role in how we restore and retrieve memories, as Flaubert's "madeleine episode" so aptly demonstrates.

Have you ever had a similar experience? The smell of a certain laundry detergent might take you back to your childhood, for example, as you envision your 10-year-old self tucked under the covers in your cousin's bed, where the sheets smelled different and foreign compared to the ones at home where your mother used a different brand of laundry detergent.

Our sense of smell is the most "primitive" of our five senses, which means that it has had the most time to evolve, according to scientists. It's also connected to the part of the brain that deals with memory, creativity, and emotion, so it's no wonder we react strongly to smell and, correspondingly, to taste. Interestingly, we can smell at least 10,000 different odors, according to researchers.

One way to make your scenes come alive is to think through your senses: what you're feeling, seeing, smelling, tasting, hearing. Conveying this to your readers can put them right into the action.

JUMPSTART

Think of a food or a meal that you associate with a pleasant family memory. Visualize sitting down at the table. What do you see, hear, smell, taste, and touch? Describe the scene.

Capturing Place

You also think through your five senses when you're writing a description. You want to show, not tell, the reader about a physical place or the world you're trying to bring to the page. And yet, you know how sometimes when you're reading long passages of description, your eyes glaze over? (At least mine do at times.) What goes through my mind is: writer, will you please get to the point!

Of course you want to add color and description to your nonfiction, but you must always ask yourself: to what end do the details serve? Your description in nonfiction can do double duty: not only capturing a place but also a point of view, mood, or tone. How do you do that? With well-chosen details.

Using Details

Take a look at this passage in Dave Eggers' memoir, *A Heartbreaking Work of Staggering Genius,* which starts with a brief description: "Through the small tall bathroom window the December yard is gray and scratchy, the trees calligraphic. Exhaust from the dryer billows clumsily out of the house and up, breaking apart while tumbling into the white sky."

The brief description does a couple of things with an economy of words. It puts us in the narrator's shoes (as we are seeing what he sees), and it sets the tone: grey, winter, deathlike. Indeed, Eggers' mother is dying of cancer inside the house, and the wintry description reflects the somber mood.

Let's say instead of this brief description, Eggers began his memoir with three or four paragraphs describing not only the bare trees but also birds in the branches, a touch of blue in sky, the sun peeking through, a slight breeze. What would these details do to the bleak, wintry mood? Chances are they would pull you in another direction, perhaps one of hope, sunshine, rebirth. But that would be false to the feeling and content of the memoir, which is about how the narrator's mother, having just had her entire stomach removed due to cancer, has no such hope of living until springtime.

You want the details of your description to contribute to a unified overall mood and point of view, to work for you and not against you. You're not making up details to establish a mood and a setting as you would in short fiction, but you also are not including every single detail because that would overwhelm the reader.

WRITERS' WORDS

"The beginning of human knowledge is through the senses, and you cannot appeal to the senses with abstractions."

—Flannery O'Connor, American novelist, short-story writer, and essayist

The first line of description, like the first lines of all good nonfiction (and fiction), should provoke a response in the reader: curiosity, anger, surprise. William Least Heat-Moon, a Native American travel writer, begins his essay "A List of Nothing in Particular" with this line: "Straight as a chief's countenance, the road lay ahead, curves so long and gradual as to be imperceptible except on the map. For nearly a hundred miles due west of Eldorado, not a single town. It was the Texas some people see as barren waste when they cross it, the part they later describe at the motel bar as 'nothing.' They say, 'There's nothing out there.'"

The essay is part of Least Heat-Moon's bestselling book *Blue Highways*, which chronicles the 13,000 miles the author traveled across America on back roads avoiding cities. In the work, Least Heat-Moon demonstrates the process of looking closely and deeply at the physical world, a crucial skill for any writer.

The author makes a list of "nothing in particular" that includes 30 such specificities, including the following:

> Small rodent (den full of seed hulls under rock)
>
> Snake (skin hooked on cactus spine)
>
> Prickly pear cactus (yellow blossoms)
>
> Hedgehog cactus (orange blossoms)
>
> Barrel cactus (red blossoms)
>
> Devil's pincushion (no blossoms)
>
> Catclaw (no better name)
>
> Two species of grass (neither green, both alive)
>
> Yellow flowers (blossoms smaller than peppercorns)

Least Heat-Moon's essay is almost a primer in how to observe and write about the natural world. He describes the "nothing" that most people miss when they're driving through the desert, and he describes the plants and animals in such a way that you can see them. His point? We miss the beauty of the desert when we don't train our eyes to see and observe closely.

Ask yourself when you're writing a description: What is the dominant point of view you're trying to capture? Disgust? Beauty? Wonderment? Peacefulness? Gloominess? What details jump out at you? Just listing all of what you see, hear, smell, taste, and touch would be sensory overload for the reader. It's your job, not the reader's, to sort out these details.

JUMPSTART

Describe a place you know well—your kitchen, a beach, a park—conveying your love for this place. Think of all the details that show how much you love being there. Now try this with a place you dislike. See the difference?

Mapmaking

In his useful book *Writing Life Stories*, memoirist and instructor Bill Roorbach has his students make a map of their earliest neighborhood, including all the "secret places," those "[w]here the weird people live," and anything else that comes to mind. I've borrowed Roorbach's exercise in my own classes, and it never ceases to amaze me how my students will come in with elaborate maps filled with details they didn't remember until they started drawing: forgotten street names, hangouts, neighbors, friends, and enemies. It all comes flooding back to them, as if they've opened a mainline to memory through drawing. Roorbach then has his students tell a story from that map, and this too has yielded amazing results in my classes.

I use a version of this mapmaking exercise both for writing personal history and for enriching nonfiction writing in general. Don't worry. You don't have to be a skilled artist or have any drawing experience to do this. I don't have either. But when you draw as opposed to write, you're accessing another part of your brain, the visual or spatial side, which might help you remember details you wouldn't ordinarily if you just listed them.

> **WRITERS' WORDS**
>
> "A fool sees not the same tree that a wise man sees."
>
> —William Blake, English poet

Sometimes we take for granted that the image we see in our head as we write and transfer it to the page is the one that the reader will have, too. For instance, when writing about teaching in a jail, most readers probably think of jails as cells with bars on them. But the jail I worked in for nearly a decade had no such bars; it was constructed on the pod system. To explain this, I drew a map. I'd been working at the jail for so long that I took basic logistics and spatial relations for granted. But one day I drew a map of the pod: where the corrections officers sat overlooking the women below, where the communal tables were, the classrooms, the bathroom, the laundry room, and bunk beds. Suddenly, I could see what my students were complaining about: that they had no privacy. There was no place to hide in this "new generation" jail to be out of sight of the corrections officers or of other inmates. Making a map helped me "see" things that I took for granted working there every day.

> **JUMPSTART**
>
> In the spirit of Roorbach, make a map of the place you are writing about in your nonfiction, whether a neighborhood from memory or a current location that is part of your story. Fill in as many details as you can: street names, stores, parks, people. Just keep adding details.

Tips for Writing About Place

When you're writing about place, you want your reader to really "see" what you're seeing. You're painting a landscape with words so the reader can visualize being there. To do that you must think through your senses, keeping in mind your point of view or what you want the reader to think about what you're describing. Otherwise, why include it?

Here are some tips for writing about place:

- Think through your five senses: what you see, hear, smell, feel, touch, and taste.
- Use details to establish a point of view.
- Use the most vivid details you can with specific words.
- Draw a map to help you "see" or remember more details.
- Use concrete and specific words in description.

Showing and Telling: Yes, You Can Do Both

One of the beauties of nonfiction is that you get to show and tell. You don't merely paint scenes; you also get to provide background material in exposition or summary and to reflect on the action, to try to make meaning of the experiences you write about, and not only for the reader's sake but also for your own.

How do you know what should be dramatized in scenes and what is best left for exposition, summary, or reflection?

DEFINITION

Exposition is the opening information that introduces the character, plot, setting, or conflict.

Take the Scene Test

One way is to do what Lee Gutkind calls the "yellow test." Grab a stack of your favorite magazines or collections of essays or even a nonfiction book. Reread a few essays as a writer, highlighting the parts that are cinematic—the scenes. Notice which parts are best left for summary, background information, or exposition. How much of the essay or passage is devoted to scenes? How much to exposition?

Gutkind says about 75 to 95 percent of each essay or story will be given over to scenes. Do your figures match this amount?

Even if they come close, you'll see that much of nonfiction (and fiction) is constructed as a series of scenes predominantly. The rest is summary, exposition, or background, which is slower paced and doesn't occur in "real time." Keep in mind too that scenes don't necessarily need to be an entire paragraph or more; they can be a few sentences within a paragraph.

Telling: The Reflective Mode

Something that can't be captured in a scene is reflection, musing about your experience. Reflection is internal; it takes place in the mind of the writer, so it can't be dramatized. Personal essays often end with reflection, with the writer thinking back on the past and coming to a new insight or acceptance.

The late writer Lucy Grealy wrote *Autobiography of a Face,* an honest, poignant collection of essays about being diagnosed with a rare cancer at 9, which resulted in losing a third of her jaw and disfiguring her face, and the lifelong series of operations to restore her face. She writes about the peace she makes with her appearance in "Mirrors." After not looking at herself in the mirror for over a year, Grealy has a moment of acceptance when she's sitting in a café with an attractive man: "That afternoon in that café I had a moment of the freedom I had been practicing for behind my Halloween mask as a child. But where as a child I expected it to come as a result of gaining something, a new face, it came to me then as the result of shedding something, of shedding my image."

Grealy goes on to reflect that truth is not eternal but rather unretainable, and for the first time in over a year, she recognizes herself in the "night-darkened glass" of the café and is at peace with her reflection.

Skim through almost any personal essay or moving nonfiction piece and look at the concluding paragraphs. What you'll find is most likely a reflective passage that is not cinematic but internal, quiet, and reflective—the opposite of a scene.

WRITERS' WORDS

"Scene occurs in a place and at a time. Exposition has no place and is out of time."

—Bill Roorbach, American novelist, memoirist, and instructor

When to Use Scene vs. Summary

How do you know when something should be dramatized in a scene or if you should tell it through summarizing? There are no hard and fast rules. Ask yourself these questions:

- How much time elapses? If it's in real time, you want to write a scene. If the action takes place over weeks or months, you want to summarize rather than dramatize.
- If you were filming the event, would you need a close-up shot or a voice-over?
- Do you have enough sensory details so that the reader can "see" the action?
- Do you have dialogue?
- Do you need to convey a lot of background information? If so, you need to summarize.

The Least You Need to Know

- Scenes are the building blocks of nonfiction: they convey action and plunge the reader into real time and place.
- Scenes show your character in conflict and move the narrative forward.
- Thinking through your five senses—what you can see, smell, touch, hear, feel, and taste—is crucial for writing about place.
- Understanding when to write in scenes—or to dramatize— and when to summarize information is crucial in nonfiction. If you need to convey a lot of information or are reflecting on an experience, you summarize.

Drafting

While half of a nonfiction writer's job is writing, the other half is research. In this part, you learn how to do research, whether you're researching your own life or that of another person. Nonfiction writing is all about imparting useful information to your reader. You must become an expert on the topics you write about, and your readers trust that you've done your homework and scoured libraries, the internet, and government sources to the best of your ability to bring them information that matters.

I also cover the art of interviewing, another essential skill for the nonfiction writer, and discuss drafting your nonfiction (hint: no one, not even famous writers, gets it right the first, second, or even third time), providing tips for getting it down, hooking the reader, and writing memorable conclusions. I address the shorter and longer forms of nonfiction more specifically, such as personal and travel essays, profiles, and food writing, as well as how to write and sustain book-length works like memoirs or biographies.

Just the Facts: Doing Research

In This Chapter

- Doing research about your own life
- Researching the lives of your subjects
- Immersing yourself in the world you're writing about
- Combining narrative and research to tell a fascinating true story

Do you like to learn new things? Do you enjoy poking around in libraries and online or perusing old documents and photographs to uncover information? Research is a big part of being a nonfiction writer. Even memoir and personal essay writers do research by interviewing friends and family members where appropriate or by finding information that's relevant to the time and place they're writing about.

When we read nonfiction, we trust that the writer has done his or her homework. And whom do you trust more? Someone who has done the legwork, ferreted out the facts, and tried to get to the truth? Or someone who guesses and leaves holes where information should be? Chances are you'll do more research than you need, but it won't be wasted work; when you write a nonfiction piece you become the authority on that subject, and the research you do shores up that authority. In this chapter, we'll cover how to research—whether that means digging into your own past, or uncovering important material from libraries and other sources.

Researching Your Own Life

When journalist David Carr decided to write his memoir, *The Night of the Gun: A Reporter Investigates the Darkest Story of His Life: His Own*, he spent three years conducting over 60 interviews with people from his past (including his ex-wife), and researched hundreds of medical files, legal documents, journals, and published reports, to write his own personal history. Why did he do this? Carr was chronicling his past as a drug addict, important chunks of which he didn't remember, and though he probably could have constructed a book from his journals and the parts he could recall, the journalist in him called for fact-checking and accuracy and the "truth" about his past.

You don't have to go quite this far when you write personal history, whether in a memoir or autobiographical essay. But all good non-fiction writers strive to be as truthful and thorough as possible, and that means doing research, even when you're writing about yourself. Think of the research as a trip down memory lane in case you've forgotten important signposts and landmarks. You might be pleasantly surprised about what you turn up.

Journals, Diaries, and Letters

Did you keep a journal or notebook from the time you were 10 or perhaps all throughout college and graduate school? Maybe you started a diary during the first year of your son's life, when being a new mother was both exhilarating and overwhelming. Do you have emails to a best friend during the time of your divorce, where you laid bare your soul every night? Or letters that you wrote by snail mail before the internet made this kind of communication almost obsolete?

These documents are primary sources, meaning they are firsthand testimonies or accounts and not secondary sources, which are written after the fact and analyze the events, like most history books. The good news is that if you have any of these sources, you can use them for writing nonfiction. The not-so-good news is that just rereading these letters or journals and copying them verbatim onto the page is not enough to turn the material into good nonfiction.

Many of my students who have kept decades' worth of journals are dismayed when they go to write about their lives that these sources don't somehow transmute into personal essay or memoir-writing gold. They don't. But they can be mined for salient details and for how you felt about things at that time in your life.

Other Documents

If you haven't kept journals religiously (and I'm in that category), more than likely you have tax records, old credit card and bank statements, even notes scribbled on random pieces of paper. These too are valuable primary sources that can help paint a picture of your life by providing telling bits of information that can help make your memories and recollections sharper.

For instance, recently I came across a recipe for biscotti scribbled on a statement for a joint bank account that I'd shared with my then-husband. Seeing that recipe, which I'd hastily scribbled down, brought back a flood of memories. I was broke that Christmas, we were getting divorced, and I decided for the first time in my life to make homemade presents. And for some reason, chocolate hazelnut biscotti were what I just had to make, though I'd never made them before. I can still picture myself, alone in the tiny kitchen of my new apartment, chopping hazelnuts through my tears and trying to forge a new life and identity even as I mourned the old. I've done nothing with that memory (until now), but I keep the statement in a recipe binder, and every time I come across it I think of that holiday full of hope and sadness, symbolized in a recipe.

What documents do you have that might be helpful in researching your own life?

JUMPSTART

Skim through your diary or journal from several years ago. If you don't have one, peruse your sent email folder as far back as you've kept one. Pick one incident. Write about how you felt at that time. Then reflect on what this incident means to you today. What have you learned since then? How do you feel about this incident today?

Social Media

These days we're much more likely to have electronic source material spanning at least the last year if not several. Do you have a Facebook page with a wall of comments? Or perhaps you tweet regularly and have a year or two of tweets. Reading through these primary sources can also help you remember the past. I've kept the emails that I exchanged with my then-boyfriend (now husband) when we were first dating, as well as the emails I sent to my good friend during the first year I was a new mother. I've not done anything with these yet either, but if I do, I'll have a chronology for how I felt at both these pivotal times in my life—full of wonder and hope and new love.

Let's say you have emails and tweets from other people or chat postings you'd like to use. Can you use them in your nonfiction piece? Though things are lifted from the internet all the time, and though I am not a lawyer, I say no. Copyright still applies.

One way to avoid infringements of copyright is to get permission, even for emails. When I wrote a travel article about visiting Graceland, I wanted to begin with a line a friend had emailed me about how visiting the King's home was not only every American's duty but also "a requirement for salvation in the next life." I wanted to use his exact words but felt squeamish about using them without his permission, even though they were written to me. I asked him if I could use them; he was quite flattered and said yes. I would always ask permission before using anyone's words, whether from a casual email or elsewhere, just to be safe.

Using Photographs

If you haven't kept written records of your past, chances are you have a cache of old photographs. And while you've no doubt heard the adage that a picture is worth a thousand words, for the nonfiction writer it's not quite that easy. Photos don't necessarily yield their meaning; it's up to you to get to and write the story behind the photograph.

I remember one student who wanted to write about her late parents' colorful and peripatetic lives. She had two large trunks full of photographs of their travels, and though many of these pictures were labeled, making sense of them was a difficult job.

Try this: Find an old family photograph, particularly one where you don't know the whole story. Free write about this photograph. Who or what do you see in the frame? What were they doing? What mysteries remain? What do you imagine happened just before and just after the photographer snapped the photo? Who was the photographer? What do you think happened in the photograph? And what do you have to research?

Nonfiction writers are like detectives looking for clues and piecing them together to tell a tale of what happened and why. But you may not be able to find all the clues or the entire story, and that's okay. If you admit what you don't know or don't remember, your reader will still find you a trustworthy narrator. Using words like "it might have been that" or "I don't remember"—when not used too often—shows you to be attempting to find the truth and will make you a more, not less, credible narrator.

Memory is a fickle faculty. Photographs can help jog your memory and are excellent primary sources, but like diaries and journals, you have to piece together their meaning and reflect on these sources to tell the tale.

Interviewing Friends and Family Members

One of the advantages of being a nonfiction writer is it gives you an excuse to interview people, like your family and friends, and ask them questions you might have always wanted to. If you're like me, you may have always listened with only half an ear to your aunt tell the story of how your immigrant grandfather was so thrilled to see Ellis Island that he jumped overboard. I've heard that tale many times, but until recently I never thought to ask: Is it really true? What happened next? Did he swim to shore? How did he go from jumping off a boat to becoming a short-order cook and then opening his own restaurant?

These are the questions I want to ask my aunts and my father while they are still alive, or most likely this oral family history will die with those who know the story. Is there a particular story or person in your family you've always wondered about? Do you have friends and relatives who are amenable and approachable to interview? If you do, the time is now.

When interviewing someone, it's important to ask open-ended questions and be respectful. I'll discuss interviewing in detail in Chapter 8.

> **JUMPSTART**
>
> Write a family story about an event or person where you don't have all the information. Just speculate about what you think happened and let the reader know you are doing this. What additional information do you need? Where could you find it?

It took memoir writer James McBride 14 years of asking his mother questions for him to get the story of her past for his memoir, *The Color of Water: A Black Man's Tribute to His White Mother*. Though he expected to sit down and conduct rambling interviews for six weeks or two months where she would spill her mysterious past, what he got instead were years of his mother saying, "Mind your own business … leave me alone. You're a nosy-body!" But McBride persisted, for as he says, "I *had* to find out more about who I was, and in order to find out who I was, I had to find out who my mother was."

It's certainly an understatement to say it would not be easy to persist in the face of being told to go away, especially by your mother. But McBride's determination paid off, both in the moving tribute that became his memoir and in his goal of understanding himself and his racial identity. I think of McBride's example whenever I feel fearful of asking questions.

Researching Other People's Lives

When you are writing about other people, as you would for a profile, biography, or other character-driven nonfiction piece, you need to interview not only the subject (if he or she is still alive) but also those closest to him or her. Ask yourself: who is important in this person's life? Who did she spend time with? The list may include employers, employees, friends, cousins and other family members, acquaintances, or schoolmates. "[A]nybody at all," says master nonfiction writer John McPhee, "the more the better."

When I was working on a profile of author Isabel Allende and her namesake foundation, I interviewed not only her daughter-in-law, Lori Barra, who is executive director of the foundation, but also someone from the women's and girl's organizations that Allende had helped fund. In my medical writing, if I'm doing a profile of a new cancer center, I'll interview patients, nurses, radiologists, and surgeons to get a complete picture of the center from multiple points of view.

In the hopes of learning more about his mother and her mysterious past, McBride set out to find her childhood friend, a woman named Frances. It took McBride 12 years "and a ton of good luck" to find this high school friend, for it had been 50 years since his mother had seen Frances, who was married and no longer was listed anywhere by her maiden name. How did McBride find her? He went back to Suffolk, Virginia, his mother's hometown, and asked around. No one remembered a girl named Frances. But finally, he found someone who did, though he couldn't locate Frances in any directory. Fortuitously, it was while McBride was visiting the local library that a librarian handed him a slip of paper with Frances's name and phone number. Luck, hard work, and persistence: this is what research is all about for the nonfiction writer.

Doing Archival Research

Though we are so used to going online to find information, there's no substitute for digging around in physical libraries. If your profile subject is famous, there may be an archive of letters and other documents you'll need to read through. For biographers, letters to and from the person are absolutely crucial for getting a sense of your subject's life. Where are the letters housed? How can you get access? I often tell my students to look at the Wikipedia entry and scan the footnotes. Though Wikipedia is not a completely reliable source (anyone can update the entries), the footnotes are often very valuable for pointing you in the direction of articles and archives.

When you're researching, you put on your detective hat. If your subject isn't famous and there aren't letters or other documents housed in a research library, you still need to do archival work. Perhaps you need to read through newspapers on microfilm to find out what life was like in the early 1940s when your mother was growing up in Brooklyn. What topped the news headlines then? What were the popular movies or songs? What was life like at that time? You can't necessarily find this information through an internet search.

When I was writing my dissertation on female adolescence in the nineteenth century (before the term "adolescence" was used), I'd spend days reading through Victorian newspapers in the New York Public Library. I was looking for any news items about young women, but also I just wanted to absorb the feel of life at that time, to see what preoccupied the Victorians in the period in which I was writing about.

I also traveled to a small London library that housed conduct manuals for middle-class women. I wrote to the librarian and got permission to look through these manuals. I wanted to see what the Victorians were thinking about the slippery slope between childhood and womanhood, a place that was absent from much of the literature but addressed in the conduct manuals.

Did I use all of this material when I was writing? No. But just as you write far more in your drafts than you'll actually use in the final version, you will research more than you need. But after all, you are the expert, and you will need to show your reader that you are. Truman Capote stated that he didn't use 80 percent of the research he conducted for his nonfiction novel *In Cold Blood*. "But it gave me such a grounding that I never had any hesitation in my consideration of the subject," said Capote in a 1966 interview.

Where can you get help finding information? Librarians are also useful founts of information and, in my experience, often vastly underutilized. For instance, one of my students wanted to write about the ghosts that apparently haunt the school tower where I teach. A search in the online catalogue turned up nothing. But when she asked the director of library services, a man who had been at the college for 30 years, it turned out he'd kept a file of newspaper clippings, letters, and other articles related to the alleged ghosts.

Not all manuscript collections are catalogued, he explained. Nor are they all online. What's more, different university archives house information by subject, though they don't always agree on what that subject heading should be. Actually going to a library and talking to people, as my student and McBride did, can turn up unexpected and vitally important information.

No one is born knowing how to do archival research. You learn by doing. You search under subject headings and keywords, you ask questions, you look at other researchers' footnotes and follow in their footsteps, you nose around, you uncover, and you meet a lot of dead ends. But you never know when you will get lucky. And you're only going to get lucky when you're digging in the first place.

Using Statistics and Government Resources

"The government throws nothing out," says nonfiction writer Philip Gerard. That's great news for the nonfiction writer. A good statistic, even in a personal essay, can help make the theme universal or might be indicative of a trend. And if the statistic is startling or arresting, it might also make for a good lead.

When I began teaching literature at the county jail, I started doing research on the incarceration rates of women. I found that even though women made up only about 7 percent of the inmate population in jails and prisons, they were the fastest-growing segment of that population, increasing nearly eightfold since 1985 and doubling that of men. I also found that, in 1994, the year I received my PhD, California began spending more on prisons than on colleges, so it was no wonder I could get a job teaching at a jail far more easily than at a university. I poked around on the Bureau of Justice Statistics (BJS) website and also found information on the American Civil Liberties Union (ACLU) website. For health articles, I always look to sources like pubmed, the National Institutes of Health (NIH) database of the latest medical research articles, as well as the Centers for Disease Control and Prevention (CDC) to see what health issues are on the rise.

The idea is not to just drop the statistics into your writing, but to make the information useful in some way. If it's not useful, if it doesn't illustrate the theme, take it out. You don't want to burden your reader unnecessarily.

The late writer Caroline Knapp used this statistic in her personal essay "Solitude in the Culture of 'We'" to show that she is not alone in her love of solitude: "In fact, 25 percent of the adult population lives alone today—that's almost double the number that lived alone 35 years ago—and although plenty of us may end up on our own for unhappy reasons (divorce, fear, geography, any number of quirks of fate and timing and circumstance), it seems both simplistic and erroneous to assume that solitude is an inherently sorry state, something you wouldn't choose if you had a better option."

Next time you are searching for information, see what records the government keeps. I know one health writer who regularly checks the statistics on morbidity looking for trends to write about.

JUMPSTART

Take out one of your essays or other pieces of writing. Look for a place to add research, whether in the form of a statistic or scientific research study or government report that would help shore up your idea. See what you can find and weave it into your essay.

Traveling: Being There

Now for the fun part: traveling. Nothing beats traveling to the place where your subject lived or worked. How else could you get the feel of a life lived if you didn't travel to London, Paris, or a small town in Virginia to find out how your subject lived? When you're walking in the footsteps of your subject, you want to show what you see. What do you see around you? What are the sights, sounds, and smells that capture a place? What are the distinguishing details? You want your reader to "see" what happened, whether you're describing the inside of a jail or life for a diesel truck driver on the wharf. That kind of vision requires that you observe the physical world in depth.

Though you should check with your accountant, most research trips are tax deductible, another bonus of being a nonfiction writer. "[A] lot of the joy of writing nonfiction comes from having an honorable excuse to go out into the world and find out interesting things," says Philip Gerard in his excellent guidebook *Creative Nonfiction: Researching and Crafting Stories of Real Life.* "Lay your hands on the stuff of the world and feel its heft, its weight of meaning, to meet fascinating people and talk to them about the things they care about most deeply."

You can't feel this weight if you are home doing only internet research on your couch. You need to get out and about. Even if you're not particularly gregarious, nothing beats experiential research—going to the place you're writing about, whether it's a warehouse that recycles mattresses from landfills or the nonprofit organization you're profiling for a magazine piece. What do you notice about a certain place? What details strike you as revealing? What is happening there while you're visiting? Bestselling writer Mary Roach, whose interview you can read in Appendix B, goes on research trips looking for scenes; she needs to see the scientific topics and the people she writes about in action, and you can't get that from library research.

Immersion Journalism

Immersion journalists like Ted Conover, Tracy Kidder, or Adrian Nicole LeBlanc, who spent a decade following her subjects to write *Random Family: Love, Drugs, Trouble, and Coming of Age in the Bronx,* absolutely must immerse themselves in the world they are writing about. You can't write about the Sing Sing corrections officers in the kind of depth and truthfulness that Conover did unless you work as one of them. You can't understand what really goes on in American elementary school education unless you spend nine months in a fifth-grade classroom, as Kidder did. You can't relate to intergenerational cycles of poverty and drug use unless you spend an inordinate amount of time with the people who are caught in these traps.

Immersion journalism is a specialized field that usually requires a long research time commitment. You have to be willing to plunge yourself into the world and subculture you are writing about and be engrossed. Of course, you first have to get access and permission (or go undercover). You spend a lot of time listening and observing and being a fly on the wall. And you collect a lot of information. If you're lucky and work hard, you will be able to write about a world in depth that few people have seen or read about.

 DEFINITION

Immersion journalism is the process of immersing yourself for months or years at a time to understand and capture the "felt life" of your subjects.

Putting It All Together

You've done the research, collected information from libraries and archives, conducted interviews, and observed the world you're writing about in great physical detail. Now you have to put it all together in writing. Where to start? How do you know when you have enough research or too much? The bestselling writers interviewed in Appendix B have their own methods: some write and research simultaneously; others, like *The New Yorker* writer Susan Orlean, research first and then write.

How do you hook the reader? Start with a scene. What interested you in the material? Begin by showing the character, problem, or subject matter in an action-filled way and you'll have your reader interested in hearing more.

Take a look at some of your favorite nonfiction writers. Look at their openings. How do they begin? With background information? A scene that dramatizes the subject? How and where in the narrative do they weave in research? Once you start reading like a writer, you'll pick up techniques like transitions, or how to weave in research so it doesn't bog down the narrative. And you'll definitely figure out where the holes are in your research as you're writing. I suggest that after you have done all the research, you just start writing and fill in the facts later. You could assemble all your research notes and write from them as well. I've done both. For me, it works better to write the narrative or nonfiction piece first with what I know, and then go back to my interviews for quotes or my research studies for statistics. See the interview with bestselling writer Mary Roach in Appendix B for her tips on how to incorporate the research and the writing.

The Least You Need to Know

- Nonfiction writers are like detectives who must do research into their own lives and the subjects they write about.
- Diaries, journals, and notebooks are all primary documents, written about the event as it was happening from an eyewitness point of view, and valuable sources for writing personal history.
- Emails, tweets, Facebook postings, and photographs also count as sources for research and can help you add color and detail to your nonfictional work.
- Nonfiction writers must do online, library, and in-person research to become experts in their subjects.
- Looking at your favorite nonfiction writers to see how they combine narrative and research can help you structure your own material.

Honing Your Interview Skills

Chapter

8

In This Chapter

- Conducting effective interviews
- The art of the interview
- What to do with information from interviews
- How can you avoid libel?

Interviewing is an artful skill and an essential tool for any nonfiction writer. But you needn't have gone to journalism school to hone this reportorial tool. Practice will do it. And the reason to interview people? Not only to find out information but also because quotations add color and depth to any story you're writing. Though you may fear you're being nosy or intrusive, I've always found that the contrary is true: people generally love to talk about themselves and their work and are often quite flattered when you ask for an interview.

Interviewing is also a form of research. You are after information that you can't get any other way. Good quotations from your sources can enliven your nonfiction piece. They certainly make your job easier. With training, during the interview you can pick out the telling quotation, the choice phrasing, the just-right remark that can help capture character, make a point, explain, or lend authority to the subject you're writing about.

How to Conduct Interviews

You can interview people by phone, email, or in person. When I just need information quickly—say, from a doctor or medical expert for an article—phone interviews are best because they are quick and efficient. If you're describing the person for a profile, writing about the place he works, or need to observe, then you must do an in-person interview.

Many writers conduct email interviews as a last resort because it's harder to capture conversation in an email. People tend to respond in bullet points with answers that often sound canned or condensed, which makes it harder to pull good quotes or capture the personality of your interviewee. Also, you don't have the chance to ask follow-up questions on the spot or let the interview go in a different direction, as you would in person or on the phone. But whatever method you choose, you'll want to know whom to interview and what to ask.

Deciding Who to Interview

Interviews are essential for gaining information that you couldn't get any other way. The first questions you'll want to ask yourself are: who are the people who have this information? How can they help me? Why is this person an appropriate source? And what do I hope to gain by talking to the person?

Let's say you're doing a story on a homeless shelter. You probably want to talk to the director of the shelter, perhaps another employee who handles check-in or checkout or other services, and after getting permission of course, some of the people who use the shelter.

As previously mentioned, there are three ways to do interviews: by phone, email, or in person. Because you need to see the shelter so you can describe it in the piece, you need to visit. That's also the only way you're going to be able to talk to the homeless who use the shelter and find out their stories.

Preparing for the Interview

I always think of the Girl Scout motto—be prepared—when doing interviews. You want to do your homework and find out as much as you can about the person, the place, the organization, and the topic so you don't waste anyone's time.

Let's say you're interviewing a food-truck vendor for a story on the rise of mobile eateries in your city. You might do a newspaper search to see what's already been covered. Perhaps the vendor has a website. Start there and read everything you can. Do an online search on the topic of food trucks and see what comes up. You might find a controversy about permits for food trucks or an opinion piece from a restaurateur about how these vendors are siphoning business from brick-and-mortar establishments. Read everything you can find on the topic. This not only will prevent you from asking just informational questions, but also can help you formulate the questions you'll need to ask.

A lot of pre-interviewing is also doing the research to find out who the best person to talk to is and his or her contact information, and setting up a good time to talk. You can find out a lot of information—names, phone numbers, titles—through online searches, but there's no substitute for calling a place and saying, "I'm writing a story on homeless shelters. Who would be the best person to talk to about this?"

People are very helpful. Usually. When I was writing the story about two Catholic nuns who opened a daytime homeless shelter, I kept getting put off. One sister didn't want me to come and didn't want me to talk to any of their clientele. I kept calling. And calling. Finally I just went down there and interviewed the homeless women outside. I also eventually got permission to come inside, talk to the women, and interview one of the sisters, but it was only because I was persistent. Later I realized that the sister was only being protective of her clients and was not denying me access because she didn't want me to do the story.

Even if you're interviewing a family member for a personal narrative, you still need to do some research beforehand. Perhaps you've found an old photograph that you'd like to know more about. Maybe you need to write down what you remember from your past so that you know what to ask or where there are holes in your family history.

JUMPSTART

In any interview situation, you want to be professional and courteous, and treat it like a job (which it is for the nonfiction writer).

Listening and Asking the Right Questions

I like to have about five open-ended questions for an interview, though I've had as many as ten. More than that, I find, is too much for one interview and one source.

You've done your homework. You have your questions. You've set up the interview. Now the fun begins. But nothing can wreck an interview more than not listening to your source. Though it may be tempting to break in with a question, wait until the person has finished speaking. The art of interviewing has much to do with listening, really listening to your subject. It's often hard to be quiet or not interrupt, and the times I have interrupted, I've regretted it because it takes the interviewee away from what he or she was just about to say. So you listen. Is there a phrase you don't understand? A bit of jargon? Make a note to ask about it later. Do you have more questions? Or did you miss something? There's no harm in saying, "Excuse me, I didn't get that part. Can you repeat it?"

Do's and Don'ts for Interviewing

Like any skill, interviewing gets easier the more you do it. And believe it or not, your source might be just as nervous or anxious as you are. You'll want to put your interviewee at ease. Tell her or him to think of it as a conversation. I usually ask my sources if we can "chat," which sounds far less intimidating than the word "interview."

Here are a few interviewing tips to help you:

- Don't ask questions that can be answered with a simple yes or no. Instead, use phrases that will get your source talking, such as "Can you describe …," or "Tell me more about …," or "What's it like to …."
- Do use words that begin with "How" or "What" or "Why" rather than "When" or "Who."
- Don't be afraid to repeat a question in a different way if your interviewee doesn't understand or respond.
- Don't interrupt. You might miss something good, and you risk having the interviewee lose his or her train of thought.
- Don't use the interview to talk about yourself.
- Do ask follow up questions, particularly if you don't understand something.
- Do be courteous and polite, even if you disagree with your source.
- Do push for specific details. You want to add color and texture to your piece, so ask your source to describe something for you.
- Don't be afraid to let the interview go off track from your questions. Often you get even better material if you let the conversation unfold naturally. But do steer the conversation back if you need to get an answer.
- Do offer encouragement such as "That's very well said," or "That's very helpful," or "That's very interesting." This lets your source know you are engaged and listening.

Recording the Interview

If you did the eavesdropping exercise in Chapter 4, you saw that people speak much faster than you can possibly record by hand. Unless you know shorthand or are able to write quickly, you might want to use a tape recorder for your interviews. There are so many ways to record conversations now: digital recorders, small handheld tape recorders (available pretty cheaply at electronics stores), or smartphones. There's even a recorder app on the iPhone that lets you record conversations and then download them to your computer. Though I have a digital recorder and have used my iPhone for telephone interviews, I prefer to use a tape recorder hooked up to my landline that uses a cassette tape.

I always record my interviews, and I ask my subjects beforehand if they mind that I record the conversation. If I'm doing this in person, I try to place the recorder in such a way to make it unobtrusive, and I always explain that I'll be taking notes as well but that I can't possibly write as fast as people talk. Of course, when someone says that something is "off the record," I turn off the tape recorder. You want to build trust with your interviewees, and being upfront about your need to record the conversation and your willingness to respect anything that they want to keep private goes a long way to establishing trust.

While the Federal Communications Commission (FCC) has no rules governing individuals recording conversations, according to its website (www.fcc.gov), "federal and many state laws may prohibit this practice." If you are calling between different states or overseas, you cannot record conversations unless you (1) get written or verbal consent from all parties before you record the conversation, or (2) get verbal consent that you record at the beginning as part of the phone call, or (3) there is a beep tone at regular intervals during the conversation that identifies the call as being recorded. The FCC also states that "a recording device can only be used if it can be physically connected to and disconnected from the telephone line or if it can be switched on and off."

To further complicate matters, federal law requires that at least one party (which can be you) be notified of the recording. But there are 12 states that require "all-party notification," which means just what it says: all parties have to agree to be recorded. I live in one of those states. You can check the FCC website for the laws governing your state.

PITFALL AHEAD

Avoid libel issues and be fair to your sources by *always* getting permission to tape your interviews, regardless of what the laws are where you live.

Beginning and Ending Your Interview

I always start my interviews by asking for the source's name, title, and contact information, including email or phone number in case I need to get back in touch with that person. I also use the opportunity to double-check the spelling of the person's name and to ask how he or she prefers to be addressed: Dr., first name, etc. This does two things: it assures you of getting the necessary contact information, and it serves as a warm-up to help get the conversation started.

Sometimes a source will need to be put at ease. You might be surprised that people are nervous talking to you, even those with advanced degrees and much research and experience under their belts. I recently interviewed a doctor who is director of a medical center, and he confessed that he was nervous, saying, "I've never done this before." When I assured him that we were just going to chat and promised that I "wouldn't make him look stupid," which he was worried about, it helped put him at ease.

I usually end my interviews with a question I picked up from prolific article and book writer Kelly James-Enger in *Ready, Aim, Specialize! Create Your Own Writing Specialty and Make More Money*: Is there anything I haven't asked you that you'd like to add or think is important for readers to know? Like James-Enger, I often get the best information from this last question—and ideas for other articles. One of the great things about interviewing in real time is that your source will often share other interests, hobbies, or thoughts that can be spun off into another nonfiction piece.

I always thank my sources for their time, and before I hang up or end the interview, I ask if it's okay to contact them by phone or email with follow-up questions. Almost everyone says yes and most prefer email, which, if it's just a follow-up clarification, is often the best and fastest way to get additional information.

Immediately after the conversation, I send my sources a quick thank-you email, which includes my contact information in case they don't have it or deleted it somehow. This also gives them a chance to add information in case they think of something they forgot to add or that pertains to the topic of the interview. I've had sources send me links to articles or sometimes files with more information, which makes my research so much easier.

Interviewing as an Art Form

Who is your favorite media interviewer? Is it Jon Stewart from *The Daily Show* or Leslie Stahl from *60 Minutes?* Perhaps you love to listen to Terry Gross on NPR's *Fresh Air* or Barbara Walters on any of her shows. Maybe you watch reruns of *The Oprah Winfrey Show* because you like both her and the way she asked questions of her guests.

Interviewing is an art form that can be learned. The more you pay attention to others who do this for a living, the more you can hone your own skills. You might also see how even these famous interviewers often break the rules by interrupting their guests, talking over them, asking yes/no questions, or by not asking good follow-up questions. Try this for yourself: watch or listen to a talk show, whether it's on late night TV or on public radio. What questions do the interviewers ask? How do they get their sources talking? What questions get the best answers? You will undoubtedly pick up tips you can use to improve your own interviewing techniques.

Letting Your Subjects Reveal Themselves

The interviews that run the most smoothly occur when I've done my homework, asked good questions, and just listened. If you let your subject talk for long enough, chances are you will get the goods: the perfect quote, a deeper history, a great explanation.

Don't rush in if your subject pauses. We're a noisy culture, and most people are uncomfortable with long silences. But try not to be. Let the person gather his or her thoughts. Or just say, "Can you tell me more about this?" Try not to fill the space; let your interviewee do so.

WRITERS' WORDS

"This is what is so uplifting and satisfying about creative nonfiction: you can be a reporter and a *writer,* too."

—Lee Gutkind, American author and editor

Paying Attention to Body Language

If you're conducting an in-person interview, look at the person's body language. Is he hunched over the tape recorder like he is given a confession? Is she nervously twirling her hair throughout the entire interview? I record notes about posture, body language, and characteristic tics like laughing after revealing a very traumatic episode. What is he doing, or how is he saying what he's saying? What does the body language reveal about character? If someone is nervously looking above or around every time, that may be an indication that she is uncomfortable or evasive. You decide.

After the Interview

After the interview, I check the tape or recording first thing, and then I try to transcribe it right away while it's still fresh in my mind. Often I type as I'm interviewing, if it's over the phone, and since I'm a fast typist, I've usually gotten about 80 percent of it.

Transcribing Your Interview

You can pay to have the interview transcribed, and there are many transcription services to do this. If you use a transcription service, know that it is not infallible. I've gotten transcripts back with words wrong or missing. If at all possible, I suggest you do your own transcribing. You'll save time because you'll be able to pick out the most interesting quotes as you do so. You're also training your ear to pay attention to what is most important, what will make it into dialogue, as well as what could be said indirectly or cut.

Do you need to transcribe the entire interview? I usually do because you want to make sure you are quoting people in context, meaning you're not plucking out quotes that make people seem like they're saying something they're not. I also like to have it all in case I need to go back for clarification on a point or to find another quote.

Just like when writing dialogue (see Chapter 4), use only "said" or "says" or "explains" or "adds." Don't be too dramatic and use "exclaims" or "sobs" or "shouts" or "gushes." Such tag lines are distracting. People "say" something, but they don't "gush" when they speak.

Editing Quotations: What's Allowed?

Like editing dialogue, editing interview quotes for readability is perfectly allowed. You are permitted to remove redundant words, change the verb tense to make sense (we often begin speaking in one tense and then sometimes mistakenly slip into another), or clarify a statement with your own words in square brackets ([ ]) if it's only a word or two.

But what you absolutely cannot do as a nonfiction writer is put words in people's mouths or add anything a person didn't say. If you do, you not only can lose your reputation as a nonfiction writer, you can also be sued for libel, which is discussed later in the chapter.

The Relationship with Your Interviewees

Your interview subject might ask if she can see the quotes you are using (or the entire interview or even the entire piece) before it goes to press or you send it out. You don't have to agree to this. Most writers I know would not dream of sending the quotes to their interviewees before publishing the piece. Too many things can go wrong: the person can retract what she said; he may disagree with something you've written and tell you to take it out; she may suggest other "improvements" or additions. But if you have gotten your source's permissions in advance, any and all objections are moot.

What do you gain by showing it to someone else first? Not much. The few times I've shared quotations with a source, I've regretted it. I've been asked to include more material with "additional" paragraphs, or I've waited days or a week to find out that everything was fine but worried in the meantime that it wasn't. The only time I run quotations by my interviewees is when an editor asks for clarification. I do a lot of health writing for magazines, and sometimes I think I understand something, but then my editor will have a question, such as what does "experientially produced pain" really mean? Is it the experience of pain? Pain produced in a laboratory experiment? I thought I knew but now I'm not so sure, so I must contact my source asking for more information.

I have no problem running these kinds of quotes by my source. But if you show more quotes than absolutely necessary, your source may want to see the entire piece or may have "editing suggestions" for you to follow.

It's your piece and your story, and if you quote accurately and fairly, then you have done your part and acted in good faith. Anything else, in my opinion, is just asking for trouble.

Libel

We live in a litigious society. On the one hand, we have our First Amendment rights to protect freedom of speech. On the other hand, we have libel laws to protect those whose characters are deliberately injured through false published statements.

In 1984, in a famous legal saga that went all the way to the Supreme Court, *New Yorker* journalist Janet Malcolm was sued for libel. The charge? She'd interviewed psychoanalyst Jeffrey Masson, who was fired as project director of the Sigmund Freud archive, and he claimed the journalist fabricated quotations in her *New Yorker* article about him. Malcolm turned over her tapes, but several of the quotations were not on those tapes. Though the journalist claimed she took notes instead of recording those portions, she couldn't find her original handwritten notes, only the taped versions. She was eventually cleared of libel because the court found that while there were differences between the taped quotations and the ones in the article, Masson could not prove that Malcolm "deliberately" or "recklessly" fabricated the quotes.

What Is Libel?

Libel is a legal term that one dictionary defines as follows: "to publish in print, writing, or broadcast … an untruth about another which will do harm to that person or his/her reputation." While *slander* is the spoken version of libel, libel refers to written statements that injure a person or institution by exposing them to public hatred, contempt, disgrace, or ridicule.

To be libelous your statement must (1) clearly identify the other person or institution, (2) be false and defamatory in nature so that it actually harms the other person, (3) show fault such as negligence or malice, and (4) be published.

DEFINITION

Libel is a published false statement that damages another's reputation. **Slander** is the oral communication of false statements that injure another's reputation.

Protecting Yourself Against Libel

Libel is not a usual occurrence for nonfiction writers who are thorough and accurate in their research and reporting. The best way to protect yourself against libel is to ask yourself if what you are writing is absolutely true and verifiable, and to get consent from your sources prior to publication. It is not enough to simply change the names in your work, or to use the words "alleged" and "allegedly." Consider also the following points:

- You can express your opinions about public figures (including actors and those who put themselves in the public spotlight) under the Fair Comment and Criticism aspect of libel law, which allows you to write your opinion (such as an actor was terrible in a movie).

- You can protect yourself through privilege, which means that statements given as evidence in a courtroom are not usually considered libelous, nor are journalists who report on things related to the public interest (such as local government or police chief meetings) held for libel.

If you have questions, or just to be safe, you should check with your attorney or go to www.nolo.com, which has helpful legal resources written in straightforward language.

The Least You Need to Know

- Interviewing—whether face-to-face with your subject, through the telephone, or by email—is an essential skill for the nonfiction writer that can be learned and honed with practice.

- Asking good questions is part of the art of interviewing, but equally important is listening to your source and picking up cues from body language when conducting interviews in person.

- When you use quotes from the interview, you're allowed to edit them to make them read better grammatically, but you're not allowed to add new information.

- Libel is malicious defamation of a character or an institution in print form. The best way to avoid libel is to always write and print the truth, and get consent from your sources prior to publication.

Composing Your Nonfiction

In This Chapter

- Establishing a writing routine
- Learning how to avoid procrastination
- Getting it down in the first draft
- How to write satisfying opening paragraphs and conclusions

Do you write in long hand or on the computer? Is the morning or evening best? Do you retreat to the quiet of your own office or prefer to write amidst the noise in a neighborhood café? Do you listen to music or shutter yourself in a soundproof closet? Do you light candles, drink tea, or perform some other ritual before you write? At almost every single author's reading I've attended, someone will ask the $64,000 question: "Just how exactly do you write?" What the person really wants to know is: What's your secret for getting it down?

The truth is there is no secret: you just have to sit down and write. Every day. Or every other day. Anne Lamott in *Bird by Bird* advises sitting down "at approximately the same time every day. This is how you train your unconscious to kick in for you creatively." While this may not be possible if you have a day job, learning to make time for writing is essential to actually becoming a writer. It's not enough to simply want to write.

Establishing a Writing Routine

How do other writers do it? The prolific Victorian novelist Anthony Trollope wrote 47 novels (3 times as many as Charles Dickens) and produced some 60 volumes of writing, all while holding a full-time job as a civil servant in the British post office. Trollope paid his groom an extra 5 pounds a year to wake him up at 5 A.M. so he could be at his desk and write from 5:30 to 8:30 A.M. before going off to a full day's work at the post office. He set his watch to write 250 words every 15 minutes, producing about 10 pages a day. Trollope's discipline and work habits were legendary. He wrote even while traveling for work: on trains, where he fashioned a writing desk, and on storm-tossed seas, where he'd rush from his room to be sick and then come back to writing. His secret? "I was once told that the surest aid to the writing of a book was a piece of cobbler's wax on my chair," he wrote in his autobiography. "I certainly believe in the cobbler's wax more than the inspiration."

Few writers are as prolific or as disciplined as Trollope, but most successful writers set page limits and treat writing as a job where you show up to work whether you feel like it or not. "Appealing workplaces are to be avoided," writes Annie Dillard in *The Writing Life*, where she describes her writing rooms of choice: "a cinder-block cell over a parking lot" and a prefabricated tool shed. She, too, was interested in other writers' schedules. Jack London would wake himself up after 4 hours of sleep and write for 20 hours. The poet Wallace Stevens woke up at 6 A.M. to write for 2 hours before heading off to work in an insurance company where he would dictate his poems to his secretary.

WRITERS' WORDS

"The secret to getting ahead is getting started. The secret of getting started is breaking your complex, overwhelming tasks into small manageable tasks, and then starting on the first one."

—Mark Twain, American author and humorist

Nonfiction writer and novelist Po Bronson wrote his first work listening to the rock band R.E.M. continuously while holed up in a supply closet in his office, a 30-inch-deep by 40-inch-wide space that was barely big enough to hold his chair. Essayist and novelist Jonathan Franzen is also known for completely shutting out the distractions of everyday life by wearing earplugs and writing in a darkened room—even going so far as to permanently disable the internet connection on his laptop by plugging the Ethernet port with a cable and crazy glue. I have one friend who writes only on Fridays; she takes off from her job every Friday to work on her book, and she's finished it that way.

There is no one way to write, no one ideal location or method that works for everyone, but every successful writer writes almost every day, whether it's two pages or two paragraphs. "A schedule defends from chaos and whim," states Annie Dillard. Establishing a routine of writing helps make writing a harder-to-break habit.

But finding your writing routine, the day and time that works best for you, is part trial and error and part understanding yourself and your biorhythms. Do you write better first thing in the morning? Or late at night? Can you get up at 5 A.M. to meet a deadline with no problem, or are you a night owl who produces better work after 2 A.M.? The answer to these questions, scientists are increasingly finding, may be due to genetics. Researchers recently uncovered what they called an "after-hours" genetic mutation, which may help explain why some people truly are more nocturnal than others.

Understanding your own most productive periods can be a huge help in structuring your writing life. If you're an early riser, for instance, and prefer to write first thing in the morning, you may want to save the afternoon for less creative tasks such as transcribing interviews, making phone calls, or doing research. Vice versa for those who write best after the late evening news.

But whatever time of day and place you work, make sure you are consistent.

Dealing with Procrastination

Now that we know the secret to getting it down in writing—that there *is* no secret—we have to address the elephant in the room: procrastination. Every writer procrastinates. Or at least every writer I know. The trick is to minimize it. My family can always tell when I'm under a crushing deadline because I'll have the sudden urge to clean the oven or wipe down the refrigerator shelves, anything that involves intensive domestic labor. It used to be that I'd give in to these cleaning urges and exhaust myself cleaning out a closet. Now, while I allow myself some time to procrastinate, I know from hard experience that writing doesn't get easier by putting it off.

Here are some tips for overcoming procrastination:

- Turn off your cell phone.
- Turn off the siren sounds of social media. If you're still tempted to be distracted, you can download Freedom, an internet-blocking productivity software that works with PCs and Macs, or Anti-Social, which blocks the social media aspect of the internet for Mac users.
- Give in to the urge to procrastinate but set a timer. Allow yourself 2 or 5 minutes to have a snack or do a few stretching exercises. But when the timer goes off, you have to get to work.
- Conversely, you can set a timer and work for 30 minutes or an hour and refuse to get up from your chair until the timer goes off.
- Make a writing to-do list of even tiny goals. This helps when you're overwhelmed and don't know what to do first. Check them off as you go along.

- Do the most unpleasant task first. Say you need to make phone calls to track down a source, start the lead of an article, and begin a personal essay. Which one of these things is your least favorite? Do that first and your day will go smoother.
- Change writing locations. If the internet is too seductive or the refrigerator too tempting, go to the library or a quiet place where you won't be distracted.
- Give yourself a deadline. If you have a writing buddy or group (see Chapter 17), that's even better: promise to email your day's work (even if they don't read it) at a certain time.
- Reward yourself with a walk, a cookie, or whatever treat you decide after you write.

JUMPSTART

List all the things that get in the way of your writing. Anything from the external factors to the internal ones, put them down here. What can you cross off this list?

For more tips to overcome procrastination, check out *The Complete Idiot's Guide to Overcoming Procrastination* by Michelle Tullier, PhD (Alpha Books, 2012).

Overcoming Writer's Block

Setting out to work on any writing project can seem insurmountable; it can be hard to get your footing, and you can wind up feeling panicked or stuck before you even begin. But the way out of this is to focus not on the product—the entire story or article or book you're writing—but the process of writing.

Know that you are not alone in these feelings. I often think of the short story writer Dorothy Parker's famous quote: "I hate writing. I love having written." Most writers feel that way at least some of the time. Fortunately, there are strategies to help get you unblocked.

- Start small. Just as you can't scale a glacier all at once, you can't write everything all in one sitting. "[A]ll I have to do is to write down as much as I can see through a one-inch picture frame," suggests Lamott. Start with one paragraph, one scene, or one tiny step on the foot of that glacier and forget about the rest.

- Start writing in the middle. Beginnings are hard to write because there's so much riding on producing an opening that is brilliant and captivating and will hook the reader right away. So don't begin at the beginning. Pick a place, any place, and just start writing.

- Write about not writing. How are you feeling at the present moment? How does it feel to be stuck?

- Take comfort in the words of other writers. When I'm feeling stuck, I reread Lamott's familiarly frank confessions. Or I take writer and editor William Zinsser off the shelf and am cheered by his assurance that, "If you find that writing is hard, it's because it *is* hard."

- Chronicle your day so far. What have you done or seen? Just list the events of your day and see what comes up.

- Write a terrible first draft. "Anything worth doing is worth doing badly," wrote the prolific English author G. K. Chesterton. Most writers know there's no such thing as "good" writing the first time; there's only rewriting, so let yourself off the hook.

- Get some exercise. Several recent studies show that 30 minutes of aerobic exercise can improve brain function, mood, and creativity for up to two hours after you exercise.

- Understand why you want to write. What are your writing goals in general and for this particular piece you want to write? Putting them down is the first step to making them become a reality, and once you're clearer on why you're doing it, the obstacles may not seem as great.

- Leave off writing at a place that you can easily pick up again.

WRITERS' WORDS

"The best way is always to stop when you are going good and when you know what will happen next. If you do that every day … you will never be stuck."

—Ernest Hemingway, American author and journalist

Banishing Your Internal Censor

Perhaps, when you sit down to write, you imagine the ghost of English teachers past huddling around you with their red pens ready to pounce on any grammar mistake or infelicitous word choice. Perhaps you hear your mother telling you not to divulge family secrets. Or your own voice admonishing you to give it up and stick to your day job. These are the voices of an internal censor. All writers have these voices in their heads, but the trick is to turn down the volume, move them politely aside, and get to work.

One writing teacher of mine advised that, when you write, you need to turn off the bird on your shoulder that sits there chirping away in your ear, "This is terrible. This is terrible. This is terrible." There will be plenty of people ready to reject your work, but you should not be one of them.

Similarly, you have to turn off the editing part of your brain. Now this may seem to contradict the fact that you need a story and a structure in nonfiction, as well as a conflict and interesting characters, all the things we've covered in the first six chapters, but you can't think about these when you are first writing. There will be plenty of time to edit and rewrite, but the time to do that is after you've produced a draft or two. For now, when you first start a piece, just let the creative part of your brain take over. Turn off the editor, turn down the volume on the internal critics, and let yourself see what comes up.

Drafting

There seem to be two main Hollywood versions of "the writer": the glamorous version, where the writer sits at her laptop with a muse pouring words into her ear, which she transcribes onto the computer effortlessly and for which she is rewarded handsomely; and the tortured version, the writer who sits at his desk blocked, unable to write a word, tearing out both his hair and his manuscript pages. The reality is much more mundane: there is writing and rewriting and more rewriting. Rarely does anyone get it right the first time. All writers know that part of writing is rewriting.

The Iceberg Draft

Right next to my desk, I have a laminated picture of an iceberg that I photocopied from novelist Lynn Freed from one of her writing workshops. The photo is beautiful with its range of blues and whites, from the deep purple blue of the ocean to the bright white iceberg and milky blue of the sky, but what interests me is not the color but the concept: like all icebergs, only 10 percent is visible above the water. Most of the iceberg is submerged under water, and in the photo, I can see the bright caves of ice underwater like an upside-down mountain range.

The photo is to remind me that the first draft is the iceberg draft: you are just writing to get the whole massive thing down on paper so you can see what you have. Anne Lamott calls it "the child's draft, where you let it all pour out and then let it romp all over the place, knowing that no one is going to see it and that you can shape it later." Whether you think of it as an iceberg or child's draft, you need to let yourself get it all down so you can fix it up later. No word is too terrible. No sentence is too simplistic. No idea is too cringeworthy.

I take comfort in knowing that so much of what I write in the first, second, third, or even fourth draft will later be submerged under water: no one will see it. But if I didn't write it, I wouldn't know where the water line was: I wouldn't know yet what should be submerged (what I should leave out) and what should be visible (what I should keep in). Think of piloting a ship: wouldn't you like to see that entire iceberg, to know the depth of it, so that you can steer around it? Writing an iceberg draft is like that. It can help keep you from sinking into despair.

Finding the Theme

Once you have the iceberg draft down, it's time to ask yourself, "What's it all about? What am I really trying to say?" The answer to these questions is the overall *theme* or focus of the piece. Think of your theme or focus as the spine of any piece of nonfiction writing: it is what holds all the elements—characterization, setting, conflict, description, plot—in place.

DEFINITION

Theme is the central topic or unifying concept of a piece. It answers the question: What's this about?

One way to think about the theme is to phrase it as your "elevator pitch": what can you say in a sentence or two? Anything longer than what you can say between floors on an elevator ride or scribble on the back of your business card is probably too long and too unfocused.

Another way to find the theme is to ask a question of the piece. For instance, Jon Krakauer's *Into the Wild* asks this question: what possesses an intelligent young man, Christopher McCandless, to journey to the Alaskan wilderness where he dies of starvation? The answer is the theme of Krakauer's book, where he tries to make sense of this quest in particular and of youthful dreams in general.

Investigative journalist Ted Conover wonders if the stereotyping of prison guards is true, a question he answers in his book *Newjack, Guarding Sing Sing*, when he spends a year working undercover in Sing Sing prison. Denied journalistic access to the New York State Corrections Academy, Conover wants "to hear the voices one truly never hears, the voices of the guards—those on the front lines of our prison policies, society's proxies." The answer, that the penal system brutalizes both inmate and corrections officer—is the theme.

The theme of Vivian Gornick's memoir, *Fierce Attachments*, is the antagonistic, entwined relationship between a mother and daughter. Annie Dillard writes that her memoir, *An American Childhood*, "is about the passion of childhood. It's about a child's vigor, and originality, and eagerness, and mastery, and joy." Anything that doesn't fit this theme would be left out. Once you know the theme, you can go back and ask of each paragraph: is this in keeping with my focus? If not, submerge it or open a new document on your computer and stick it in there as fodder for another story.

Finally, you can always ask a trusted writer friend to help articulate the theme for you. We'll cover how to form a writing group in Chapter 16, but if you're lucky enough to have someone whose opinion you trust, ask that person to sum up the theme of your nonfiction piece and see if it matches your intent.

JUMPSTART

Read through all the responses to the exercises you've done this far. What themes or patterns emerge?

The Importance of the Lede and the Conclusion

In journalism, the opening paragraph is called the lede (also spelled lead), and it's the most important paragraph of the piece. Here you have only a few seconds to capture the reader's attention, convince her to keep reading a while, and encapsulate the essence of your piece. No wonder the lede "is the hardest part of a story to write," says journalist and master nonfiction writer John McPhee.

But once you have written your lede, "you have in a sense written half of your story," says McPhee. The introduction is also your promise to the reader: it says where you're going to go with the piece while not giving too much away. Think of your opening as being akin to a first date. You want to reveal enough exciting information to keep your date intrigued and have him call again, but you don't want to get into so many personal details that you've revealed too much.

Hooking the Reader

Here is a lead I wrote for an essay that appeared in *Glamour* magazine. I wanted to give information—the five Ws in newspaper writing: who, what, where, why, when—and also hook the reader:

> Twenty-four women are waiting when I enter the classroom. In their bright orange sweatshirts and sweatpants, my students look like fluorescent ice pops. They are all bigger and taller than I am at 5'2" and 105 pounds. I feel vulnerable, but I try to stride in confidently: It would be a mistake to show fear on my first day teaching at the San Francisco County Jail.

To write captivating leads, you might begin with one of the following:

- An arresting fact or statistic
- An intriguing quotation or bit of dialogue
- Something humorous
- A story or anecdote
- A provocative question

There's only one real test to tell if you have a successful lede: does it work? Does it make you want to keep reading? If so, you've done the job.

Here are three ledes that I find compelling. What do you think?

> I've always wondered about dog food. Is a Gaines-burger really like a hamburger? Can you fry it? Does dog food "cheese" taste like real cheese? Does Gravy Train actually make gravy in the dog's bowl, or is that brown liquid just dissolved crumbs? And exactly what *are* by-products? (From Ann Hodgman's story, "No Wonder They Call Me a Bitch," printed in *Spy Magazine*)

A man sits in a room, manipulating his kneecaps. It is 1983, on the campus of the University of California, Los Angeles. The man, a subject study, has been told to do this for four minutes, stop, and then resume for a minute more. Then he can put his pants back on, collect his payment, and go home with an entertaining story to tell at suppertime. (From Mary Roach's *Bonk, The Curious Coupling of Science and Sex*)

As soon as the 2003 World Taxidermy Championships opened, the heads came rolling in the door. There were foxes and moose and freeze-dried wild turkeys; mallards and buffalo and chipmunks and wolves; weasels and buffleheads and bobcats and jackdaws; big fish and little fish and razor-backed boar. (From Susan Orlean's story, "Lifelike," printed in *The New Yorker*)

Writing Satisfying Conclusions

Think of the conclusion of your piece as ending a conversation like you would on the phone: you don't want to end too abruptly, nor do you want to drone on repeating things you've already said. Rather, you'd like to leave the conversation with the other person wanting to come back for more.

Here are five tips for writing satisfying conclusions:

- Circle back to your introduction and see if there's something you can "echo" back to, which will give your work a nice sense of symmetry.
- End with a memorable quote.
- Reflect on what the experience means to you now.
- Offer a new insight.
- Surprise the reader with humor, if appropriate, or something emotional.

Like the perfect dinner party host, you want to leave your guests (readers) satisfied yet wanting to come back for more of your work. In nonfiction magazine writing, editors often talk about "the takeaway," information that the reader can put to use or some new idea or understanding of a problem. Think of the takeaway as something that the reader didn't know before reading the piece.

Just like with the lede, there's no one way to write a good ending. I ended my essay on teaching at the jail at the end of the semester at Christmas time:

> We read the O. Henry story, "The Gift of the Magi,"
> and watch a tape of "A Charlie Brown Christmas" that
> I brought in on a lark. They all think Lucy is a pain, feel
> bad for Charlie Brown with his puny tree, and laugh at
> the jokes. "On earth peace, good will toward men," Linus
> says. "And women," I say softly. "And women," one of my
> students repeats more loudly. "And women," say the others
> in unison. It sounds like a blessing.

One way of testing your ending is to look back at your introduction. What did you promise the reader? Did you arrive where you said you were going to?

Reflecting on the Experience

Personal essays often end with an *epiphany*, a moment of enlightenment usually provoked by some commonplace event or the result of musing about a topic. James Baldwin ends his essay "Notes of a Native Son" with an epiphany, reflecting on a biblical verse his father used to preach and realizing that his own hatred of his father and of other men is corrosive. "The dead man mattered ... blackness and whiteness did not matter," writes Baldwin, "to believe that they did was to acquiesce in one's own destruction. Hatred, which could destroy so much, never failed to destroy the man who hated and this was an immutable law."

DEFINITION

An **epiphany** is a change in perception or sudden insight into the meaning of something. It's from an ancient Greek word *ephiphaneia*, signifying a manifestation or sudden appearance, usually of a god.

Pick up almost any magazine that has a personal essay feature and read the last paragraph. Does the author reflect on his or her experience, often coming to some new understanding? More than likely, the answer is yes. This new insight need not be life-altering necessarily or sum up whatever the writer was wrestling with in a tidy, moralistic conclusion. Life is not like that.

Essayist Scott Russell Sanders ends his essay "Under the Influence" with his attempt to understand his father's alcoholism and its effect on his own life, stating, "I write, therefore, to drag into the light what eats at me—the fear, the guilt, the shame—so that my own children may be spared." But the essay does not resolve these issues completely; it cannot. Still, the reader feels that the act of writing the essay was cathartic and that the essayist has left no stone unturned in his effort to come to terms with his father's drinking and his legacy. This is what the reader wants at the end of a nonfiction piece: the assurance that the writer has investigated the topic thoroughly and arrived somewhere new at the end.

The Least You Need to Know

- Find a writing routine that works for you and stick to it. This is essential to being a successful writer.
- All writers procrastinate; learn to limit procrastination by turning off social media, setting a timer, or rewarding yourself after writing.
- Writing an "iceberg" or first draft can help you see your entire topic; you can fix it up later.
- To hook the reader, you want to begin with an arresting lead paragraph that may include an interesting quotation, story, statistic, or provocative question.
- A satisfying conclusion will leave the reader with a surprising idea, fitting reflection, or gratifying sense of symmetry.

Short Forms of Nonfiction

In This Chapter

- Writing an effective personal essay
- What makes a good travel essay?
- How to write a good profile
- Getting a taste for food writing

Open up almost any magazine or even newspaper these days and you'll see examples of short-form narrative nonfiction: first-person travel essays, food writing that includes recipes and reminiscences about family dinners, profiles of ordinary people doing extraordinary things, and personal essays often found in sections called "Connections," "Reflections," or "Personal History." There seems to be no shortage of space devoted to capturing a true story in a literary and captivating way, and that's what narrative nonfiction is all about.

So whether you're writing about food, travel, people, or something else, the ingredients of nonfiction apply: you want to have a story where something meaningful happens, you want to include the best descriptive details to capture that place or meal, and you want to have real flesh-and-blood people in your tale so that the story comes alive.

This chapter will cover some of the shorter forms of nonfiction—personal essay, travel essay, profile, and food writing—with tips on how to write each one.

The Personal Essay

I introduced the personal essay in Chapter 1, a form that has its roots in the French word *essai*, or "attempt." Unlike the formal essays you might have written in school, where you had to argue a point and prove your thesis, the personal essay is more meandering, less about arguing than about showing the reader the writer's mind at work. In the words of nonfiction writer Lauren Slater, "[e]ssay writing is about transcribing the often convoluted process of thought, leaving your own brand of breadcrumbs in the forest so that those who want to can find their way to your door."

A personal essay is intimate, informal, and candid. It is also dialogic; the writer is having a conversation mostly with himself but also with the reader. You feel as if the essayist is talking into your ear, letting you into her confidence and speaking honestly about something that is on her mind, like a friend would.

Although personal essays can be about any topic, often they are about humble subjects, what Phillip Lopate, an authority on the form, calls the "snail's track." You don't want to tackle big ideas such as "love," "truth," or "freedom" in a personal essay, but you may come to an essential truth about these big ideas by focusing on something smaller and more particular. It's as if in a personal essay you can't get to the universal themes by taking the major interstate highways, but rather only by traversing the smaller back roads.

Yourself as Subject

Personal essays, as the name implies, are about the writer. And often they are more about explorations than solutions. I turn to the personal essay when I have some problem I'm wrestling with that hasn't been fully resolved. You want the reader to experience the problem with you, to come along on your twists and turns of thought as you puzzle something out. If that problem or conflict is already resolved in your head, chances are it will sound predigested to the reader.

The personal essayist must also be vulnerable and reveal herself on the page; there's no holding back, though that doesn't mean you offer up everything about yourself, only what is crucial for the particular subject you're wrestling with. And what is the payoff for you as a writer of a personal essay? In Lopate's words, "the writing of personal essays not only monitors the self but helps it gel." In other words, you create yourself on the page when you write.

In her poignant essay "A Few Words About Breasts: Shaping Up Absurd," screenwriter and essayist Nora Ephron writes about growing up in the gender-rigid 1950s feeling that nothing would turn her into a woman except breasts. However, Ephron remained small-breasted, a subject she explores with candor in the essay, from her preadolescent self to her adult life, including a conversation she had with the mother of a man she was engaged to marry, who told her, "Always make sure you're on top of him so you won't seem so small."

JUMPSTART

Write about something that is taboo to you personally. It could be anything—the credit card debt you keep from your spouse, the envy you feel about a friend's promotion—anything. Don't worry about showing this. No one has to read it, and you can burn it afterwards. Just write for two pages or more.

At the conclusion of the essay, after doing everything short of getting breast implants—sleeping on her back, splashing cold water on her breasts, buying a breast developer, none of which worked—Ephron writes that she is still obsessed by breasts. Yet she is aware that the reader may wonder what all the fuss is about. "Here I have set out to write a confession that is meant to hit you with the shock of recognition," states Ephron, "and instead you are sitting there thinking I am thoroughly warped. Well, what can I tell you? If I had them, I would have been a completely different person. I honestly believe that."

It's that "shock of recognition" with the reader that you want to achieve in a personal essay. Though male readers perhaps cannot relate to the specific anxiety about breasts and femininity that forms the theme of Ephron's essay, they may perhaps feel a similar shock of recognition about being self-conscious about their bodies in other ways. It's the candor, the truthfulness, the no-holds-barred discussion about this particular topic that characterizes the narrator of the essay. Yes, you may think she's crazy, but you are absolutely convinced that she has explored this subject in depth in a way that is honest and intimate.

> **JUMPSTART**
>
> Think about something you didn't have growing up, whether it's large breasts in Nora Ephron's case, or a sober father in Scott Russell Sanders', or something else you desperately wanted. Title your essay, "On Not Having _____." Write two or more pages of a personal essay on how not having this affected your life growing up and how it affects you now.

Your Voice

Personal essays are distinctive, and this is due mostly to the writer's voice. Though many of my writing students worry about whether or not they have a "voice" in writing, I tell them that when you write passionately and honestly about something that matters to you, you can almost be assured that you're writing in your own voice.

Sometimes it takes many revisions to get down to the level of honesty required in a personal essay. The form is more vertical than horizontal; you are diving deep into a subject rather than just telling a story chronologically.

You don't need literary flourishes—long multisyllabic words, cute metaphors, or clever turns of phrase—in a personal essay. Many times students worry about developing a literary style, and what I think they mean is their voice. Tell your essay in your authentic voice—you at your most honest—and it then cannot help but be told in your style.

Marjorie Williams, the late opinion writer for *The Washington Post* and politics profiler for *Vanity Fair*, wrote plainly about the discovery of her cancer in "The Woman at the Washington Zoo," a collection published after her death. Williams discovered an apricot-sized lump on her abdomen one day while talking on the phone. "You know how you've always wondered about it: would you notice if you had a sudden lump? Would you be sensible enough to do something about it? How would your mind react?" writes Williams. There's nothing melodramatic about her prose. In fact, when you have something this serious to say, you almost want to get out of the way and say it as simply as possible. It isn't until many months later, when a CT scan reveals Williams' body is riddled with a lethal cancer, that she stated, "This is the moment when I know for certain that I have cancer."

Williams' essay, later collected into her memoir, is distinctive for its voice, honesty, and lack of self-pity. You don't need literary flourishes in a personal essay, just honest thought.

> **WRITERS' WORDS**
>
> "Good writing has two characteristics. It's alive on the page, and the reader is persuaded that the writer is on a voyage of discovery."
>
> —Vivian Gornick, memoirist and nonfiction writer, quoting one of her writing teachers

The Questioning Mode

Because a personal essay is about portraying the process of thinking, it's perfectly okay to be contradictory, uncertain, paradoxical, or questioning. Personal essays thrive on these impulses. How else to "best reflect the moving, morphing human mind, which is what the essayist wants to capture," says Slater.

You're asking yourself in a personal essay: What do I think? What bothers me? What are my pet peeves? What keeps me up at night and why? And you answer these questions through writing. The essay is like a quest.

Consider the poet and essayist Katha Pollitt's candid essay "Webstalker," which first appeared in *The New Yorker* in the Personal History column. "After my lover left me, I went a little crazy for awhile." What did she do to show she was a little crazy? She became obsessed with webstalking her ex-lover (and anyone else connected to him), looking online for information about him, trying to break into his email account, and scouring the web for any crumb of information about what he might be up to. In the process, Pollitt asks not only "How well does anyone really know anyone else?" but also just what was it about herself that made others believe she approved of her ex-lover's philandering ways.

At the end of her exhaustive internet searching, Pollitt realizes she's no closer to understanding the answer to her real question: "Why?" Why did her lover cheat on her and leave? She'll never really know. And for the reader, and for Pollitt herself, that's okay. For it's the questioning, the search, that really forms the spine of the personal essay. Not the answers, as you might have told when you wrote essays in college or high school.

WRITERS' WORDS

"Do I contradict myself? Very well, then I contradict myself, I am large, I contain multitudes."

—Walt Whitman, American poet

Tips for Writing Personal Essays

Personal essays are not the place for grand themes. Instead, personal essays are about "the irritations, jubilations, aches and pains and humorous flashes we experience as we go through life," writes essayist Adair Lara in *Naked, Drunk, and Writing: Writing Essays and Memoirs for Love and Money*. The essay shows the writer's mind at work, illustrating and analyzing a conflict or a problem, allowing the reader to live the experience.

Here are a few tips for writing personal essays:

- Start with a small problem, not a large theme.
- Write in the first person ("I").
- Use examples to illustrate the struggle or problem you're having.
- Be vulnerable and open; you don't have to portray your "best" self in an essay or try to be likeable.
- Make sure that you've changed or reached some new understanding at the end of the essay. You don't have to have solved your problems, but if you don't end up at a different place than where you started, the essay will be flat on the page.

The Travel Essay

When you picture your fantasy writing job, what comes to mind? For many, that ideal job is being a travel writer. After all, what could be better than traveling to the Australian Outback or Ixtapa, Mexico, and getting paid to write about it?

Well, the travel writers I know who work for guidebooks will tell you it's not all that glamorous. They are often paid a flat fee and to save money often spend their nights in the cheapest hotels, not the four-star ones they write about. Or they spend most of their "sightseeing" time tracking down addresses, phone numbers, and websites of the restaurants, hotels, and attractions they'll list in the book. But yes, they get to travel and get paid for it.

Far more likely is that you'll travel somewhere on your own dime and sell the story to a magazine or newspaper afterwards. What's more, travel writing seems like it would be the ideal job, but in some ways the stakes are higher than for other forms of writing. After all, what can you say about Athens that hasn't been said before?

Autobiographical Travel Stories

"What happens in a travel story has to be more than you went there," says travel writer and memoirist Laura Fraser, whose complete interview you can read in Appendix B. Would-be travel writers generally commit two basic sins, says Fraser: one is not having a story, and the second is not having a unified tone or voice. "The most deadly thing in travel writing is when people start [from] taking off on the airplane: 'On our first day we went to the Parthenon, and on our second day we ate here and here,'" says Fraser. "It's like sitting through someone's slide show that they haven't edited."

The other sin besides having a story where nothing happens is not keeping a consistent voice. Say you start off in the first person: "In keeping with my newly formed belief that people and life were the reverse of what they seemed, I decided to visit a friend in Australia, a place where things are notorious for being upside down." My essay starts with a first person point of view and with an autobiographical slant. But if I then continue, "The Commonwealth of Australia is the sixth largest country inhabited by almost 23 million people and was 'discovered' by Dutch explorers in the seventeenth century," I would sound like a dry guidebook. What happened to the personal voice? The sense of autobiography that underpinned the travel story? Keeping a unified tone makes the essay readable and consistent.

So how do you avoid these sins? Though you may think you're writing about Lima, Peru, or even the last undiscovered beach on the California coast, you're really writing about yourself in most nonfiction travel pieces. The story is what happened to you on this trip, not necessarily what you saw and ate and where you slept. To that end, ask yourself these questions for a travel essay:

- What is your motivation for going?
- How did the place change you?
- What surprised you?
- What did you feel when you were there?
- What were the people like?
- How is the culture similar or different from your own?

Poet, memoirist, and travel writer Patricia Hampl writes about Italy in her book *Virgin Time: In Search of the Contemplative Life,* but though she describes the Umbrian landscape, her real subject is herself and the memories of her Catholic high school past that come back to her when she stays in Italian monasteries. "I spent most of my time not viewing the Giottos, guidebook in hand, but sitting on the balcony of my room, gazing down at the nuns who were cultivating the garden, dressed in their heavy habits, which were hitched up slightly. They had broad straw hats over their veils," writes Hampl. Through her eyes, we picture the peace of the convent garden, the timelessness of the landscape that Saint Francis of Assisi once roamed. These are the things that are important to Hampl. Another writer, one not steeped in Catholic school and tradition, would no doubt write a different travel essay that focused on what was distinctive and important to him.

Your particular story and the kind of lens through which you see the place where you're traveling is really what the reader wants to read about.

Travel Writing Close to Home

You don't have to go far to be a travel writer. "One of the richest travel books written by an American is *Walden,* though Thoreau only went a mile out of town," writes William Zinsser in *On Writing Well.*

Part of what makes travel writing (and other nonfiction writing) memorable is distinctive details that capture "the central idea of the place," in Zinsser's words. You want to find what is idiosyncratic about the place you're writing about. To do that you must observe closely, looking for the most colorful, telling, and salient details.

JUMPSTART

Think about the town where you grew up or take the town that you live in now. Pretend you're a stranger seeing it for the first time. What is distinctive about your town? What qualities make the people and place unlike any other?

What Are the People Like?

Central to the idea of capturing a place is capturing the people who inhabit that place. What kinds of things do they say? How do they view the world? Just as you can use dialogue to help capture a person's character, you can also use it to capture the inhabitants of a city, country, state, or town to show the reader what it's like to live there.

When I wrote my first travel piece on a trip to the Australian Outback, I tried to write about the odd Australian sense of humor, which to me typified the people. "It's like the American West, but it isn't," I wrote. "It's not only the kangaroos, which move incredibly fast (up to 75 kilometers an hour) when they're not staring at you, it's more a feeling you get from the people you meet there: they approach life with an ironic sense of humor that seems so distinctive it almost constitutes a national character. If you have red hair, for instance, the Australians will call you Blue, just to be perverse."

Life in the Outback is harsh; it rains only a few scant inches per year, which to me seemed reflected in how people greet one another. "Because there is no physical escape from the extremes of cold and hot, the dryness of the cracked, dusty red earth, and the feeling that you get that the land just doesn't want you there," I wrote. "It is telling that one of the most common ways people greet you is to ask how you're battlin'."

I didn't know what or if I would write when I set off to Australia on the heels of getting divorced, and that really is the great boon of travel writing: "it's the serendipitous finding of what you're not looking for," I wrote in my essay. The best travel stories have this sense of discovery and surprise—not about the place, necessarily, but about the person who travels there.

Tips for Writing Travel Articles

Whether you venture abroad or explore your own city, keeping your eyes and ears open is a must for travel writers, as is being curious about people you meet and how they live.

Here are some tips for writing travel stories that will transport readers:

- Tell a story.
- Keep a consistent voice.
- Find the most fascinating and significant details.
- Locate the central idea of the place.
- Choose your words with care. If a cliché pops into your mind, don't use it.
- Edit to include only the experiences necessary to show the central idea. Otherwise, your story can read like a series of unedited slides from your trip.
- Capture people through dialogue.
- Tell your reader one central thing, not many.

The Profile

A profile, whether a paragraph or a page, tells the story of a person who has done something of note. You might have seen magazine columns (usually open to freelancers) devoted to profiles with names like "Women Making a Difference" or "Local Heroes" or "Vital People." Profile writing is difficult: it combines all of the narrative nonfiction skills—dialogue, description, characterization, storytelling, scenic action—usually in a very condensed short form to illuminate someone's life. Profiles are usually pretty condensed and run anywhere from 500 to 1,000 words on average. That's why good profile writing requires good interviewing skills (see Chapter 8) and good editing (see Chapter 13).

Your Choice of Subject

Profiles don't have to be about famous people. In fact, celebrities have been profiled so many times that there's probably not much new to say even if you did have the opportunity to interview one. But your choice of subject is crucial. Profiles are about a person, but they're also about what that person has done that can make us think or feel or see differently. "The best profiles teach the rest of us something about life," writes *Esquire* journalist Chris Jones in his blog on writing. "They're about beauty or art or the fragility of life. They're inspirational or devastating."

How do you find good subjects to profile? Just as you would for nonfiction in general: reading your local paper; talking to friends or even strangers, store owners, or the people at your gym; keeping your ears open at meetings and events; and basically poking around and exploring.

What you're looking for in a profile is someone who has done something remarkable and has a good story to tell. I'm drawn to unsung heroes, those people who do good deeds that go unnoticed or unpublicized, and I'm always on the lookout for those who fit this mold to profile. How do I find my subjects? I call up people I used to work with at the jail to ask what new programs they've started or what nonprofits they might be partnering with. I look at the community leaders who've won local awards. I keep my ears open at events, usually those that have to do with women and girls. I read a story in a newspaper and think I'd like to know more about this businessperson, leader, or exceptional student. How did he get started? What made her do this remarkable or noteworthy thing?

If you're interested in sports, you may be drawn to an up-and-coming high school basketball player, one whose life would make a good profile because of her perseverance through hard times or injury. Perhaps you know a teacher who was beloved by students for 60 years who might make a good profile or a woman who rescues dogs from foreclosed houses.

Researching and Writing Profiles

You will probably begin by interviewing your subject profile, but to get a good story, you'll need to ask the right questions. "You must ask deep questions," advises journalist and profile writer Jacqui Banaszynski. "What has defined this person? What is this person's motivation? Value system?"

You also may need to jolt people out of their comfort zones, their habitual ways of talking about their lives, to get the color and depth of information you need. One way to do this is to ask leading questions, as discussed in Chapter 8, such as: Describe the moment you knew you were going to devote your life to helping get young women off the streets. What was going through your head the morning you founded your nonprofit? What were you thinking and feeling? What did you think would happen?

In addition to interviewing your subject, you'll want to interview those people closest to him. What about the recipients of the scholarship your subject established? Or others who may not hold the same view of her charitable work? You want to dig deep and find these sources, too, so that you paint a 360-degree view of your profile subject.

The profile itself will have the ingredients of the best nonfiction writing: memorable quotes that reveal character, a scene or story that shows the character in action, a physical description that lets us see the person and what she's done, and a moving takeaway for the reader, something that gets us to look at life differently. It's a tall order for a short form, but the best profiles read like "minidramas" says Melvin Mencher in his classic text *News Reporting and Writing*.

> **WRITERS' WORDS**
>
> "Writing a profile is like writing someone's obituary before they're dead."
>
> —Chris Jones, journalist, *Esquire Magazine*

Tips for Writing Profiles

In addition to following the interviewing techniques discussed in Chapter 8, the following tips can help you write in-depth profiles:

- Prepare by reading everything you can on your subject, but don't assume everything you read on the internet is true.

- Interview people around your subject (getting permission from your subject first, of course): family members, co-workers, and friends.

- Ask probing questions about who or what most inspired your subject or what her most memorable experience was. What turned out differently than she expected? What most influenced her? You want to get beyond the facts and to the emotional life of your subject to help make this person come alive on the page.

- Ask your subject to describe what he was feeling or thinking on a certain day when he won that award, or started the nonprofit when the odds were against him. You can't describe the thoughts of your subject unless you find out what they were.

- When writing, use the 5Ws to help write your lede—who, what, why, where, when—so that the reader will know the essentials about the person right away.

- Avoid too much description, which will drown your subject rather than make her come alive.

- Use anecdotes (mini stories) to show your subject in action.

Food Writing

Like travel writing, food writing is not so much about the thing itself, the food, but about the person describing it. Of course we want to know if a certain restaurant is worth the two-hour wait on weekends and which dishes are absolute must-haves, but that kind of food writing is what restaurant reviews are for. If you want to know more—in a sense, if you want to know what food means—you turn to food writing.

Filling Your Soul

One of my favorite food writers is the late Laurie Colwin, whose books are part cookbook and part memoir. Colwin wrote about food but also about what food represented. "When I was alone, I lived on eggplant, the stove top cook's strongest ally," Colwin wrote in her essay "Alone in the Kitchen with an Eggplant." "I fried it and stewed it, and ate it crisp and sludgy, hot and cold. It was cheap and filling and was delicious in all manner of strange combinations. If any was left over, I ate it cold the next day on bread."

The story is a meditation on the joys of living alone in a tiny apartment with a tiny counter and the two electric burners that constituted Colwin's kitchen. And yes, it is about eggplant, but only in the sense of what it represents: the freedom to be young and living in New York and eating what pleases you and you alone. "Now I have a kitchen with a four-burner stove, and a real fridge. I have a pantry and a kitchen sink and a dining room table," Colwin stated in the last paragraph of her essay. "But when my husband is at a business meeting and my little daughter is asleep, I often find myself alone in the kitchen with an eggplant, a clove of garlic and my old pot without the handle about to make a weird dish of eggplant to eat out of the Meissen soup plate at my desk."

For a few years, I wrote an "Adventures in Dining" column for my local parenting magazine. The premise was to take my then very picky 7-year-old, who ate mostly white-colored food, and expose him to different cultures through cuisine. The pieces were fun to write, and in truth I did very little describing of the food, other than to indicate price and specials and what was featured on kid-friendly menus. Each column had conflict—required in nonfiction—which was the fact that we could barely get our son to eat anything other than pasta with butter. And there was the element of surprise and novelty as our family tried different foods, everything from eating Ethiopian food with our fingers to sampling rich German cuisine. I wrote about the culture and my family first and only secondarily about the food itself.

When you are writing about food, you're writing about something that matters to you. Good food writing is about more than just filling your stomach; it's about filling your soul.

Tips for Food Writing

Good food writing reveals the personality of the writer as well as what's distinctive about the food. I asked Tori Richie, food writer, blogger (www.tuesdayrecipes.com), and instructor (and former student of mine), for her best tips on strong food writing:

- Don't try to sound like you think you should sound; write in your own voice.
- Avoid the lazy "ious" words: *delicious, luscious, scrumptious.* Also try to avoid *tasty* and *yummy*; they tend to sound juvenile.
- Adverbs are weak, so choose strong verbs instead; for example, "shingle the bottom of the pan with the potatoes" vs. "attractively arrange the potatoes in an overlapping pattern" (from Judy Rodgers, *Zuni Café Cookbook*).
- Three adjectives is too many.
- Use all the senses when describing the food, not just taste and smell: "Choose very fresh green chard, just mature enough to issue a comforting scrunch when you squeeze the leaves" (from Judy Rodgers, *Zuni Café Cookbook*).
- Think of someone asking you, "Why am I interested in this story/recipe/blog post?" Keep asking yourself this throughout the writing process to determine what to leave in/take out.
- Don't be afraid to use humor if it's appropriate to the subject matter.

The Least You Need to Know

- Personal essays are often about small problems that resonate with the reader, creating a "shock of recognition."
- Good travel writing has a unified voice and tells a story.
- Profiles are "minidramas" encapsulating the elements of nonfiction writing—storytelling, characterization, action, dialogue, and description—often in a condensed form to illuminate a person's life and teach us something.
- Good food writing does more than list ingredients and recipes; it shows that food matters to the writer.

Long Forms of Nonfiction

In This Chapter

- Why do you want to write a book?
- Writing a memoir
- Writing an autobiography
- Reporting and writing effective long-form journalism
- Deciding to write a biography
- Tips for sustaining long-form work

Nonfiction writing encompasses many genres, as we've seen, from personal essays to profiles to biographies and book-length memoirs. How long should your piece be? How do you know whether you have enough material for a book or for an essay? My students often ask me whether the nonfiction piece they're writing should be 5 pages or 15. I'm always tempted to give the answer a zen car mechanic once gave me when I asked him how long it would take to fix my old VW Rabbit. "How long is a piece of string?" he replied.

My belief is that the material will tell you how long it needs to be. If you let your piece evolve organically as you research and write, you'll know whether you need 500 words or 50,000 to tell the story. Unless you've been given an assignment by an editor who has a very specific word length in mind, then your piece will be as long as that particular piece of string, or as long as your story needs. But then there are times when you just know that only a book-length story will do.

This chapter will cover longer forms of nonfiction writing—memoir, autobiography, long-form journalism, and biography—with tips on how to write each one. You'll see that the same principles of writing compelling shorter nonfiction—good storytelling, characters, conflict—are at the heart of book-length nonfiction as well.

Why Write a Book?

Many people say they want to write a book. For some, they've always dreamed of writing the great American novel. For others, writing a book is on their bucket list. For nonfiction writers, writing a book means you have a story to tell that requires anywhere from 50,000 to 100,000 words.

Say you want to write about your childhood, your crazy family, and the fact that your grandfather had a secret second wife and family in another state. It would be hard to fit this into a magazine article in any meaningful way. Or perhaps you want to write a biography of nineteenth-century photographer Julia Margaret Cameron, as my friend Victoria Olsen did. Only a book could contain the life of a woman who was given a camera on her forty-eighth birthday as a gift from her daughter and who became obsessed with the new medium, spending hours in the blinding sun arranging her subjects and staining her hands by processing wet plates.

The Memoir

Memoir is perhaps the most popular form of nonfiction writing today. Sales of personal memoirs increased more than 400 percent between 2004 and 2008, according to Ben Yagoda in his fact-filled book *Memoir: A History*, leading him to proclaim that fiction is a twentieth-century form. It's passé. It is nonfiction in general and the memoir in particular that is the leading form of the twenty-first century. Though I find this to be slightly exaggerated—take a look at what the *Harry Potter*, *Twilight*, *The Girl with the Dragon Tattoo*, and *The Hunger Games* series have done for fiction—you do have a better chance of publishing your first book as nonfiction rather than fiction.

Although every memoir tells a unique personal story, memoirs tend to fall into larger subcategories: relationship, illness, travel and adventure (think Elizabeth Gilbert's *Eat, Pray, Love*), childhood, addiction and recovery, business, or a combination such as travel and romance (such as Laura Fraser's *An Italian Affair*). For an excellent detailed look at these memoirs and in-depth advice about how to write one, see Victoria Costello's invaluable *The Complete Idiot's Guide to Writing a Memoir*.

Unlike autobiography, where you are writing the chronology of your entire life and leaving almost nothing out, a memoir requires you to be selective and focus on a particular time or theme. You can write many book-length memoirs but only one autobiography.

WRITERS' WORDS

"Memoir is the art of inventing the truth."

—William Zinsser, writing teacher and nonfiction writer

Deciding What Your Memoir Will Be About

To figure out what kind of memoir you'd like to write, ask yourself these questions:

- What are the major turning points in your life?
- What are the most significant things you've accomplished?
- What are you obsessed about?
- What haunts you from your childhood?
- What notable things have you done in your life?
- What would you like people to remember you for?
- What have you struggled with your entire life?
- What relationships have you had that have most shaped you?
- What inspires you?
- Where have you traveled?
- What insights about your life have you gained?

- What themes run throughout your life?
- What would you like to make sense of?

Perhaps you have a general idea of a topic or period in your life you'd like to focus on, but nothing from this list jumps out at you. That's okay. We write to discover what we know, not to transcribe fully formed thoughts from our brains to our keyboards like Athena springing from Zeus's forehead. Just start writing whatever comes to mind, and soon you may see a common theme start to appear.

The Reflective Mode

Writing down your memories is the first step in writing a memoir, but there's another part and that is: What do they mean? Why do you remember some things and not others? When you're writing memoir and nonfiction, you get to both show and tell. You can describe in vivid detail with action-filled scenes so your reader can visualize being there, but you also can comment on the action.

"We store in memory only images of value," writes Patricia Hampl in her collection of essays on memoir, *I Could Tell You Stories.* It is the memoirist's job to suss out these meanings. Hampl tells the story of writing a memory about a piano lesson with a nun, Sister Olive, who looked indeed like an olive, and of having a red music book. After writing the first draft, she finds that there are many inaccuracies in her memoir, including the fact that she never possessed a red piano book. But the detail is a clue to a mystery that Hampl will solve in future drafts: it will tell her about longing and belonging and what she wanted as a child. That's the kind of work the reflective mode does: it looks back on the experience, or the memory, and tries to understand its importance.

WRITERS' WORDS

"Memoir is the intersection of narration and reflection, of storytelling and essay writing. It can present its story *and* consider the meaning of the story."

—Patricia Hampl, poet and memoirist

Tips for Writing Memoirs

So how do you get started writing a memoir? Here I must defer again to William Zinsser in his excellent *Writing About Your Life*, who states that there's no advance road map for writing a memoir, but there is a process for the journey.

Zinsser advises sitting down and writing about memories or events that are very vivid, the ones you might tell at parties or the easily accessible remembrances when you hear a certain song or think of your first kiss. Write those down in all their vivid detail: how you felt; what you remember seeing, hearing, and tasting, anything you can think of for as many pages as you can. Then put it away.

Repeat this process every day, "preferably, at the same time of day," for several months, advises Zinsser. Don't worry about finding a theme or overarching story yet: just write. You might be surprised to find that memory begets memory. The more you write, the more you'll remember. After a while, you'll probably notice that you sound much more like yourself. Your voice will emerge, the place where you sound most like yourself: authentic, candid, real.

At the end of several months, you may have a hundred or more pages. Read these through and see what themes emerge: what patterns do you notice? What are you most concerned with or consumed by? You will no doubt have found a theme for your memoir.

The Autobiography

Autobiography differs from memoir in that an autobiography is the story of your whole life rather than a window into a certain period in your life. Why write an autobiography? Because you've led an interesting, difficult, challenging, fulfilling, _____ (you fill in the blank) life and you have a story to tell. Or perhaps you want to record your life experiences as a gift for your children or relatives. Maybe you want to understand yourself better by writing about what has shaped you into the person you are today. Famous people often write their autobiographies, such as Bill Clinton did in his 2004 autobiography, *My Life*, for which he reportedly received the highest-ever book advance. But you don't have to be famous to write an autobiography; you only have to want to do it.

Chronology in the Autobiography

Most autobiographies are told chronologically and leave almost nothing out. Clinton's autobiography, at slightly over 1,000 pages, begins with his birth and ends when he left the presidency. But just like with any long-form work, you want to write a story that will keep the reader interested, and you do that by writing in scenes and seeing patterns, the cause and effects of events in your own life. So though you may be chronicling everything that has happened to you, you still want to weave the events into a story, to shape what had previously been shapeless.

Digging into the Past

Just like writing memoir, you need to do research when writing autobiography. Journals, photos, or family documents are great primary resources. Consider researching your ancestors, for as the late American writer Harold Brodkey wrote, they set the stage for your own tale. Perhaps your grandparents were immigrants.

You might explore what life was like for recent immigrants to the United States at the turn of the twentieth century or research what life might have been like in their country of origin. Are there relatives you could interview? Or can you get hold of legal or other family documents? I was given my grandfather's notebooks when he was trying to learn English. He had emigrated from Greece, and was working two jobs and going to school at night. He wanted to become a U.S. citizen. The notebooks don't tell me much about him, other than his determination to succeed and build a life for his family. But seeing his writing as he copied letters, much like a child in grade school would, evokes a world of difference from my own life and makes me imagine what his world must have been like.

WRITERS' WORDS

"True stories, autobiographical stories, like some novels, begin long ago, before the acts in the account, before the birth of some people in the tale."

—Harold Brodkey, American short-story, novel, and nonfiction writer

Tips for Writing Autobiographies

Writing autobiography can help you understand your own life and the forces that have shaped you. It can be a fun thing to do. If you don't want to show anyone your work, you don't have to, of course. If you want others to read it—family, friends, or the world at large—you'll have to pay more attention to storytelling techniques and felicitous language.

Whether you write 10 or 1,000 pages of your life story, here are some tips that may help you write your autobiography:

- Write an outline of your life, much like a table of contents, with major and minor chapters to help you get started.

- Brainstorm a list of the major turning points of your life and use them to help organize your material.

- Start with your childhood and everything you can recall about each year.

- Look at photographs, listen to songs from the era you're writing about, cook food that you associate with your family, or pore through any kind of relic from your past, whether it's clothing or toys, to help jog your memory.

- Write a little each day. Memory begets memory, and you might be surprised at how much you start to remember when you write.

- Read other autobiographies to see how writers structure their material.

Long-Form Journalism

Immersion journalists like Tracy Kidder, Ted Conover, and Adrian Nicole LeBlanc (whose books are listed in Appendix C) spend months or years in the world of the people and places they write about, which of course lends itself to a book.

Finding a subject for long-form journalism means finding access to that world. For many years I taught women prisoners at the jail, and it was a world that many people were curious about but few had access to. Even though I worked at the jail, I was hesitant to write about the women there at first and approached the sheriff to get permission from him and, of course, later on from the women themselves. The sheriff trusted me, had seen what I'd written, and thought more people needed to know about not only what went on inside a rehabilitative jail but also about the people housed there. "These people are your neighbors," he said. "They'll be living next to you when they get out." I spent a year interviewing women and then almost another year following a handful of them outside the jail as they tried to rebuild their lives. Unfortunately, every single woman I followed went back to doing drugs and turning tricks. And though I followed them to places I would not go to now, such as alleys where they were doing drugs, in the end I never published the book. I have all that material: the tapes of the women, the draft of the book I wrote. Although I never published it, I got firsthand experience of the do's and don'ts of immersion journalism.

PITFALL AHEAD

Just like writing memoir and biography, when you're writing long-form journalism you want to resist including all of the research you've done and every piece of information you've uncovered. Instead, use only the material that serves your narrative, your story. It's okay to collect much more information than you'll use. It will help you write a better book. Just don't feel you have to use every piece of information.

Immersing Yourself in the Subject

For their award-winning nonfiction book *Nightlife NYC*, married writers Russell Leigh Sharman and Cheryl Harris Sharman spent a year awake at night in the "city that never sleeps," shadowing night shift workers. From fry cooks to cabbies, emergency room doctors to fishmongers, 1 in 10 New York City workers are on the night shift, and the Sharmans tell the stories of some of these "people who sleep too little and work too much" to keep the city pulsing 24 hours a day. Their in-depth reporting and vivid narration take the reader into this world, where day is night for the more than 200,000 men and women on the "graveyard shift." But the reporting and shadowing required that they too lived this graveyard shift.

Seeing the Forest for the Trees

As in biography or other long forms of nonfiction, once you've done all the research, it's tempting to put everything you know into the book. But remember that you want to write about the "big picture" in long-form journalism so that your reader can see the forest and not just the trees. That means you want to make sure that you sustain a narrative other than "this happened, then this, and then this …" which is an episodic structure—one episode after the next. Instead, tell a story. What the Sharmans do so well in their book is tell the stories of people, so that the chapters come alive with conflict and characters, rather than simply relate a collection of facts about what the characters do.

Tips for Writing Long-Form Journalism

When you're working on a book that requires months of investigative research, dozens of interviews, and shadowing your subjects, it's like a marriage. You want to make sure the subject is something you're interested in and can see through the long haul of the research and writing.

Here are some tips for writing long-form journalism:

- Make sure you have access to the world you want to write about.
- Allow enough time—weeks if not months—to immerse yourself in that world.
- Resist using all the information you've uncovered and use only the material that serves the larger story.
- Allow the story to emerge from your interviewing and observations, even if it's a different story than what you thought it would be.
- Spend time doing research even if it looks like it may not go anywhere.

The Biography

A biography is the story of someone else's life. It could be about someone famous, a relative, a business leader, someone living or dead, anyone whose life you think would make a good story. The marriage analogy is one I've often heard biographers use: if you're going to spend years researching and writing about a person, you want to make sure that person is interesting to you.

Why Choose This Person?

Perhaps you want to write a biography about your grandfather or great-grandfather. Similar to writing a memoir, you might start by asking questions: What makes your grandfather interesting and special? What major events or turning points marked his life? What has he accomplished? Who were his parents and ancestors? His children? What influenced him, and how did he influence others?

Nonfiction writers often begin biographies with many more questions than answers. When I was in graduate school, I came across a then relatively unknown nineteenth-century British novelist, Rhoda Broughton, whose life I thought would make an interesting biography. Broughton published her first two novels anonymously in 1867, *Not Wisely But Too Well* and *Cometh Up as a Flower,* both of which were considered scandalous for their portrayals of young women in love. These novels were sort of the Harlequin romances of their day; they had a freshness and frankness about female sexuality that seemed far more twentieth than nineteenth century. Broughton never married but lived with her sister and her pugs, turning out a novel every two years (25 novels in all) and becoming something of a celebrity, known for her witty conversation and decades-long friendship with the more famous British novelist, Henry James.

I wanted to know more about Broughton. Did she have an early love affair like the ones she described in her fiction? Why did she never marry? How was she able to write so frankly about romance and female desire? What was her friendship with Henry James like? I couldn't imagine a more unlikely pairing. What was her relationship with her sister like? With the other literary figures of the time?

JUMPSTART

Brainstorm a list of 10 people you think would make good subjects for a biography. Think of your friends and family, business associates, or acquaintances. Whose life are you most interested in finding out about?

I never wrote the Broughton biography. I went on to write a different book, though I read all her novels that I could find. Reading her work would be one way to start if I were to finally write her biography. Then I would begin researching her life, looking to see if there are any surviving letters written by her or to her. I'd start scouring online sources looking for archives. I'd write to the libraries that might house collections of her letters or know of other libraries that do (which would no doubt be overseas in England, perhaps in Oxford, where Broughton lived). Then I'd try to track down relatives, perhaps her sister's great-grandchildren, to see if they had any personal collections of letters, manuscripts, or other documents, and I'd interview them as well.

Researching for a Biography

As we saw in Chapter 8, when you write a biography or any non-fiction work, you need to do a lot of research, even if you're writing about a relative. You'll want to find all the documents you can—birth certificates, marriage licenses, school yearbooks, letters, journals, newspaper articles, photographs, scrapbooks—and then you'll need to interview family members, friends, employers, and anyone connected with your subject who could help shed light on his life.

When writing a biography, you're like a detective hunting for clues about a person and interviewing others for insight; a scholar sifting through documents, analyzing them, and making sense of the information you find; a historian examining cultural influences and different time periods; and of course a nonfiction writer weaving together the story of a life with scenes, profiles, description, dialogue, and summary, all in a literary and compelling way.

WRITERS' WORDS

"Writing a novel is like driving a car at night. You can only see as far as your headlights, but you can make the whole trip that way."

—E. L. Doctorow, American novelist

Tips for Writing Biographies

Because writing a biography is a big undertaking, and one that I've never undertaken, I've asked my friend Victoria Olsen, New York University writing instructor and author of *From Life: Julia Margaret Cameron and Victorian Photography*, for some tips on writing biographies:

- Read recent biographies and reviews of biographies. Not all biographies are written "cradle to grave" any more, and your subject may suggest a different form for your book.
- Write as you research. If you plan to write when you are "done" researching, you will never write a word.

- Keep a file about photos, illustrations, and permission to publish as you work on the book. When your publisher asks you for that information, it's easier if you don't have to start from scratch.

- Consider how your book may be timely several years from now. Biographies take a long time, so an anniversary coming up will help you pitch and sell the project.

- Don't worry about other biographies on "your" subject. Reviewers like to group books and events together, and that can create more publicity for you.

- Enjoy the process! Your subject will surprise you and your book will take you in directions you didn't expect ... go with it!

JUMPSTART

Consider joining the Biographers International Organization, which promotes interactions among biographers and runs a popular conference every year. Go online to biographersinternational.org to learn more.

Sustaining a Book-Length Work

Writing a book is daunting. But when you realize that a book is merely made up of chapters and that those chapters are made up of shorter scenes and summaries, it may not seem so insurmountable. I remember the first time I realized this truth: I didn't have to write the entire book on female adolescence all at once. I only had to write one chapter at a time. That I could do. It sounds so obvious, but I know from my students who want to write books and get overwhelmed: knowing books that are composed of manageable parts and really taking it in are two different things. It's like the old joke: how do you eat an elephant? One bite at a time.

Outlining

You'll be doing a lot of research and writing for a book. Do you research everything first and then write? Research and write each chapter as you go along? For an interesting discussion of these different methods, take a look at Susan Orlean's and Mary Roach's interviews in Appendix B. They are both bestselling writers and both write books differently.

There's no one way, and finding a system that works for you can involve a bit of trial and error. Some writers start with an outline to sketch out chapters and areas for research. Others create a table of contents and see the book take form that way. Still others dive into the research and outline later. For me, the book begins to take shape and seems real when I do a table of contents, complete with chapter titles. I find this part fun; I'm creating something out of nothing. There's so much promise in the table of contents, and it seems like a real book. Of course, everything may change as I go along: I'll add new chapters that I hadn't thought of before, I'll delete others that never developed, and I'll rearrange material.

Your outline needn't be fancy, no roman numerals and subheadings unless you want them. Just the briefest of road maps will do.

Organizing Your Material

You'll need to develop a system for keeping track of and organizing your research. You might start different folders for each chapter and put in everything that belongs in that chapter: interviews, research notes, vague scribbling about further research.

Perhaps you like index cards because you can take research notes and shuffle the cards around, as I did for a book once. Every morning, I'd read through the cards and then start to write. I liked the feel of these cards; I liked how substantial they felt with all my notes.

Whatever system works for you is the one that is best, but having no system is not going to work. You'll just have too much material and perhaps be too overwhelmed to go on.

Staying Motivated

So how do you keep from getting discouraged when writing long-form nonfiction? Check out Appendix B for interviews with bestselling nonfiction writers who share their struggles.

Keep these tips in mind:

- Write a little every day, even if it's only a paragraph or two.
- Start a book by outlining or creating a table of contents. You can always change it as you go.
- Find an organizational structure that works to keep track of all of your research.
- Know that books are nothing more than chapters and that chapters are nothing more than scenes and summaries.
- Don't look at the big picture; take it a little at a time.
- Join or start a writing group (covered in Chapter 16).

The Least You Need to Know

- You write a book usually because the material warrants it. Writing a book is also a great accomplishment.
- A memoir is a story of your life at a certain point in time or a story about a theme that runs through your life.
- You can write many memoirs but usually only one autobiography, which is a book that contains everything about your life.
- Long-form journalism requires you to immerse yourself in the world you're writing about, and it requires time, patience, and research.
- A biography is the story of another person's life, and it requires finding both a good subject and a research commitment on the part of the writer.
- Writing a table of contents or outline before you begin a book-length work is like drawing up a blueprint for a building: it can help you create structure.

Crafting Memorable Nonfiction

In this part, you get tips for crafting better sentences, including a look at the importance of grammar and punctuation and using metaphors, similes, and other techniques to make your sentences sing.

Every writer knows that the secret to writing is revising. I also share how you can revise your piece to find your focus and pacing, and tell you how to declutter your sentences and avoid common writing mistakes. All of the information in this part is designed to help you write memorable prose and stay true to your own voice.

How to Make Your Sentences Sing

In This Chapter

- The importance of grammar and punctuation
- Add interest by varying sentence length
- Fixing run-on sentences and fragments
- Choosing strong action verbs
- Using metaphors and similes, and avoiding clichés
- Making your prose more musical

Have you ever had a conversation with someone who talks very quickly, never pauses between sentences, and makes it impossible for you to get a word in? Or with someone who speaks in clichés but whose meaning still remains cryptic? In each of these cases, your unhelpful conversationalist is ignoring the rules of not only etiquette but also grammar—the relationship between parts of the sentences and how they fit together to make meaning.

This chapter is about how to make your writing more interesting. It's not intended to be a full review of grammar, but rather about specific ways you can improve your writing and craft better sentences. There are excellent grammar books out there (like Strunk and White's classic, *The Elements of Style*) that cover more ground; this chapter is about things like why punctuation matters and how you can use it to make your writing stand out. It also covers some common grammar mistakes with the goal of helping you see that you can break the rules as long as you know what those rules are. More common writing mistakes—and how to fix them—are covered in Chapter 13.

Why Grammar and Punctuation Matter

Grammar refers to the rules governing how words are put together in a sentence to make sense. Grammar is really all about relationships: relationships of words to sentences and relationships with your readers so they can understand what you're saying. Knowing these grammar relationships can help make you a better nonfiction writer.

Even if you don't know the names of all of the rules of grammar, you know the basic rules. Consider this sentence written by English specialist James Delaney at Cayuga Community College:

> The porturbs in the bigger torms have tanted the maret's rotment brokly.

What is the subject of this sentence? The porturbs. Notice how it's the first two words in the sentence. What have these porturbs done? They have tanted. That's the verb, the action word and second major part of the sentence, also called the predicate.

Even if you don't know what "porturbs" or "bigger torms" are, or what "have tanted" means, you can probably recognize the bones of the sentence and see how it is put together.

Grammar is hardwired into our brains; we are a language-using species, after all. We refer to languages as being part of families— Germanic, Greek, Latin—using the model of a biological family tree. We speak in our "mother" tongue. Linguists talk about "daughter" languages being offshoots of a "mother" language.

Language is a living thing. It changes and grows. Think about how new words come into our language, such as *fax*, *email*, and *crowdsource*. Or how older words, such as *cougar*, take on new meanings. The Global Language Monitor, a group based in Austin, Texas, that tracks new words, estimates that a new word is born every 98 minutes.

Punctuation is important in your writing, too. It's been said that an English professor wrote this sentence on the board and asked his students to add punctuation: "Woman without her man is nothing."

Rumor has it that the men in the class punctuated the sentence this way: "Woman, without her man, is nothing." The women punctuated it like this: "Woman: without her, man is nothing." See the difference?

This sentence can be interpreted to offend on many levels, but as an example of how punctuation can dramatically change the meaning of a sentence, it works—even if the story is of dubious origin.

Varying Sentence Length

All writers know that varying sentence length is a key to keeping your reader interested. Take this paragraph from Mary Roach's *Stiff: The Curious Lives of Human Cadavers*, in which she describes what the book will be about and some of the "odd, often shocking, always compelling things cadavers have done." Lest the reader disagree, Roach writes:

> Not that there's anything wrong with just lying around on your back. In its way, rotting is interesting too, as we will see. It's just that there are other ways to spend your time as a cadaver. Get involved with science. Be an art exhibit. Become part of a tree. Some options for you to think about. Death. It doesn't have to be boring.

If you count up the number of words in each of these sentences, they are: 12, 11, 14, 4, 4, 5, 7, 1, 6. There is a rhythm to this prose. Long. Long. Long. Short. Short. Short. Very short. Short (and funny).

JUMPSTART

Pick any nonfiction book you're reading and choose one paragraph that you find particularly memorable. Count the words per sentence in that paragraph. What do you notice?

If all the sentences contain approximately the same number of words, they may lull the reader to sleep with their sameness. If you want to wake up the reader, make your prose sing: vary the lengths. This is not to say that a writer sits there thinking to herself, "Hmmm.

I have a 12-word sentence here; now it's time for a 27-word one."
Rather, we vary our sentences instinctively. If you think your prose
is falling flat on the page, count the word lengths of your sentences
and see if you can change things up.

Run-On Sentences and Fragments

Two of the biggest offenders in clear writing are *run-on sentences*
(or run-ons) and *fragments*. In English, sentences must have a subject
and a verb and express a complete thought. "I am" is a sentence.
"I am writing" is also a sentence. "Am writing" is not.

DEFINITION

A **run-on sentence** is an ungrammatical sentence in which two or more
independent clauses (which could be complete sentences on their
own) have been joined together without the appropriate punctuation.
A **fragment** is a group of words that is missing a subject, verb, or
complete idea and thus cannot stand alone as a sentence.

You might have heard the phrase "sentence boundaries" back in
school. That refers to the beginnings and particularly the endings
of sentences. You can get into trouble with your readers if you have
sentences that are run-ons, meaning they have more than one subject
and verb and don't use enough punctuation. Think of a run-on as
the inebriated dinner guest who goes on and on with one story after
another and you want to tell him to leave but you can't because you
are a good host but if you hear the story one more time of how he
had a terrible childhood and thought he wasn't good enough his
whole life and no one gave him a break until he met this one woman
who turned his life around but then she left him for another man
and now he's miserable again and …. You get the point. That's a
run-on.

The other end of that spectrum is writing in fragments. We speak
in fragments all the time. We don't include either a subject or a verb.
"Walking the dog now," we may text someone. Well, that's fine. Our

friend understands who is walking the dog, but that is not a sentence. It's a fragment; it's missing a subject.

Take the Fragment Test

Sentences are made up of independent clauses, which are noun-verb predicates that can stand alone as complete sentences, and dependent clauses, which cannot. One way to test whether you have a fragment is to put "I realize" in front of the sentence and see if it makes sense as a new grammatical sentence, a tip I picked up from Larry Beason's and Mark Lester's book *A Commonsense Guide to Grammar and Usage*. It won't work with questions where the subject is implied, but let's look at a few examples:

> Walking the dog.
>
> Nonfiction writers get to live twice.
>
> Getting to live twice.

Which one sounds like it makes sense when you put "I realize" before it? The second one. That's a complete sentence. The other two are fragments. You might have noticed that I just wrote a fragment: "The second one." Are all fragments bad? Absolutely not. Writers use fragments purposefully to give rhythm to their prose, to add emphasis, or to make their prose punchier. In fact, the beauty of knowing the rules of grammar is being able to break them. However, if someone writes only in fragments or run-ons, it looks like that person doesn't know the rules.

How do we fix these particular fragments? Usually by adding a subject, verb, or auxiliary verb (forms of *be, do, have,* or *will* followed by another verb) such as "Henry was walking the dog."

Fixing Run-On Sentences

Remember the inebriated dinner guest? His story might have been a little more palatable if he'd used the pauses and stopping points that punctuation provides. We use punctuation—periods, commas, semicolons, colons, exclamation and quotation marks, apostrophes—like traffic signs, telling our reader to slow down, stop, or "note that this is important."

Say you have a run-on sentence (two or more independent clauses that could stand alone as complete sentences). There are three main fixes: you could add a period and make separate sentences; you could add a comma and a conjunction, or you could use a semicolon.

First, let's add periods to fix the run-on sentence:

> Think of a run-on as the inebriated dinner guest who goes on and on with one story after another. You want to tell him to leave. But you can't because you are a good host.

We could also add commas with a *conjunction*. One way to remember the conjunctions we use most often is the acronym FANBOYS: *for, and, nor, but, or, yet,* and *so* are all conjunctions.

DEFINITION

A **conjunction** is the part of speech that joins words, phrases, clauses, and sentences.

You can use a comma with a conjunction to join two independent clauses, but a conjunction by itself is not strong enough and leads to a run-on. Here's how we'd fix the sentences with a comma and a conjunction:

> Think of a run-on as the inebriated dinner guest who goes on and on with one story after another, and you want to tell him to leave, but you can't because you are a good host.

That sentence, with all three complete clauses, is grammatically correct.

Another way to fix run-ons is to use the semicolon. I tell my students to think of the semicolon as holding hands. Would you go up to a stranger on the street and grab her hand? No. If you see two people holding hands walking down the street, what does that imply? That they have a relationship. The same rule applies with the semicolon; you use it to show that the two independent clauses on either side have a relationship. Perhaps that relationship is cause and effect.

Perhaps it's one of illustration. Here's how we'd fix that dinner guest passage using semicolons:

> Think of a run-on as the inebriated dinner guest who goes on and on with one story after another. You want to tell him to leave, but you can't; you are a good host.

Using Strong Action Verbs

The average high school graduate knows about 45,000 words, according to Stephen Pinker in *The Language Instinct: How the Mind Creates Language*. But according to some linguists, we use only a fraction of these in everyday speech if we are native speakers of English—somewhere between 1,500 and 2,000 words. I'd bet that we use even fewer verbs and that the ones we do use tend to be the same ones over and over: *got, went, are, am,* and so on.

Strong verbs can make all the difference in your writing. Beginning writers often think that the more adjectives (descriptive words) and adverbs (which modify or change nouns and usually end in *-ly*) they use, the better. But think of adjectives and adverbs as your penny words: they're cheap. They don't usually add much more than garish decoration.

Your verbs, on the other hand, are the $500 words. You want to put your money on them. Because we tend to get in a verb rut, I tell my students to keep a list of strong or arresting verbs when they're reading for future use.

For instance, I love the way Dave Eggers turns a noun into a verb in this passage from *A Heartbreaking Work of Staggering Genius*, in which he is recalling how he and his siblings were hit by his mother and sometimes by his father:

> In my case, I guess, it was imagination more than anything, my morphing him into the murderers and monsters I *nightmared* [emphasis added] about every night, to a degree that I became convinced that there was a better than average chance that, given the wrong set of circumstances, that someday, it would be an accident, but that someday he'd kill one of us.

Using a noun, *nightmare*, and turning it into a verb, *nightmared*, as Eggers does, is certainly more arresting than saying something like, "I had nightmares about …," where the verb is the run-of-the-mill "had."

Consider Jo Ann Beard's verb choice in the following passage, taken from her unique nonfiction piece, "Undertaker, Please Drive Slow," about a real woman, Cheri Tremble, who is undergoing a mastectomy:

> This time there's a tray of knives, she sees them right before the anesthesia erases her. When she awakens her breast is gone, melted into a long weeping scar across her chest.

Use of the verb *erases* to describe the feeling of undergoing anesthesia, and the chilling *melted* to describe Tremble's missing breast, is remarkable, memorable, and does more to describe the scene than any amount of adjectives and adverbs could do.

JUMPSTART

Brainstorm a list of verbs associated with a particular profession different from your own, like a chef, fashion designer, poker player, or surgeon. Try these verbs in place of the ones you habitually use in your writing.

Metaphors and Similes

You may have heard the eighteenth-century Scottish poet Robert Burns' famous song:

> O my Luve's like a red, red rose
> That's newly sprung in June;
> O my Luve's like the melodie
> That's sweetly play'd in tune.

Or the nineteenth-century poet Christina Rossetti's poem "A Birthday," which begins:

> "My heart is like a singing bird
> Whose nest is in a water'd shoot;
> My heart is like an apple-tree
> Whose boughs are bent with thick-set fruit; …

You might already know that when you compare two things using "like" or "as" you have a *simile*. But if you were to say, as Shakespeare did, "All the world's a stage," you'd have a *metaphor*.

 DEFINITION

A **simile** is a figure of speech in which two unlike things are compared, usually introduced with the word "like" or "as." A **metaphor** is a figure of speech where one thing is said to be another for the purpose of comparison.

Why use metaphors and similes in your writing? Because they make your writing memorable. Surprising similes and metaphors stick in the craw of memory.

What if you're not a poet and don't consider yourself to be particularly metaphorical? I've never felt that using metaphors or similes was my strong suit. Yet I've seen people, not all of them writers, who seem to effortlessly unspool surprising comparisons when they speak that would take me weeks to think up.

Fortunately, there are some tricks to help you write more metaphorically. One is to notice how often we speak in comparisons. If you've ever been around children, you might have fun watching how they literalize metaphors. For instance, I remember a friend telling her daughter to show my son "the ropes" at school, meaning, of course, to help him feel comfortable. "What ropes?" she asked quite rightly. You get the point. We often speak in metaphors without realizing it.

Pay attention to any newscast and see how we talk about "front lines of defense" in a "war against cancer" or some other disease. Comparisons are all around you; the trick is to come up with new ones.

Writing teachers tend to share exercises that work, and this next one absolutely does. In his book *Writing Life Stories, How to Make Memories into Memoirs, Ideas into Essays, and Life into Literature*, Bill Roorbach calls it "The Old Chinese Restaurant Menu Exercise." In one column, list a number of abstract ideas like *love, marriage, friendship, romance, hatred, illness*, or whatever topic you want to write about. In the second column, list some concrete nouns like *truck, fire, knife, dishwasher, pen*, and *tree*.

Here's an example:

Column A:	Column B:
Love	Truck
Marriage	Fire
Friendship	Knife
Romance	Dishwasher
Hatred	Pen
Illness	Tree

Now take one item from Column A and one from Column B, such as "Love is like a truck" for a simile or "Love is a truck" for a metaphor. Write one or two paragraphs, extending the metaphor for as long as you can. "Love is a truck, an 18-wheeler, barreling down the highway of life without any brakes." Or something like that. Keep going. Don't censor yourself. Don't worry if what you're writing doesn't make any sense. I promise you that somewhere, if you keep writing long enough, you'll come up with something original, something surprising and fresh.

Instead of nouns in column B you could put verbs, suggests Roorbach. Let's say you had *wash* as a verb in the second column. You might begin "Love washes …" and let yourself write for a paragraph or two and see what comes out.

PITFALL AHEAD

Although using some metaphors and similes can make your writing more interesting, take care not to overuse them. Too many metaphors or similes will detract from rather than enhance your prose.

Avoiding Clichés

"She had a heart as good as gold." "It was a piece of cake." "I could see the handwriting on the wall." These *clichés* are overused expressions. At one time they were fresh, but that may have been hundreds of years ago. Many clichés come from the Bible; others are from Shakespeare. The problem with clichés is that they shut our minds down. If someone said that going through a divorce was not "a walk in the park," we'd know it was difficult. But how difficult? If, on the other hand, that person described being so upset by the divorce that he "lost 40 pounds and couldn't eat more than breakfast in any one day," we'd get more of a sense of the toll the divorce was taking on him.

DEFINITION

Clichés are trite or overused figures of speech. They should be avoided because they cause the reader to gloss over rather than understand what you are trying to show.

Do you recognize the following clichés? They all come from William Shakespeare's work, and while they were novel in the sixteenth century, they are worn out in the twenty-first century. Avoid these in your writing:

- It's all Greek to me
- Dead as a doornail
- Heart of gold
- Love is blind
- Set my teeth on edge
- Star-crossed lovers
- Wear one's heart on one's sleeve

- (He won't) budge an inch
- Tongue-tied
- In a pickle
- Slept not a wink

How to Make Your Prose Musical

Just like in music, your words have a beat on the page. You may not even realize this until you read your work out loud, when you can hear how it sounds. This is one of the tips for developing your voice, as discussed in Chapter 3. One way to beat out a tune is through repetition, using either words or clauses that are similar.

In *Hard Times*, a critique of the industrial revolution that was polluting British cities and turning men and women into automatons, Charles Dickens describes the fictional town of Coketown this way:

> It contained several large streets all very like one another, and many small streets still more like one another, inhabited by people equally like one another, who all went in and out at the same hours, with the same sound upon the same pavements, to do the same work, and to whom every day was the same as yesterday and to-morrow, and every year the counterpart of the last and the next.

What is the effect of this on the reader? We understand the numbing sameness of life in Coketown; the routine is underscored by the repetition of the phrase "like one another" and by continually repeating "same," which beats more persistently and ominously as the passage closes, much like the continually beaten-down life of the workers who live in Coketown. In this example, the sound echoes the meaning and underscores Dickens' theme: a condemnation of capitalism and the darker side of the industrial revolution.

Here's another example, from John F. Kennedy's 1961 inaugural speech: "And so, my fellow Americans: ask not what your country can do for you—ask what you can do for your country." Do you feel the rhythm in that sentence?

Or hear the ringing notes of another sentence in this speech: "Let every nation know … that we shall pay any price, bear any burden, meet any hardship, support any friend, oppose any foe, in order to assure the survival and the success of liberty." Note the strong verb clauses, particularly the *alliterative* ones, where there is a repetition of consonants as in "pay any price" or "bear any burden." These are strong clauses made that much more serious and pounding by the repetition of sounds.

DEFINITION

Alliteration, the same letter or stressed consonant sound at the beginnings of words in a group, is often used in poetry and for emphasis in prose.

The Least You Need to Know

- Grammar is about the relationships of words to each other in a way that makes meaning possible. Punctuation is important not only for changing the meaning of sentences, but also for letting your reader know when to stop, slow down, pause, or if there's something important ahead.

- Varying the length of your sentences is a simple way to make your writing more interesting.

- Run-on sentences can tire your reader and should be avoided; fragments, which are missing a subject, verb, or complete idea, are okay when used sparingly.

- Choosing strong action verbs add impact to your writing.

- Metaphors and similes are comparisons that add freshness and surprise to your writing, but take care not to overuse them. Do avoid clichés in your writing, which are overused or trite expressions.

- You can make your prose musical by using repetition of words, clauses, or consonants.

Revision: Your Best Friend

In This Chapter

- Revising to find your central focus
- Revising at the paragraph level
- Pacing your paragraphs
- Doing line-by-line or sentence editing
- Revising at the word level
- Avoiding common writing mistakes

No writer gets it right the first time—or even the second or third. Almost all writers subscribe to editor and writer Harry Shaw's theory that "There is no such thing as good writing. There is only good rewriting." Supposedly even the ancient Greeks practiced a form of this philosophy. Upper-class boys learned to write by rewriting: they'd carve letters on wax-covered tablets, etching their words with a wooden stylus or pen, then heat the wax, smooth it over, and begin writing again.

Though students often see revision as punishment, revision is really a gift. In speech, we can't take back things we've said in anger or in a moment of carelessness other than by adding more speech and saying, "I'm sorry." But we can in writing because we can revise. How do writers revise? I know writers who perfect one paragraph, which can take anywhere from an hour to six or seven, and then move on the next. Other writers revise as they go along, unable to pick out where one draft ends and another begins. For others, revision happens at the end of an entire draft and continues for several drafts after that. There's no right way to revise; whatever works for you is the right way. But there is no writer who doesn't revise.

Revising for Focus

Revision in writing is all about knowing what to leave in and what to take out. Simple, right? Well, it can be once you know what you're writing about and if you follow a few principles for revising.

When you're revising, you're usually doing one or more of these operations: adding, deleting, substituting, or reordering, according to Harvard Writing Program Director Nancy Sommers, whose prize-winning article, "Revision Strategies of Student and Experienced Writers," shaped the way so many writing instructors think and teach revision. These operations are performed at several levels: thematic, paragraph, sentence, and word. Before you revise at the sentence level, you need to figure out the central focus or the theme of the piece. Then work on making sure all paragraphs adhere to your central focus before you begin decluttering your sentences or substituting words.

Finding the Central Focus

If you're making chocolate chip cookies and decide to put in shredded coconut, raisins, oatmeal, and ginger, you've got too much going on for one cookie. The same is true in writing: good nonfiction pieces have only one central focus.

In the words of master nonfiction writer William Zinsser, "every successful piece of nonfiction should leave the reader with one provocative thought that he or she didn't have before. Not two thoughts, or five—just one." The late Pulitzer-prize winning journalist and lifelong writing teacher Donald Murray puts it another way: what distinguishes "the successful writer and the unsuccessful one is that the successful writer says one thing. One idea dominates."

WRITERS' WORDS

"The beautiful part of writing is that you don't have to get it right the first time, unlike, say, a brain surgeon. You can always do it better, find the exact word, the apt phrase, the leaping simile."

—Robert Cormier, award-winning American journalist and novelist

But how do you find that one idea? When you're writing the first draft of an essay, you shouldn't worry too much about the theme—or anything really; you're just trying to figure out what you have to say. But after you've done one or two drafts, it's time to put on your editor's hat and ask yourself: What's it all about? What is the one thing I'm trying to say here? In other words, what's my main focus?

To help find your theme, ask yourself these questions:

- What did I learn in this piece?
- What one thing am I trying to show the reader?
- What surprised me in writing this?
- What leaps out as being the most important?

If you have a trusted writer friend, something we'll discuss in Chapter 16, you might ask that person to read the piece with these questions in mind:

- What do you remember most about the piece?
- Where were you most interested?
- What do you want to know more about?
- What dragged in the piece?
- What do you think it's about?

WRITERS' WORDS

"Revision is where fine art begins."

—Barbara Kingsolver, American novelist and nonfiction writer

Beginnings and Endings

Another way to find the focus is to look at the beginning and ending of your draft. In college composition classes, students often write their way toward their thesis—their central focus—which is contained in the last paragraph of their essay. Though they're often dismayed when I point this out and tell them that almost everything but the last paragraph has to go, I try to get them to see the upside: they've done the hard part, finding their focus, and now have the backbone on which to build.

In writing nonfiction you may not have an argument, but it still may take a few drafts to figure out the one thing you want to say in the piece. Take a look at your beginning and your concluding paragraphs. Do you have a single focus? Did you write your way to a more interesting idea? And if so, what do you need to keep and take out to keep this unity of focus?

Novelist, nonfiction writer, and activist Barbara Kingsolver writes that her "best writing tool is the Delete key." She counts the first hundred pages of a new novel in negative numbers from –100 to zero, as she knows she will write them but throw them out.

It helps not to get too wedded to the beginnings of what you've written. I often think of the first few paragraphs or pages as building a bridge to what I want to say but being expendable afterwards. If you're stuck on what your focus is, take a look at the last several paragraphs and see if you've built your bridge to it.

JUMPSTART

"Writing is like a piece of pie," says essayist Adair Lara. "Let it cool before touching it with a knife." Time is on your side in revision—unless you're under a deadline. But even so, you should let your piece rest for a few hours, days, or even a week. Then come back to it with fresh eyes when you're more objective and can see what's working and what's not.

Revising at the Paragraph Level

Once you have your main focus, it's time to see if every paragraph advances the main idea. Some writers compose outlines before they begin a nonfiction article or chapter, which helps them write paragraphs that stick to the main idea. Others, like me, outline after the fact. I look at every paragraph and ask myself: What am I really trying to say here? Does it illustrate the central theme? Is it off-topic? If so, I delete it.

When I'm revising, I find it much easier to print out my entire piece so I can see it all. You can't see more than a page at a time on a computer screen. Yes, it's not ecologically sound (however, you can print out subsequent drafts on the backsides of the paper), but I need to hold what I'm working on in my hands, read it through several times, and see how everything fits together.

JUMPSTART

Take a nonfiction piece that you've written and outline it afterward. In the margin next to every paragraph, write two or three words of what that paragraph is about. Do they all fit your focus?

Pacing in Your Paragraphs

I'm sure we've all had the experience of listening to someone relate a story and saying silently to ourselves, "Come on. Get on with it." That's pacing, which in narrative nonfiction refers to how slowly or quickly you tell the story. And, of course, you want your readers to be sitting on the edge of their seats, neither impatiently hurrying you to get to the good part nor nodding off because you've got too much extraneous material.

How do you know if the pacing is working? I think it's easier to know when pacing is *not* working. When pacing—the way the events are told—unfolds in just the right way, you don't think about it.

Here's where it's helpful to have good readers give you feedback. These are questions you want to ask of yourself or a writing group or buddy:

- Where do you want me to slow down and tell more?
- Where do you want me to speed up?
- Where were there too many details?
- Is there too much telling and not enough showing?
- Where were the most exciting parts of the piece?

If you can answer some of these questions, you'll see where you've gotten the pacing just right and where you need to pick up (or slow down) the pace.

You may be able to delete entire paragraphs that slow down the pacing. Does one paragraph contain a so-so anecdote? Cut it out. Does another add nothing to your central focus? Again, cut it out.

How can you pick up the pace of your narrative? You can add dialogue or substitute a scene for a summary. You can cut extraneous material like description if it's irrelevant to your focus. You can also plot out the events in your piece and see how they contribute to the narrative arc: the conflict, rising tension, climax, and resolution, which I discussed in Chapter 2. If an event is not part of this arc, get rid of it.

When you look at your piece as a whole, seeing how all the parts work, you can see which paragraphs support your theme and add to perfect pacing and which paragraphs need revision or excising. You can also rearrange your paragraphs. Does the paragraph containing the conflict need to be moved closer to the opening? Does the order of the concluding paragraphs need to be changed? There's nothing that says you have to keep your paragraphs in the order you initially wrote them if changing them will improve the pacing.

 PITFALL AHEAD

Don't be afraid to get your hands dirty and revise your work. You can always save different drafts on your computer. Just make sure you label them 1.1, 1.2, and so on, or whatever scheme works for you, and that you don't delete anything you might want to put in again later.

Revising Your Sentences and Getting Rid of Clutter

I talked about getting rid of run-ons and too many fragments in Chapter 12, and now it's time to take a closer look at the individual sentences of your piece in the revision process.

If you're writing for a specific magazine that has word count guidelines, you learn how to edit pretty quickly. Nothing ticks off an editor more than turning in a piece that's twice as long as it should be. Not only will she return it to you to do the hard work of revising, but she also will probably never assign you anything again.

Part of getting something right on the page is examining your sentences and making sure they are all doing the work they are supposed to: advancing the central idea. Shorter sentences, punchy fragments, and dialogue all speed up the pace. Longer sentences, full of clause after clause, slow down your reader.

Somewhere along the line, particularly in academic writing, we subscribed to the notion that the more difficult or impenetrable the writing, the more intelligent the author. The contrary is more likely true: it takes great skill to write simply. Just as Olympic ice skaters make performing double and triple axels look easy, experienced writers do the hard work of revising so that readers can glide effortlessly through their prose.

How do you make your sentences easy to read? In William Zinsser's words, you get rid of the clutter. Our language is full of clutter. Take the fine print of your credit card statements, health insurance coverage, or a car or apartment rental agreement. How much of the meaning comes across plainly? How much do you understand? What's included or excluded in your coverage? Who's to say?

WRITERS' WORDS

"Any fool can cut a bad line. It takes a real pro to cut a good line."

—Theodore Roethke, American poet

Clutter in a sentence is any word that is not doing important work. But getting rid of clutter, pruning your sentences to make them work efficiently, is done during the last phase of revision. I don't worry about sentence-level or line-by-line editing until I have a close-to-final version.

The following are some examples of clutter:

- Extra prepositions, as in "head *up* a committee."
- Superfluous adjectives. Poet Theodore Roethke would advise his poetry students to "take out all the adjectives" and "see which ones are absolutely essential to the poem"—or nonfiction story.
- Habitual expressions that don't mean anything, such as "as a matter of fact," "at this point in time," or "needless to say."
- Adverbs, those words ending in *-ly*, such as walked *slowly*. Instead, choose a more descriptive verb, such as *ambled*.
- Euphemisms, such as the phrase "collateral damage" when used by the military. Isn't it more accurate and stronger to say "civilians were killed and their property damaged"?

Revising at the Word Level

I tell my students to use what I call the Titanic metaphor when looking at their sentences: you only have so many lifeboats to use, and those lifeboats can only hold so many words. Which words will be cut loose, buried undersea? (It's okay; they're only words.) Which words are worth saving? It's do or die time, and you must decide.

Many writers take to heart this famous quote from British journalist, critic, and novelist Sir Arthur Quiller-Couch: "Whenever you feel an impulse to perpetrate a piece of exceptionally fine writing, obey it—whole-heartedly—and delete it before sending your manuscript to press. *Murder your darlings.*" In other words, indulge your urge to write whatever you want, to fall in love with your prose, but then have the ruthlessness to excise your favorite lines. It's difficult to "murder your darlings"—to get rid of the sentences or passages that you're inordinately fond of—but it's often necessary. Why? Because you most likely can't be objective about whether they work or not. I suggest not murdering them entirely; just take them out, open a new file on your computer, and label them "darlings" or whatever subject you'd like.

When I'm writing a first or second draft, I'm less likely to fall in love with my words and more likely to think of them as understudies standing in for the real stars: the Academy Award–winning words. I have a friend who actually worked at Hollywood award shows as a "seat filler": he'd take the seat of a star who went to the bathroom or got up to make a phone call so it wouldn't look like there were any empty seats. And I think of my words in a first draft as similar to my friend's job: some words are just placeholders for words that are more precise, accurate, revealing, distinctive, telling, or memorable.

Now it's time to fill these seats with the real stars. Use proper nouns, specific words, fewer adjectives, and no adverbs at all. Rethink your verbs to use strong ones.

Perhaps there is no better advice about how to write succinctly than George Orwell's in his 1946 must-read essay, "Politics and the English Language." Here are Orwell's six rules:

> (i) Never use a metaphor, simile, or other figure of speech which you are used to seeing in print.
>
> (ii) Never use a long word where a short one will do.
>
> (iii) If it is possible to cut a word out, always cut it out.
>
> (iv) Never use the passive where you can use the active.
>
> (v) Never use a foreign phrase, a scientific word, or a jargon word if you can think of an everyday English equivalent.
>
> (vi) Break any of these rules sooner than say anything outright barbarous.

Checklist for Revision

Revision: the word itself means "to see again." Revision is your chance to get it right on the page. One way to do that is to let it sit. I forget which writer said that revision happens in your desk drawer. I've found that to be true. Letting your piece marinate for a day or two or a week allows you to come back with fresh eyes, to literally see it again. With time, you may find that parts you were very fond of are more easily deleted and that parts you thought were good could be made better with another example or two.

Continually ask yourself, "How can I make this better? How can I sandblast off the extra writing?" in journalist Anne Hull's words. Take your hardcopy and your pen, and sandblast the excess words, the meaningless phrases, the jargon, the flabby writing that takes up space but doesn't advance the narrative. This kind of sandblasting can take the writing from 70 to 90 percent finished, says Hull. "Cut as close to the bone as possible," she says, which is good advice.

How many drafts are enough? When asked this question, *The New Yorker* humor writer S. J. Perlman purportedly said 37: 33 drafts were too few but 42 too many, he quipped. How many should you do? As many as it takes.

What you're doing when you're revising is not only seeing it with fresh eyes but also anticipating the readers' eyes and their questions. To make revision easier, here is a checklist to help you see your work in a new light:

- ❏ Do you start at the most interesting place? Perhaps close to the conflict?
- ❏ Does the opening hook the reader with an interesting quote, anecdote, statistic, question, or other surprising opening?

- ❏ Does the piece have one central focus?
- ❏ Do all the paragraphs relate to that focus?
- ❏ Does the pacing work to move the piece along?
- ❏ Does it have a voice?
- ❏ Are your sentences decluttered?
- ❏ Are your facts right?
- ❏ Is it easy to read?
- ❏ Have you taken out anything—dialogue, description, information—that doesn't add to the focus?
- ❏ Do you use the absolute best word?

Avoiding Common Writing Mistakes

In addition to revising at several levels, there are other things to look out for as you're writing or rewriting. These common writing mistakes can sink your piece and prevent your reader from sticking around to the end or even the middle. If your piece just isn't working, ask yourself if you're committing one or more of these errors.

Changing Point of View

As we saw in Chapter 10, one of the sins travel writers often fall prey to is not keeping a consistent point of view. You might start off with an autobiographical account of going to Ixtapa with your mother and sister, and suddenly you change tone by providing historical details about the Aztec Indians and the Nahuatl language they spoke. In one sentence you're a first person narrator recounting how you're struggling to get along with your nuclear family on the first vacation the three of you have taken together since high school, and in another you're recounting the history of Mexico and her people from the third person perspective of a history tome.

You have to decide who is telling the story. Is it a first person narrator using "I"? Or are you going to recount the events from a third person point of view?

It's okay to vary the point of view once in a while. I often use the second person "you" (as in the previous paragraph) to draw the reader into the piece. So though you don't have to always use "I," you do need to be aware of changing the point of view so that it doesn't completely change the tone of your piece. If you switch too often from first to second to third, you risk losing your readers to a kind of verbal whiplash as they look around trying to see who's on first.

PITFALL AHEAD

Though you might have been told in high school English class to always use "one" and never "I," that rule doesn't apply in narrative nonfiction. Using "one" often makes the voice of the piece sound disembodied or absent.

Not Having a Voice

Pick up almost any instructional manual for your DVR, DVD player, computer, or smart phone, and what do you find? Probably no voice at all. Government documents, credit card instructions, and other "impersonal" writing often doesn't have a voice. It's easier to hide information and not take responsibility if there is no actor, no voice, no one in command of the language.

But a good nonfiction piece cannot thrive without a voice; it will wither on the page. If you can't hear your voice—where you sound like your real, vibrant, warm, authentic self—try reading the piece out loud. Where do you sound like yourself? What parts sound like you're trying too hard or speaking with an accent? Get rid of those and keep only the parts that sound like a real human being. Like you.

Not Keeping the Facts Straight

As a nonfiction writer, you impart information. It's part of your job. The reader trusts that you've double- and triple-checked all your statistics, quotations, sources, government documents, and journals to give as accurate a representation as possible. If you don't know something, admit it. The reader will trust you more. If you do state a statistic, provide a fact, use a quotation, or impart information, you have to make sure it's accurate to the best of your ability. You have to be your own fact-checker. Your reputation as a nonfiction writer, both in a particular piece and in general, is on the line.

> **WRITERS' WORDS**
>
> "Only editors know the awful truth: how bad even the best narrative stories look in the beginning. Successful rewriting requires a fierce sense of competition with yourself, not anyone else. You must be dogged in reaching for your personal best. When you begin a story's first draft, you must ask yourself hard questions."
>
> —Anne Hull, *Washington Post* reporter

Holding Back from the Reader

Sometimes in a personal essay or narrative nonfiction piece, a student will hold something back from the reader. The other students can always tell that there's something missing. It's uncanny. Maybe the writer does not mean to be untruthful or to omit relevant information. Maybe there's more to the story that will be uncovered by pressing on this particular area. But the rule is, if you know more, spill it. When you spill it is up to you. But holding back—both of information and of yourself on the page—will cause your reader to retreat.

As Annie Dillard advises in *The Writing Life*, "One of the things I know about writing is this: spend it all, shoot it, play it, lose it, all, right away, every time. Do not hoard what seems good for a later place in the book or for another book; give it, give it all, give it now."

The Least You Need to Know

- Every piece of nonfiction should have one central focus, one thing that unifies all the material in that essay, article, or chapter.

- You can outline your draft after you've written it to see how all the paragraphs relate to your focus and delete those that do not move the story along.

- Pacing refers to how quickly or slowly you tell the story in your piece. You can pick up the pace of the narrative by shortening your sentences or adding dialogue and pruning description and summary.

- Revise your sentences by pruning excess words and using only the best or most precise word.

- Revision means seeing your piece with fresh eyes; leaving it for a few days or a week can help you get the distance you need to revise.

- Avoid common writing mistakes such as changing the point of view or tone of the piece, not having a voice, holding back from the reader, and not getting your facts straight—all will cause you to lose your reader.

After the Writing Is Done

Congratulations! You've done the hard part, and now you want to send your nonfiction out into the world. In this part, I introduce you to both paying and nonpaying markets and show you how to break in. Often the rules for breaking into consumer magazines (which do pay) and literary magazines (which might not pay) are the same: for personal essays, for example, you send the entire piece and follow the magazine's guidelines for submission. I address how to submit your work, how long to wait to hear back, and how to deal with rejection, which is part of life for any writer.

I also talk about setting up a successful blog with tips for writing content and attracting readers, as well as other venues for DIY publishing. You also find out how to market your writing. Finally, I share tips for building and sustaining a writing life over the long haul. By the end of this book, you'll have all you need to start, hone, and establish your nonfiction writing career.

Breaking into Nonfiction Markets

In This Chapter

* What markets are there for narrative nonfiction?
* How to break into literary and online magazines
* Sending out simultaneous submissions
* Understanding query letters
* How to deal with rejection
* Answers to frequently asked questions

Congratulations! Your nonfiction piece is written and revised; it's your best work, and now you'd like to get it published. What do you do next? Today all kinds of publishing venues exist, from literary nonfiction magazines (online and in print) to consumer publications, traditional book publishers, and self-published e-books (which we'll cover in Chapter 15).

Knowing where and how to send your piece is key for it to reach a larger audience. And then there's dealing with rejection, which is inevitable for every writer. Being a writer takes persistence and resilience in general; multiply that a few hundred times when you start to send your work out. You must develop a thick skin and take off your writer's hat, putting on your business person's attire instead.

The Narrative Nonfiction Market

Which magazines do you habitually read? What magazines do you have piling up by your bedside table? What's the first thing you pick up when you're browsing at a bookstore? Figuring out where to send your work is part sleuthing, as you uncover new markets, and part affinity, as you think about submitting to the kinds of magazines you're drawn to. I've heard authors say they write the kinds of books they want to read; nonfiction writers also tend to write the kinds of pieces they like to read and publish them in like-minded journals.

Today there are many opportunities for the narrative nonfiction writer. Open almost any magazine, and you'll see a section devoted to personal experience, essays, travel, or narrative nonfiction. The reading public seems to hunger for true stories that are well told. It used to be that you sent out short stories to magazines; now you generally send narrative nonfiction.

Some venues, like consumer magazines, may pay $1 per word. Others, like literary and smaller online magazines, pay little or nothing at all. While seeing your byline in a magazine is a thrilling experience, it doesn't change your life—or your wallet—all that much, unless you're very prolific. The truth about writing for money is that, unlike inflation or the price of gasoline, writers' salaries have not changed much in decades: a "good" rate is still $1 per word, sometimes $2 or $3, and often less. This is not meant to discourage you. It's possible to earn a living as a freelance writer by selling your nonfiction, and it's possible to break into consumer magazines—those you see on newsstands—as a beginning writer. After all, all those bylines contain the names of writers who were once starting out just like you.

JUMPSTART

Brainstorm a list of your favorite magazines, both online and in print. Then skim these magazines to see the kinds of nonfiction they publish and what departments are devoted to essays, journalism, or articles. Make a list of your top 10 dream markets and then another 5 of your second-tier markets. Aim high: submit to your dream markets first; then go down the list.

Breaking into the Market

It's been said that experienced writers "sell first and write later," whereas inexperienced writers "write first and sell later." When you're just starting out, you will probably have to do more of the latter than the former. But when you are pitching nonfiction articles, most times you sell them first and then write them. And you do this with a detailed query letter, which I'll discuss later in this chapter.

I usually tell students who want to break into nonfiction writing to try the literary and personal essay markets first or the magazines that are taking complete travel essays or food pieces. The reason? When you're pitching these markets, you're sending the entire piece. This is your best work; you've rewritten your narrative nonfiction piece 20 times until you can't rewrite it anymore. It's your baby, and you want to get it out there.

The best-case scenario? You get an acceptance and your essay is published. The second-best-case scenario? You get a personalized rejection letter where the editor likes your work and asks you to send her something else. In the third-best case, you get a form rejection letter saying your piece is not right for the publication and wishing you luck. The worst-case scenario is radio silence. Unfortunately that happens, too. But even in this case, your essay was probably read and you've made contact (establishing a possible link to an editor who likes your work).

When you send out an essay or first-person piece, it acts as your calling card, your entrée into the world of publishing. That's one reason sending out personal essays is a good place to start; you're more likely to break in with a quality first-person piece or memoir excerpt than you are with a magazine article idea, and you can get an editor to notice your work.

Do Your Homework

The first rule when you're trying to break into any magazine, whether literary or consumer, print or online, is to study the magazine in depth. Check your local library, which probably keeps not only the most current issue but also several months' worth of back issues.

Start with the cover page. What are the cover stories? Which ones capture your attention? Then check out the table of contents. What departments and columns does the magazine habitually run? Does it have a space for nonfiction essays or personal history or first-person journalism? Look at the editorial board and note the names of writers. It's often possible to determine potential freelance opportunities in a magazine by seeing which staff writers are responsible for which sections. Check out the contributors' biographies, if there are any, and read the corresponding articles. Look at the ads to figure out the audience demographics: does the magazine target women in their 30s or men in their 50s? How can you tell? See if you can determine the socioeconomic background, median age, educational level, or marital status of the typical reader based on the kinds of advertisements that appear.

And, of course, you must read several issues to get a feel for the voice of the magazine. Is it chatty or serious? Authoritative or questioning? Funny? Sarcastic? Conversational? Where do you see your work fitting in? Which magazines match the tone and style of your work? Target those publications.

Sending Your Work

If you're breaking into nonfiction markets, particularly with personal essays and first-person pieces, you'll need to send the completed piece. Many magazines devote a department to a form of the personal essay or short memoir, and these are excellent places to send your work.

How do you find these places? Every year or so, mediabistro.com, a website for "jobs, classes, community, and news for media professionals" (and a valuable resource for freelance writers) publishes a long list of Personal Essay Markets—"45 print publications that love personal essays"—and 15 digital publications that are also looking for a moving essay. Mediabistro is free for most of the site's services, but for this list as well as its frequent "How to Pitch" sections, you'll have to pay a small yearly fee, which is well worth it.

The most recent Personal Essay Markets list has magazines from *AARP* to *Yoga Journal*, and what's more, each entry specifies exact word length, pay, assigning editor, and tips from editors about exactly what they're looking for. Many say to check the submission guidelines and to read back issues, which you should do anyway, but there are also helpful hints about the kinds of essay topics editors would like to receive or advice on how they'd like you to hook the reader and structure your essay.

Literary Magazines

As the name implies, literary magazines are focused on publishing good-quality fiction and nonfiction, where the attention to literary techniques and compelling storytelling are just as important as the subject matter. These independent magazines are often good places for the beginning writer to break in to, as their mission statements often state that they publish emerging writers and experimental work.

Some literary magazines, like *AGNI* at Boston University, are housed at university creative writing programs. For the nonfiction writer, perhaps the most well known and largest literary magazine devoted solely to publishing nonfiction prose is *Creative Nonfiction* (CNF), established in 1993 by Lee Gutkind. But there are hundreds of other literary magazines, and even those that don't focus entirely on nonfiction often have a section devoted to essays or criticism or interviews, where the aspiring nonfiction writer can submit material. As always, it's necessary to do research and read widely in different online and print journals to see who publishes work like yours.

Like all literary journals, *Creative Nonfiction* receives far more submissions than it has room to publish. But don't let that stop you.

PITFALL AHEAD

Literary magazines can be just as competitive as consumer markets and just as hard to break in to. Always send your best work, and make sure what you're sending fits the magazine.

Breaking into Literary Magazines

Most literary magazines have submission guidelines that tell writers both exactly what the magazine is looking for—such as "well-written prose, rich with detail and a distinctive voice," according to *Creative Nonfiction*—and how to send in work: whether by email or snail mail, completed manuscripts or queries, including self-addressed stamped envelopes or not, or specifying font type. Writers ignore these guidelines at their peril.

Sometimes you have to scroll to the end of a website to find submission guidelines; other times they're located in small print on the front or back matter of a journal. Still other journals ask you to send a letter and self-addressed stamped envelope requesting submission guidelines that they'll then mail to you.

Be sure to review the guidelines carefully. If they say send essays of no more than 1,000 words and you send 2,000 words, it's doubtful your essay will be read. Editors are very busy, and they don't have time to wade through everything. One easy way to reject a writer is to toss those who don't follow the guidelines. Presentation—how you send the piece, and whether or not you adhere to the submission guidelines for sending it—can get your foot in a very narrow door.

What Do Literary Magazines Pay?

You won't get rich writing for literary magazines, though of course that's not why you send your work to them. Creative nonfiction pays $10 a page and sometimes requires a $20 reading fee to submit your work (or $25, and you get a year's subscription to the journal). *Brevity: A Journal of Concise Literary Nonfiction*, started by nonfiction writer Dinty Moore (whose interview appears in Appendix B), publishes brief nonfiction essays (fewer than 750 words) and pays a $45 honorarium to those writers whose work is selected.

"No man but a blockhead ever wrote, except for money," Samuel Johnson, eighteenth-century man of letters, purportedly said. So why would you send your work to a low-paying or nonpaying market? There are many reasons, from the thrill of seeing your byline, to sharing your work with others, to making connections with editors and readers, to amassing clips, which are published pieces that could lead to other work.

Lest you think that only unpublished writers submit to literary magazines, *Brevity* states on its website that it has featured work from "two Pulitzer Prize finalists, numerous NEA fellows, Pushcart winners, *Best American* authors," and writers from around the world, though it takes "a special joy in helping to launch a new literary career."

Publishing in a literary magazine can help you build your reputation, attract the notice of other editors, and gain readers. Whatever your reason, nonpaying markets can be a good place to start sending out your work.

Where to Find Literary Magazines

How do you find literary magazines? One of the best sources is www.newpages.com, which has an extensive A to Z listing of literary magazines. You can also check out a selected list in Appendix C. And every year Writer's Digest Books puts out a huge updated tome: *The Writer's Market: The Most Trusted Guide to Getting Published*, which lists thousands of venues for submitting your work to book publishers, consumer and literary magazines, trade journals, literary agents, and more. Each entry has a paragraph or two covering contact information (though editors move to different companies regularly, so you'll want to call to get the most up-to-date information), how long it takes them to respond, tips for submitting, what the magazine is looking for, and what, if anything, they pay. *Writer's Market* is a good resource, though at over 1,000 pages, it's a bit unwieldy at times. But in addition to the listings, it has sample query letters, information on contracts, even a self-publishing checklist in the 2012 edition. It's all useful stuff that's worth a look.

Online Magazines

Online magazines can be web-based or an extension of a print magazine, like *AGNI Online*. In the latter case, you might check to see if there are different submission rules for print or web-based work. *AGNI Online*, for example, is an eclectic magazine that publishes poetry, fiction, translations, and nonfictional essays; it also publishes material online that is not found in the print journal.

The recently started *Hippocampus Magazine*, on the other hand, is "an exclusively online publication set out to entertain, educate, and engage writers and readers of creative nonfiction," as its website proclaims. *Hippocampus* has a detailed Submissions link, stating that it accepts memoir excerpts, personal essays, and experimental nonfiction. It doesn't pay, but published authors get bios and links to their blogs or websites and "can win bragging rights AND a prize" states *Hippocampus*, "if his piece is deemed Most Memorable." The site also provides a new nonfiction writing prompt each month, which can be a fun way to keep writing.

JUMPSTART

Every year, publisher Houghton Mifflin Harcourt puts out a *Best American* series, an anthology of previously published work selected by genre or theme. There's *The Best American Essays, The Best American Sports Writing, The Best American Science and Nature Writing,* and others. Not only should you read the series you're interested in to see what the best have to say, you also should check out where they were published. Scan the table of contents in *The Best American Essays* anthologies, for example, and you'll see the title of the essay and where it was originally published. Read these journals and consider sending your work there.

We're still in the midst of an informational and digital revolution, which for the nonfiction writer translates into more opportunities to sell work to online markets, including websites. The rules of reading back issues (or in this case, archived material) still apply because you want to get a feel for the website or digital publication and the kinds of articles or essays it typically runs.

One advantage to publishing in a strictly online venue? Unlike a print magazine, where the content is decided four to six months in advance (for instance, many magazines are working on their Thanksgiving issue in February or March), online magazines and websites work much closer to real time. There's often a much shorter lag time between submission and publication, which means you can pitch holiday stories or essays closer to the actual month in which they fall.

You can find a selected list of online magazines in Appendix C, and you can dig up many more with a little web surfing on a site such as newpages.com. Some online magazines, like some literary magazines, may pay a small fee if they publish your piece: anywhere from $25 to $500 dollars, or even more. You can always check *The Writer's Market* for more information.

> **JUMPSTART**
>
> Although you may not get paid very well, or at all, for publishing in literary magazines, what you will gain is invaluable. You'll join a community of writers and readers, make connections with editors and other writers, and have bragging rights whether or not you win a prize.

Sending Work to More Than One Publication

The question that beginning writers always ask (and some established writers as well) is: can you send the same piece to two or more publications? You can if the submission guidelines say that they accept *simultaneous submissions*. But first you have to make sure your personal essay or nonfiction piece really fits all the markets you're sending it to. Some journals have a political slant and won't take essays unless they relate to a current issue in the world. Others, like *Brevity*, want short nonfiction (fewer than 750 words). Ask yourself: does your essay or nonfiction piece really fit both markets? If it does, you can send it simultaneously if submission guidelines say that's acceptable.

> **DEFINITION**
>
> **Simultaneous submission** means sending the same essay or work to two or more publications at the same time with the understanding that only one will publish it.

If the submission guidelines don't specify, you can state in your query letter (something I'll discuss later in this chapter) that you're sending it out to a few different places. Then there are the questions that only you can answer: "How lucky do you feel?" and "What would you do if they both wanted to publish your piece?" I know writers who say they have neither the time nor the bank account to wait months to see if a magazine will take their work and who thus advise sending it out to as many places as are good fits. But you risk alienating the editors at two journals if both want the piece. I've never had that happen to me, however, or to the many other writers I know and writing students whom I've taught. It's your call.

The Nonfiction Query Letter

Say you've sent out your essays and first-person pieces, or you've established your blog. You've done your homework, studying the magazines you want to write for and figuring out the departments open to freelancers and not written by staff. Now what?

The next step is to write a *query letter* (also called a pitch letter). The first line of the query letter is your hook: just like in any nonfiction piece, it needs to be immediately arresting. If the first sentence or two doesn't make the editor want to read on, then you've blown it. How do you start? With a quotation, story, interesting fact or statistic, or question. Remember that magazine editors are very busy people and get lots of email, so it's important to grab their attention immediately.

DEFINITION

A **query letter** is a short (usually a single page) letter of introduction about you and work.

The second paragraph is what's called your nut graph: in a nutshell (the origin of the term), it explains what your story is about and why it's timely and important. If you can't do that in a nutshell, chances are it won't sell.

The third paragraph fleshes out the main idea more by providing an example or two, perhaps the sources you'll interview or suggestions for sidebars. This is the paragraph that lets the editor envision what the piece will look like.

The fourth paragraph is what freelancer Kelly James-Enger calls the "I'm so great" paragraph. Here you specify why you and only you are the person to write the piece. You can talk about your work experience; for example, if you're pitching a parenting article, you'd mention that you are a mother of five children. You'd list places where your work has appeared and links to that work or to your blog. You want to give the editor a reason to assign the piece to you and only you. That's why James-Enger calls it the "I'm so great" paragraph. Tout yourself and your experience, but don't overdo it.

Dealing with Rejection

J. K. Rowling, author of the hugely successful *Harry Potter* books, claims her first book in the series was rejected by "lots" of publishers. Of course, she went on to become the world's best-selling author of the best-selling series in history. All writers are rejected at one point in their career. It comes with the territory. There's rejection when you send out a personal essay and it comes back with a "thanks, but not for us," letter—or no response at all. And then there's rejection when you get a bad review or a reader or editor doesn't like something you've written and lets you know it.

If you're *lucky*, you'll get rejected as a writer. And yes, you read that right. Because if you're getting rejected it means two things: you're not dreaming of *someday* being a writer, you really are one if you're sending out your work; and you can learn to be an even better writer by figuring out what's working and what's not. Whatever you do, don't use rejection as an excuse to give up or beat yourself up.

Learn from the Experience

I once got a rejection letter from a literary agent that said, "This did not hold my attention long enough to read it." Ouch. Though I didn't keep the letter, that one line is burned in my memory. The rejection also stopped me in my tracks for a good six months. Every day I went to work to teach writing; every evening I came home, laid on the couch, and felt sorry for myself.

Though I'm not sure what got me out of my depression, one day I got angry and fired off a response to the agent (which I wisely did *not* send): "How can you tell, if you didn't bother to read my book proposal?" And then I realized something: I'd sent my book proposal to the wrong agent. Although the agent had been recommended by a friend, I'd sent him a nonfiction book proposal (and sample chapters) on teaching women prisoners when he didn't cover that kind of book. Not only that, but what if the proposal itself needed work? And finally, what is one rejection from one literary agent? How could I let it derail me?

I got off the couch, rewrote the proposal, revised it a few more times, sent it out to three agents, and heard back from all three of them within a week. All three wanted to represent me and the book. One even went so far as to leave a voicemail telling me not to sign with anyone else until she had a chance to talk to me.

WRITERS' WORDS

"Rejection is not a stage that you outgrow and get over. Every time you don't see your book in a bookstore, you feel rejected; every time you don't win a prize and somebody else wins a prize, you feel rejected; every time somebody writes a stupid review on Amazon and gives your book one star, you feel rejected. Rejection comes in many forms—but it's part of the process of writing and publishing."

—Elizabeth Benedict, novelist (quoted in Catherine Wald's *The Resilient Writer: Tales of Rejection and Triumph from 23 Top Authors*)

Tips for Dealing with Rejection

The lesson I learned from that painful experience? There are several, and I'll list them here to hopefully save you from months of misery and wasted writing time:

- Consider whether your piece was right for the magazine, agent, or publication. If not, find a market that's a better fit and send it there.

- Use the rejection as a learning process to become a better writer. Review the tips on revising your work in Chapter 13 to see how you can improve your work even more.

- Don't take it personally. Easier said than done, I know, but publishing is a business and you can get rejected for reasons that have to nothing to do with your work and everything to do with the supply and demand of the marketplace.

- Read *The Resilient Writer: Tales of Rejection and Triumph from 23 Top Authors*, Catherine Wald's interviews with bestselling writers for inspiration, or another book on writing. You'll see that all writers get rejected.

- Send your work back out again immediately. Master writing teacher and journalist William Zinsser says that whenever a piece got rejected, he "didn't waste any time crying over the fact that it had come back," but rather "made it a principle to get it back in the mail by noon."

- Get in touch with your reasons for writing. Most likely they have more to do with your desire to express yourself and less with becoming rich and famous.

- Don't let doubt, fear, self-loathing, or any other negative feelings as a result of the rejection prevent you from writing.

- Put the rejection into perspective. Chris Bojhalian (essayist and author of the bestselling book *Midwives*) received 250 rejection slips before he published his first short story.

WRITERS' WORDS

"You can waste a lot of time on self-pity, and self-pity has no part in being a successful freelance writer."

—William Zinsser, teacher, journalist, and nonfiction writer

Frequently Asked Questions

While there are many books on how to become a freelance writer (you'll find a few listed in Appendix C), some frequently asked questions apply to sending out both narrative nonfiction and nonfiction queries. Here are some questions and answers about submitting nonfiction work.

Q: Do I send my piece by snail mail or email?

A: Check the submission guidelines. Most, though not all, publications will ask for email submissions.

Q: Do I need a detailed query letter if I'm sending a complete essay or narrative nonfiction piece?

A: No. The essay or personal narrative should speak for itself. But you do need a short cover letter introducing the essay by title, with a brief description (and word count) and a short paragraph about yourself and your qualifications. Always double-check submission guidelines to see if the publication wants more information.

Q: How long should I wait after I've sent in my work before I contact the editor?

A: It depends on the magazine. If they say they respond in a month, give them a month and a few days, and then contact the editor. Check *The Writer's Market* or the publication's guidelines and follow up after their turnaround time.

Q: What's the best way to follow up?

A: Usually by email. If you sent something by snail mail, call the main number and see if you can get an editor's email. But don't call. Editors have no time to speak to every writer who submits work.

Q: What if I never hear back?

A: Email once. Wait a week. Then email again. If you still don't get a response, move on and send your piece elsewhere.

Q: What if my piece gets rejected?

A: Think about whether you sent it to the right market. Revise if need be, and send it out again to another venue. Don't get too hung up on the rejection, but look at it as an opportunity to send the piece out to a "better" venue.

The Least You Need to Know

- Dozens of excellent literary magazines—both online and in print—seek nonfiction essays, memoirs, and autobiographical narrative work.

- Studying back issues of the literary journal or magazine that you want to break in to is essential. You want to understand the kinds of articles or essays it typically publishes and see if the tone and voice of the magazine fits your work.

- Be sure to review the publication's submission guidelines and follow them to the letter to increase your chances of success.

- Before sending simultaneous submissions, make sure submission guidelines allow it, and that your personal essay or nonfiction piece really fits all the markets you're sending it to.

- The query letter introduces you and your work. It should grab attention in the opening paragraph and make the editor want to read on.

- All writers face rejection; it comes with the territory. Let rejection work for you by revising your piece, resubmitting it to a more appropriate market, and learning how to become an even stronger writer.

Self-Publishing Your Work

In This Chapter

- Thinking about blogging?
- Secrets of successful bloggers
- Do-it-yourself publishing
- Promoting your work through social media and live events

Years ago, if you wanted to self-publish your work, you turned to a vanity press, which had a rather derogatory connotation (as well as title) and which meant the author had to pay for the privilege of seeing her name in print. All that has changed now with the internet and the proliferation of blogs and e-publishing venues. No longer is self-publishing looked at askance; rather, for many writers, it's not only more practical than turning to a traditional publisher but also more lucrative.

Why would you turn to a self-publishing venue? First, you don't have to face rejection. Second, you can get your work out in front of the public eye more quickly. Third, so many traditional publishers have slashed their marketing budgets that the writer must be not only author but also PR person and marketer as well. So why not just become a one-person publisher and bypass the traditional route?

Blogging

The numbers (though they change hourly) are staggering. According to WordPress, a *blog*-hosting site, there are 71.2 million WordPress blogs read by 375 million people who view more than 2.5 billion pages per month. And that's just WordPress. Other free blog hosting sites, such as Blogger, TypePad Micro, and Tumblr (see Appendix C) as well as corporate blogs and those on personal websites, no doubt match or surpass those numbers. It's safe to say that millions of people are blogging worldwide every day, producing billions of pages.

DEFINITION

Blog (a marriage of the words *web* and *log*) is an internet journal where the writer records observations, comments, or narrative, usually in an interactive format.

Which begs the question: who is reading all these blogs? And should you start one? What are the benefits of having a blog? For the nonfiction writer, blogging can be excellent practice for honing writing skills, developing a voice, presenting research, writing captivating leads, figuring out what you have to say, and saying it in a condensed, lively form. Good blogs—those that offer interesting content and are well written—are hard to do. Writing a blog can showcase your skills, help build a platform and attract readers, and even lead to freelance work.

Brainstorming a Blogging Subject

The typical internet reader has an attention span of about six seconds or less. To attract readers to your blog, you'll have to grab their attention, be provocative, promise new information, or give them a compelling story or voice so they keep reading—all in the span of a few seconds.

Which blogs do you read? Which do you read more than once? Thousands if not tens of thousands of blogs are probably started every day, and just as many probably languish for lack of interest.

You want yours to have staying power, and to do that you need not only good writing but also a unique angle to your blog.

Just like coming up with an idea for a personal essay or other auto-biographical nonfiction piece, blogging requires that you write about something that matters to you, something you're passionate about. Are you into yoga? Do you have a child with special needs and years of experience finding resources and support for the child that you can share with others? Are you newly divorced and struggling to be happily single? Or newly retired and seeking to live off a fixed income?

You need a topic for your blog but also an angle; that's what distinguishes your blog on yoga or nonfiction writing from all the other blogs on that subject. Is it your personality and voice—humorous and intimate? Your target audience—mothers of preschoolers with special needs? Your twist on the subject—yoga for people who don't like to exercise? The more time you spend honing your topic and angle before you begin your blog, the better.

JUMPSTART

Brainstorm a list of 5 to 10 things that you are passionate about. Choose one and come up with your "USP"—unique selling proposition—or angle. What twist can you put on this topic to make your blog stand out?

Catchy Blog Titles and Tag Lines

Every blog needs a great title and a tag line, your blog's main message. The tag line is just as important as the blog title itself. Tag lines are short (10 to 12 words or less), powerful, punchy, and most of all memorable.

Think of your tag line as your Hollywood movie elevator pitch: it's the summation of what your blog is about in a few memorable words.

Here are a few blogs and their tag lines. Which ones attract your attention?

- Writer Joanna Penn's blog *The Creative Penn* (thecreativepenn.com) has this tag line: "Helping you write, publish and sell your book." Incidentally, Penn's blog was voted one of the top 10 blogs for writers in 2011.

- On an entirely different topic, food blogger Deb Perelman's *Smitten Kitchen* blog (smittenkitchen. com)—"Fearless cooking from a tiny kitchen in New York"—features photos, recipes, and autobiographical musings in a warm conversational style that makes it seem as if you're talking to a good friend in her kitchen.

- Prolific freelancer and author Kelly James-Enger's blog is called *Dollars and Deadlines* (dollarsanddeadlines.blogspot. com). Her tag line? "Helping nonfiction freelancers make MORE money in less time."

- Former journalist Julia Scott has a very successful and profitable blog, *Bargain Babe* (bargainbabe.com), with the tag line "Daily tips for savvy spenders."

You get the picture. How do you think of a great title and tag line? First brainstorm a list of words and phrases that come to mind when you think about your blog topic. Write down as many as possible. Pick one word that stands out. Put that in the center of a piece of paper. Next draw bubbles branching out from this word that illustrate your word with activities, events, or other words and phrases. Let's say your topic is "meditation." Put that in the center of a piece of paper, and brainstorm whatever comes to mind when you think of meditation.

After you've done the brainstorming exercises, try cutting out these words and phrases with actual scissors (not cutting and pasting on the computer). Next use them as building blocks and play around with them, just as a child would with actual lettered blocks. What you're aiming for here is novelty or surprise, something that captures the subject of your blog in an interesting way.

After you have your blog title, or a few candidates, it's time to think up a tag line. Try these exercises to help you brainstorm a tag line:

- List five benefits that readers can get from your blog. How will it help them?
- Draw (even if you're not artistic) the main idea of your blog. What colors would you use? What shapes or images pop into your mind?

After you have several candidates for blog titles and tag lines, choose several and poll your friends and family. Which ones do they like best? Which ones don't work as well?

Incidentally, the process of coming up with titles works for books as well. It also helps to have clever friends who can help you. Some people are great at coming up with titles; others are not. But brainstorming, meditating on your topic, and drawing images can help you. Mark Victor Hansen and Jack Canfield, authors of the *Chicken Soup for the Soul* series, knew that a catchy title would make or break their book. They apparently meditated on the subject for an hour a day until Canfield had an image of his grandmother's chicken soup, which he remembered her saying could cure anything—and a very successful brand name was born.

WRITERS' WORDS

"If you're passionate about what it is you do, then you're going to be looking for everything you can to get better at it."

—Jack Canfield, author and motivational speaker

Secrets for Writing Successful Blog Posts

You've picked your angle and topic. You've got your blog title and tag line. You've gone to WordPress or another free blog-hosting site, where you've set up your blog in under five minutes. Trust me. It's that easy, even if you're not that comfortable with technology. Now what?

You need to write your blog posts. How long should each post be? About 300 words, which is a few paragraphs and all your reader will have time for. And just like all nonfiction pieces should leave the reader with one new idea, each blog post should have one single focus. No more.

You'll also need to write an About page, which is basically your autobiography. This should also be short and sweet, just a paragraph or two that captures the part of you revealed in your blog.

Here are some secrets for writing blogs:

- Create catchy titles for posts. People really do judge blogs by their titles. You want yours to be informative and memorable; tell readers exactly what your blog is about in a succinct, striking phrase.

- Give useful information. When you're blogging or writing nonfiction in general, you're writing to express yourself, yes, but that's only part of it. You're also writing to impart useful information; in my opinion, that's where many blogs fail. The more useful the information—tips, experience, resources—the more people will return to your blog.

- Suggest resources or give tips on making life easier for your readers in some way. Can you discuss the latest research finding about your topic?

- Use bullet points or lists. Bullet points are easier on the eye, draw attention to important information, and convince readers who may only be skimming your blog to stick around for a while.

- Adopt a conversational tone. You don't want to be formal or stiff; just like good nonfiction, you want to have a conversation with your reader, as if you're chatting over drinks.

- Don't use clichés. If a phrase comes into your mind easily, question it. If it's a cliché, find another way to say it that will illustrate your point.

- Include links or URLs to other websites and blogs. The more you link to other sites, the more you join the blogging conversation and drive traffic to your site.

- Mix up the format. Tell a story one day. Use a list the next. Include images. Do a review or a roundup of advice. You want to mix up and change the format.

- Edit and proofread your posts. Spelling errors, sloppy grammar, and incorrect information are sins to be avoided when writing in general and blogging as well.

- Blog at least three times a week. Don't let your blog languish for a week or write once a month. You'll lose readers. You want to refresh your content and keep readers coming back for more.

- Include a guest blogger or an interview. Likewise, see if you can guest blog or be interviewed on someone else's blog and include a link to yours.

- Check out sites like problogger.net or a blogging bootcamp and workshop like alistbloggingbootcamps.com to hone your blogging skills and get new ideas.

Self-Publishing e-books

No longer denigrated as the province of desperate authors, self-publishing has undergone a revolution in the last couple years. Publishing a nonfiction book through a traditional publisher means writing a book proposal complete with a sample chapter or two and finding a literary agent to represent you. (If you're interested in going this route, Marilyn Allen and Coleen O'Shea's excellent *The Complete Idiot's Guide to Writing Book Proposals & Query Letters* can help you; as literary agents, they have decades of experience to share. See Appendix C for details.)

Unlike writing fiction, where you have to have the entire novel completed before you sell, in nonfiction you usually sell the book first (after having written one or two chapters) and then write it. Getting an agent is one hurdle; getting a publisher interested is another. Book advances are down, marketing budgets are slashed, and the hurdles to publication are long, so more and more authors are turning to self-publishing e-books.

In 2010 there was a fourfold increase in self-published e-books, with over $878 million in sales. The phrase vanity press no longer applies.

One Writer's Success Story

Amanda Hocking is certainly the poster child for what can be done with good writing and a lot of marketing elbow grease. In 2010, she was a penniless fiction writer who wrote mostly paranormal romance novels. By day, the 26-year-old author worked caring for disabled people; by night, she'd penned 17 novels. Hocking's work had been sent out and repeatedly rejected by traditional publishing houses and agents alike. She had a stockpile of rejection slips. Hoping to raise $300 for a trip, Hocking told her roommate that she was going to publish a novel directly on Amazon.com. Instead she raised over $20,000 in the next six months by selling her novels as e-books. "I didn't think I'd have any kind of success with e-books, but I kept researching it," Hocking wrote on her blog.

Hocking continued to write and publish her e-book novels and went on to make over $2 million through self-publishing. Last year, Hocking signed with a traditional publishing company that paid her $2.1 million for her next four books.

How did the self-publishing phenom achieve this success? She states that her "books are in a popular genre," young adult paranormal romance (think zombies and vampires), and the price (anywhere from .99¢ to $2.99) was attractive to readers. Finally, and perhaps most importantly, she discovered "book bloggers," people who read and blog about books and who recommended hers. (I'll discuss book bloggers later in the chapter.) Hocking is also a nonstop publicity machine: she states that she's on "Twitter, Facebook, goodreads, Amazon, KB. I'm anywhere I can be." She also responds to her readers.

JUMPSTART

You have to do research when you are your own publishing company. Amanda Hocking read J.A. Konrath, a successful detective writer who's sold more than 800,000 e-books and earned a handsome living bypassing traditional publishers. There are e-books, of course, on the subject, as well as lots of free information on the web, including Hocking's own blog (amandahocking.blogspot.com).

Choosing Your Self-Publishing Platform

Kindle Singles is a new service from Amazon where both published and nonpublished writers can submit their longer work. "We're looking for compelling ideas expressed at their natural length—writing that doesn't easily fall into the conventional space limitations of magazines or print books," states the Kindle Singles website (kindlesingle.net). Submissions usually are between 5,000 and 30,000 words. Like traditional publishing, Kindle Singles has an editorial process, so it's not self-publishing, but if your work is selected you can receive 70 percent of royalties (the percentage you get after the book is sold) of a Single priced anywhere from .99¢ to $4.99. Some see sites like Kindle Singles as making long-form journalism accessible on e-readers and taking the form out of the province of print magazines.

When it comes to deciding which self-publishing platform to choose, you have several options:

- CreateSpace (createspace.com), Amazon's *print-on-demand* service, gives you free tools and makes your printed book available for sale on Amazon.com.

DEFINITION

Print on demand (POD) is a digital printing technology where books are printed one at a time or "on demand." POD means your book is always "in stock" and is often a more reasonable way of producing a book.

- Amazon's Kindle Direct Publishing e-book service (https://kdp.amazon.com) allows you to upload to Amazon. com, and also distributes the book for you in electronic format.
- Lightning Source (lightningsource.com), another print-on-demand service, prints books in any quantity.
- Smashwords (smashwords.com), a free service that publishes e-books and claims to be "the largest indie e-book distributor," helps you publish and distribute your book to retailers such as Barnes & Noble and Apple iBookstore.

- BookBaby (bookbaby.com) is a site where you can upload your e-book for $99 and get it distributed to online retailers like Amazon, Apple's iBookstore, or Sony's Reader Store.

Advantages and Disadvantages

What are the advantages of publishing an e-book? First, there's the speed in getting your work out—a few months versus a year or more through a traditional publisher. Second, you get to keep more of the royalties—anywhere from 35 to 70 percent, which is far more than the 10 to 15 percent you'd earn with a traditional publisher, and that's if you earned your advance, which is not a given. And when you self-publish, you don't have to deal with the sting of rejection, or write a book proposal and wait months to hear from agents.

What are the disadvantages to publishing e-books? Traditional magazines often won't review e-books, at least for now. Also, your book won't appear in any library. But the digital revolution is changing so fast that maybe these things will change in the very near future.

You also have to wear many hats when you self-publish—copy editor, proofreader, publicist, graphic designer (for book design and any illustrations)—or pay someone else for those services. And you have to be media- and internet-savvy, or willing to put in the time to learn, so that you can market your book through social media, blogging, and other internet channels. Marketing your book can be a full-time job.

You do have to spend some money to publish your e-book. Cookbook author and writer Monica Bhide's e-book, *In Conversation with Exceptional Women: Seeds of Inspiration to Help You Bloom Where You Are Planted*, cost her about $1,500 for a 200-page book and took about six months from start to finish. "Nothing is as simple and as easy as it sounds and always costs twice as much," says Bhide, who hired a graphic designer to help her with the cover. "People do judge a book by the cover," she adds.

JUMPSTART

For more information on indie or self-publishing, turn to those who've done it—and written books about it. Sm*art Self-Publishing: Being an Indie Author* by Zoe Winters or the bestselling *How I Sold 1 Million eBooks in 5 Months!* by John Locke are both available on Kindle Singles—naturally.

When you publish an e-book yourself, you set the price. Too expensive and you risk missing out on sales; too inexpensive and you need to sell more books to make the same profit—but you may attract more readers who'll take a chance on a book priced at 99¢. Amazon Kindles, for example, has two royalty options. Books priced between $2.99 and $9.99 allow you to keep 70 percent of every book sold. For books that sell for less than $2.99 and more than $9.99, you keep only 35 percent of royalties. Check around to see what the prices are for books like yours. You can also adjust the price if you find it's too high or too low.

Marketing Your Nonfiction

As I've discussed, the biggest downside to self-publishing is that you must wear many hats: writer, creative director, editor, proofreader, publisher, and marketer. You can hire people to help design your book cover and to proofread or edit (which most of the authors I know who've self-published have done), so you can take some of the load off that way. But you must launch your own media campaign to draw attention to your work.

It's not only self-published authors who have to serve as their own PR campaign leaders. More and more it's the job of authors who have published work through traditional channels as well. Blogs; websites; social media sites like Twitter, Facebook, and LinkedIn; and bookstore and community readings all are ways to get your work out there.

Using Social Media

The microblogging site Twitter (twitter.com) is a great way to join a conversation with other writers, keep up on what's being talked about in publishing and nonfiction, and make connections.

But Twitter is not about shameless self-promotion. In fact, writers who report getting the most out of Twitter are those who retweet others' interesting posts, follow authors or magazines, and share ideas and work, all in 140 characters or less. Writing can be lonely and the urge for connection through social media strong.

But if you're part of the conversation, you may have others mentioning your work, referring to your blog, or retweeting your posts, and you can get your name out there that way.

You can also use Facebook or LinkedIn to promote your work among friends, family, and co-workers. I've posted to Facebook, for example, when I'm looking for "real people" to interview for stories. And getting people to "Like" your work can help boost your visibility.

JUMPSTART

If you don't feel particularly media-savvy or are shy or uncomfortable about promoting your book yourself, you could hire someone to help you. Check listings on craigslist.org, or a listserv like Freelance Success (freelancesuccess.com) to find someone experienced in social media and marketing. It's crucial to promote your book in the first few months after it comes out, so don't wait.

Book Bloggers

While traditional magazines may or may not review your e-book, book bloggers will. These sites draw thousands of readers and can help launch your career, as they did for Hocking. *The Book Lady's Blog* (thebookladysblog.com), started by Rebecca Joines Schinsky, a member of the National Book Critics Circle, or *Shelf Awareness* (shelf-awareness.com), a free e-newsletter about books and the book industry, are two book review sites among many in the Book Blogger Directory (bookbloggerdirectory.wordpress.com).

If you have a blog or know people who do, see if you can do an interview about your work to help market it. You may even try an incentive, like freelancer Gretchen Roberts did to promote her e-book *Full-Time Income in Part-Time Hours: 22 Secrets to Writing Success in Under 40 Hours a Week.* She asked writers to send their own "Tales from the Trenches" about writing part time, with the winner receiving a free copy of her book. Incentives can work.

Giving Live Readings

Though speaking in public requires a bit of getting used to, it can help you sell your work. You might offer to do readings at your local bookstores. Also try your library, which may host an author's night. What about a school where you can talk to students about your work?

Victor Mark Hansen and Jack Canfield, authors of the extremely successful *Chicken Soup for the Soul* series, apparently sold their self-published work from the back of their cars. They'd been rejected by more than 50 publishing companies but were determined to publish and market their inspirational book. You know how that story ended.

The Least You Need to Know

- Blogging can be good practice for honing your nonfiction writing skills. You'll need to come up with memorable titles and tag lines and present information in a compelling way to attract readers.
- Good blog posts vary in format. Think of using lists, images, or stories to alternate the format.
- Self-publishing, whether through print-on-demand services or via e-books, is a viable and often lucrative option for getting your work out there, but there are disadvantages.
- Using social media, reading your work in live venues, and getting reviews by book bloggers are great ways to promote yourself.

How to Sustain a Writing Life

In This Chapter

- Getting support from a writing community
- How to get and give helpful feedback
- Revising your work after feedback
- Tips for sticking with it

It's been said that writers get to live twice. This is particularly true for nonfiction writers, who live the experience and then get to write about it and the world around them. It's a pretty good deal to be a writer. Of course, writing comes with rejection and days of despair where, at least for me, words feel like blunt instruments that I hold rather clumsily in my hands. But then there is the pleasure of getting things right on the page, of making sense of experience, of discovery, and these things are more than worth the price of admission.

Over the 20 years I have been teaching writing—everyone from Master's students at a prestigious university to women inmates with third-grade reading levels—most everyone wants to know the secret for sticking with it. After all, there's no one knocking at your door begging for your next nonfiction piece. Even editors you might have worked with move on to working with other writers. But there are some secrets for stick-to-itiveness, if that's a word.

Building a Supportive Writing Community

The first semester I taught at the Continuing Studies program at Stanford, my students wanted to know what's next. They had taken the class because they'd always wanted to write nonfiction, and they needed the weekly class assignments and deadlines to make good and actually write. But life intervenes, jobs change, children arrive and need you, the house needs work, and writing quickly becomes last on a to-do list. How do you keep going, they wondered? How can we keep this class alive?

I suggested that they continue meeting as a writers' group. They knew how to give useful feedback (more on that later in the chapter) and were respectful of each other and each other's work. "You can't do this alone," I said. "Or you can, but it's much, much harder that way." Almost every writer I know belongs to some sort of writers' group, whether that means one or two trusted friends, usually also writers, who are their first readers, or a group that meets regularly either in person or online. I've been part of several writers' groups: they've been invaluable for getting me to be honest and write and meet deadlines. Now I have one very good friend who is my first reader. I often think of her as I write, and her kind yet razor-sharp critical ability, and that has made all the difference between being a writer and wanting to be a writer.

Incidentally, the writers' group that formed, a subset of several students from that first class, is still meeting almost 13 years later. When you find a like-minded tribe of excellent readers and critics in the best sense, it's like winning the writer lottery.

 WRITERS' WORDS

"Almost every writer I've ever known has been able to find someone who could be both a friend and a critic. You'll know when the person is right for you and when you are right for the person. It's not unlike finding a mate, where little by little you begin to feel that you've stepped into a shape that was waiting there all along."

—Anne Lamott, novelist and nonfiction writer (from *Bird by Bird*)

Forming a Writing Group

How do you form a writers' group? Where do you find fellow writers? And how do you know you'll be a good match? The first writing group I was a part of came about because I knew one member. I'd recently moved across the country, and I was writing my dissertation—or not writing it, as the case was, because I'd been stuck for over a year and hadn't written much at all. When I moved to San Francisco, I reconnected with another Victorian scholar, a woman I'd met at a Dickens conference. She and four other women had put together a Reading Group, as it was called, that met weekly to both read intellectually challenging material (that is, academic theory) and critique each other's Master's thesis or dissertations in progress. We were all women, all about the same age, but from different academic disciplines. What we shared was a love of reading, a somewhat dread of writing, and the gift of time: most of us were unemployed graduate students. In six months of meeting weekly with the Reading Group, I was able to write over 200 pages and complete my dissertation, something I'd been unable to accomplish previously. And my Reading Group, as we still call it 18 years later, still meets once a year for a retreat, where we talk nonstop for the entire weekend and read each other's lives with the same care we once read each other's work.

I've been part of other writing groups that have not worked so well, either because we never clicked, or one person dominated, or the writers who were supposed to bring written work never did so but wanted to "talk through" what they hoped to write about instead. That never works.

How do you find a writer's group?

- **Through connections.** Do you know another writer or a friend of a friend of a writer? Ask him if he is in a group or would like to form one.

- **Advertise.** Post on Craigslist or another local listserv. Be prepared to try out potential groups and candidates for your group.

- **Go to author readings.** You're bound to meet people who love books and writing at these venues. Ask around when you're there.

- **Check your local bookstore or library.** Sometimes independent bookstores in particular have a bulletin board for other writers seeking groups, or perhaps you can post a sign yourself.

- **Check out online groups,** like absolutewrite.com or writerscafe.org, where you can meet other writers virtually and make connections.

- **Take a writing class.** Colleges and universities often have extension programs where you can take a writing course and meet other writers and writing instructors.

How to Structure a Writing Group

I'm sure you know of, or perhaps belong to, a book club whose members do more talking about unrelated matters than the book itself. You don't want the same thing to happen to your writing group; it's too important. Here are some guidelines for keeping the group on track:

- **Delineate goals.** Are you all on the same page, so to speak, with your goals? What do you each want out of the group? Firm deadlines where you bring in work and get feedback? A commitment to write in the group itself? Do you want to include only nonfiction writers, or fiction writers as well? It's good to have every member write out goals to see if everyone is compatible.

- **Pick a format for the group.** Do you want to meet once a week? Once a month? At a coffee shop or someone's house? Have two people read their work or one at each meeting? Do you want someone to lead the group? Or someone to act as secretary and send out reminder emails? Or alternate responsibilities for leadership? Do you email writing beforehand and then critique in person? Deciding what format you want to follow beforehand can help your group run smoothly.

- **Set some ground rules.** Invariably, there will be weeks when people don't have work to share. Perhaps you work out a substitute system, so that someone else steps in. Or do you hold the group anyway and perhaps do a writing exercise or brainstorm together? In addition, you might plan to let each person speak without interruption to prevent one person from monopolizing the meeting. You can also have the writer hold off from responding until she's heard from everyone.

- **Limit socializing.** Of course, it's fun and natural to talk about things other than writing. Allow 15 or 20 minutes at the end of the meeting for socializing. I've tried doing this at the beginning of the group as well, but that invariably means less time for talking about writing.

- **Give good feedback.** You want to give constructive criticism and receive it as well, and that means setting up guidelines for criticizing the work. See the following section for more about giving and getting feedback.

JUMPSTART

Pick a day and time that works for everyone, schedule your writing group meetings months in advance, and mark the dates on your calendar. It's easy to say you'd like to meet twice a month, but unless you put it on the calendar, it's not likely to happen.

The Importance of Constructive Feedback

My very first semester of teaching, I had a student I'll call Eddie. Eddie rarely said a word in class and only grunted when I asked him a question. He didn't make eye contact, and I could only assume he hated taking this required composition class and wanted no part of it. But I made Eddie (and all the other students) come to a mandatory conference to talk about their strengths and weaknesses as writers and how we could work to make their writing better.

I'll never forget when Eddie walked into my cubicle. He didn't take a seat. Instead, when I asked him how it was going, he held out his paper and said, "You called my writing crappy." His head hung low. I was horrified. I told him he must be mistaken. I would never write that. "It's right there," he said, holding the essay toward me. "In the margin." I looked. The word I had written was "choppy," as he was jumping quickly from topic to topic in one paragraph, which made for choppy writing. "No," I told him. "It says 'choppy,' not 'crappy.' I'd never write 'crappy.'" Though I apologized over and over for my abysmal handwriting (which has since gotten worse, requiring me to type my comments on student work), there was no getting through to Eddie. He believed that I had called his writing crappy, and no amount of telling him otherwise would convince him.

I realized that most of us on some level probably think our writing (and, by extension, ourselves) warrants the same label. And I know this feeling is devastating. I once had a rejection from a literary agent that said, "This did not hold my interest long enough to read it," which made me lie on the couch every day for six months and swear never to write a word again. But giving helpful feedback is the opposite of soul-crushing: it's inspiring, necessary, and life affirming. That's the kind of feedback you want to get and give.

WRITERS' WORDS

"Writing can be a pretty desperate endeavor, because it is about some of our deepest needs: our need to be visible, to be heard, our need to make sense of our lives, to wake up and grow and belong."

—Anne Lamott, novelist and nonfiction writer

Tips for Giving Feedback

Even if you don't know the name Peter Elbow, writing professor emeritus at the University of Massachusetts Amherst and author of several groundbreaking books on writing, you might know the principles he helped advocate. One is the importance of freewriting, and another is giving feedback. According to Elbow, there are two kinds of feedback:

- Criterion, which is more teacher based (is there a thesis or argument, do the paragraphs stay on theme, that kind of thing)
- Reader response, which is what happens to you moment by moment as you are reading someone's draft

Are you thinking about dinner rather than concentrating on the prose? Does the writer's use of a certain word send your mind off in another direction or keep you riveted waiting for the next word? If you're thinking about something else other than the writing, chances are it's because the writer has failed to keep your interest, and that's not your fault.

What you want to do when you're giving feedback is a bit of both types of criticism: what is working (or not) structurally and on a more emotional or intellectual level. Ideally, the purpose of feedback is to help the writer understand what he or she does well along with what needs work.

Soliciting feedback takes some getting used to. It's kind of like going to a nude beach in a way, where you are letting everything show. But if everyone is sharing his or her work, then everyone is in the same "unclothed" position.

I make sure the students in my writing classes feel comfortable with each other, which takes a few weeks, and that everyone is schooled in how to give helpful criticism. Saying something is "good," for example, won't help the writer produce another piece of "good writing," for she won't know exactly what made her work good.

On the other hand, certain words like "boring" and, of course, "crappy" are verboten. You may devastate a writer by saying something is boring; you certainly won't help him. But you can say something specific like, "I was lost at this part because of …," or "I found myself paying more attention at the beginning but then in the middle, on page 2, I was confused." Circle the parts that work for you and try to explain why. Similarly, circle where you were confused and list what makes a passage difficult to follow.

There's a widely held belief that in the critique process the writer should remain silent as people give feedback on his work. This could be to prevent the writer from being repeatedly put on the defensive, saying things like, "I was going to put that in" or "I thought of starting there instead." The writer won't really be able to hear the feedback if he's too busy defending himself. On the other hand, I don't subscribe to the notion that the writer should be silent as if in front of a firing squad. I think a happy medium is best: if you're the writer, try to listen and not jump in, and if you're the person giving feedback, be as helpful as you possibly can. That means being as specific as you can, and being honest but not brutally so. You shouldn't evade criticizing if the piece isn't working, but rather work harder as a critic to articulate what about the piece needs improvement.

I use the following list for critiques in my nonfiction workshops:

- Where does the piece catch your attention?
- Where do you want to hear more?
- What parts do you remember most?
- What parts slow you down in the reading?
- Where were you confused and why?
- What words, phrases, or sentences jar?
- What does the writer do well?
- What suggestions do you have for revision?

Revise Your Work After Getting Feedback

So you've gotten feedback from your writing group, your writing buddy, or your editor—now what? If it's your editor or editors (I once had an essay edited by 18 different people over one year), you must answer their questions and fill in any gaps. But what if you get contradictory feedback? What if half the group likes your lead and the other half finds it less captivating and prefers that you begin instead with paragraph 4, where you really get going? What do you do then?

Ultimately, you have to sort through the feedback. You may always get readers who have different opinions: reader responses are subjective, after all. But if five people are telling you the lead you thought was clever was not, you probably need to delete it. I like to wait a day or two after getting comments because I find I'm more open minded and less defensive. I can step back from the work and see what my reader or readers are saying. With time, I'm also less attached.

Ultimately your goal is to make reading your work as enjoyable an experience (and informative or moving or stimulating) as possible. That's where good feedback can help. After weighing the comments, see where the piece lags, where it needs more examples, more dialogue perhaps, or less exposition. Good feedback should incite you to revise your work, not squash your desire to write again.

Writing When You Don't Feel Like It

You're sick. Or the dog is ill. You're on vacation. Or you sit down at your desk and you're not inspired. "Give it up," says one voice. "Go outside and garden. Go shopping. Pay the bills. Do anything but write. It's too hard."

"Writers write every day," says another voice. "Or almost every day. They write whether they feel like it or not." Which voice will win? I hope it will be the pro-writer voice.

WRITERS' WORDS

"You only learn to be a better writer by actually writing."

—Doris Lessing, British short-story writer and novelist

It's taken me most of my life to realize these truisms: (1) writing is hard, and (2) writers write every day. I recently went on a second-grade camping trip with my son and his class, which included another parent who is a Pulitzer Prize–winning novelist. All the parents were sitting around the campfire chatting and roasting marshmallows as the kids ran around, and we all watched as this famous writer took out his laptop and made his way back to his tent. There was no electricity. The stars were out. The fire was warm. The tent was undoubtedly cold. Another parent asked what he was doing. The prize-winning novelist said that he wrote every day. At least 1,000 words whether he felt like it or not. That was his secret, and despite the fact that we were in the middle of the wilderness with pit toilets and no electricity and it was 9 P.M., he was going into his tent to write. And he did.

Find a Schedule and Stick with It

I talked about the importance of a schedule in Chapter 9, and it bears repeating here. What separates the writers from those who want to write is that the former sit at their desks every day regardless of the obstacles that life invariably sends their way. Find out which time of the day or night works best for you and write during that time. I know writers whose most productive hours are between 11 P.M. and 3 A.M., when the kids are in bed and the house is quiet. I work better first thing in the morning, from 6 A.M. on, so I make sure I'm at my desk then.

We all know how seductive email and social media can be. Try to minimize distractions by turning off email alerts, and rather than give in to checking Twitter or Facebook, make that a reward for *after* you've written rather than before.

Ask yourself these questions:

- Does your day get better if you've written something?
- Is the pain of not writing greater than the pain of writing?
- Do you feel happier when you've written?

If you answer yes to any of these questions, you're a writer. You need to carve out time to keep you on the path. Set a date with yourself in your calendar. Write even if you're sick in bed with the flu. Write as you're waiting to pick up your child from soccer practice. Squeeze in 15 minutes before you go to bed at night. If you are a writer, you will make time. These increments will add up.

Breaking your writing schedule is like skipping three or four weeks of working out. What happens? It's hard to motivate yourself again. Or like one cookie becomes four and you think, why bother? Writing can be like that, too. Or not writing.

Think of the prize-winning novelist who took his laptop into his tent. Did he write anything good that night? I don't know. Maybe not. But he wrote, and that's the main point. As Stephen King wrote in *On Writing: A Memoir of the Craft*, give yourself permission to write: "you can, you should, and if you're brave enough to start, *you will*."

WRITERS' WORDS

"Writing, the creative effort, the use of the imagination, should come first—at least for some part of every day of your life. It is a wonderful blessing if you use it. You will become happier, more enlightened, alive, impassioned, light-hearted and generous to everybody else."

—Brenda Ueland, journalist, writer, and writing teacher

Set Writing Goals

Every year, usually around New Year's, I sit down and write out my writing goals. Usually I share them with Jane, my good friend and writing buddy who is often my first reader. We meet at a café and exchange our goals for the year. Some of them are writing related, such as "back up computer," which is essential but a task I keep putting off. Others are more specific and income related: "find three new magazines to pitch to regularly" or "make $xxx per month in freelance income." Others are more open-ended and creative: "Begin writing mystery novel." I tuck these goals away somewhere, but I usually stumble across them sometime later in the year and am stunned at how much I've achieved, unconsciously it seems, because I've forgotten about them.

There is something magical about writing down your goals, and I encourage you to regularly write down yours. You may be surprised at what comes out on the paper. You may be surprised when you come across them later and see how many goals you've realized.

Say you want to send out your essays for publication and get at least one published this year. Or maybe this is the year you are going to research and begin writing your memoir in earnest. Perhaps you want to set semi-annual goals or monthly goals to keep you on track.

Celebrate Your Successes

You don't get a lot of pats on the back for being a nonfiction writer. Sure, it's thrilling to see your name in print, but for most people, it's not life altering. Maybe not even all that bank-account altering. Yet even if you find success, you can't just sit on your laurels; you still have to get back to your desk and turn out something new and keep writing. Most writers continue to write because they can't imagine *not* doing it.

That's why it's important to celebrate your successes as a writer. If you've sent out your nonfiction to six new markets, celebrate that even if you get rejections. If you meet your deadline, take yourself out to lunch or buy a book you've wanted to read or something else small to reward yourself.

Even staff writers on magazines and newspapers, from what I hear, don't get lots of compliments from their editors. The gratification you get from writing is really the writing itself. But it helps to give yourself pats on the back for doing it.

Stay Connected to Other Writers

Another way to sustain yourself as a writer is to keep connected with other writers. Having a writing group can be a huge and necessary boon. Going to book readings, attending writing conferences, blogging or contributing to others' blogs, joining a writers' listserv and participating in online discussions, tweeting and following writers and editors on Twitter, anything that gets you out in the world and makes you part of a larger writing community is beneficial. Writing is a solitary act, but that doesn't mean it's a solitary profession. I find that writers are, in general, a helpful and generous group. We all know it's tough. I've gotten leads for work and contacts with editors through other writers. I've passed along assignments when I am too busy or the fit isn't right for me. Give back as a writer and you will be rewarded, too. Nonfiction writing is a wonderful way to know yourself and others. And as King says, "The water is free. So drink."

The Least You Need to Know

- Writing is a solitary act but not a solitary profession: finding or forming a writing support group can make all the difference between sustaining a writing life and abandoning your writing.

- It's important to set goals, a format, and ground rules for your writing group so you can get and give helpful critiques.

- Constructive criticism means giving specific examples of where the writing moved you, where it dragged, and where you'd like more information. It's important to avoid general words like "good," which won't help the writer produce another piece of good writing.

- Writers write even when they don't feel like it or life intervenes. Committing to writing on a regular schedule separates those who are writers from those who want to write.

- Writing down yearly, monthly, or semi-annual goals can help you achieve writing milestones.

- It's important to celebrate your success as a writer and to be part of a writing community whether in person or online.

Glossary

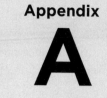

alliteration   Using the same letter or stressed consonant sound at the beginning of words in a group. Alliteration is often used in poetry and for emphasis in prose.

autobiography   An account of a someone's life told by that person.

biography   A written account of another person's life.

blog   Short for web log, a blog is an online journal, usually updated frequently, that contains commentary, narrative, advice, opinions, or anything else that the author feels like writing.

cliché   A trite or overused figure of speech.

conjunction   The part of speech that joins words, phrases, clauses, and sentences (for, and, nor, but, or, yet, and so).

creative nonfiction   A literary genre where factual information is told in compelling and literary ways.

dependent clause   Also called a "subordinate clause," a dependent clause is not a complete sentence but rather needs an independent clause.

epiphany   A change in perception or sudden insight into the meaning of something. The word comes from the ancient Greek word *epiphaneia*, signifying the manifestation or sudden appearance of something, usually a god.

exposition   Information that introduces the character, plot, setting, or conflict.

first person   A story told using the pronouns "I," "we," or "us," so that the narrator is a character in the narrative.

food writing   A genre of writing that uses literary techniques and an autobiographical mode to explore the cultural and personal importance of food.

fragment   A group of words that cannot stand alone as a complete sentence because it's missing a subject, verb, or complete idea.

immersion journalism   A journalistic practice of embedding oneself, often for weeks or months, in the world of a subject to capture the "felt experience" of that world.

independent clause   A group of words that has a subject and verb and can stand alone as a sentence.

in medias res   Latin for "into the midst of things," a narrative technique of beginning the story in the middle of the action, usually at a crucial point, rather than at the beginning.

libel   A published false statement that damages another's reputation.

lyrical essay   A hybrid form that incorporates both the lyricism of poetry and the prose of an essay.

memoir   An autobiographical nonfiction form based on personal experience.

metaphor   A figure of speech where one thing is said to be another for the purpose of comparison.

narrative nonfiction   *See* creative nonfiction.

personal essay   An autobiographical essay written in an intimate style; one of the most popular forms of creative nonfiction.

plot   The careful selection and arrangement of events to reveal cause and effect.

print on demand (POD)   A digital printing technology where books are printed one at a time or as customers order them.

profile   Usually a short biographical piece based on interviews that shows something remarkable about a person, place, or institution.

query letter   A short (usually a single page) letter of introduction about you and your work in the hopes of interesting an editor or agent.

run-on sentence   An ungrammatical sentence where two or more independent clauses (which could be complete sentences in their own right) have been joined together without the appropriate punctuation.

second person   A story told using the second person pronoun, "you," so that the reader feels as if she or he is part of the story.

simile   A figure of speech in which two unlike things are compared, usually introduced with the word "like" or "as."

simultaneous submission   Sending the same work to two or more publications at the same time with the understanding that only one will publish it.

slander   The oral communication of false statements that injure another's reputation.

theme   The central topic or unifying concept of a piece. It answers the question: What's this about?

third person   A story told using the pronouns "he," "she," or "it."

travel essay   An intersection of the personal essay with travel writing, where the writer tells an autobiographical account of the journey.

vignette   A short, literary description or scene. The word comes from the Old French word "vigne" for vine. Think of a vignette as something decorative or extra that is pleasing.

voice   The distinctive style or personality in writing where you sound like your most authentic self.

Want to know what the research and writing process is like for bestselling nonfiction writers? Where they get their ideas? How they know if they have a story worth telling, and what form it will take? Or how they write about real people without offending them? Do these writers ever feel like throwing in the towel? Read on for insights into the challenges and the joys of writing from some of today's most popular nonfiction writers. The answers may surprise and inspire you.

Susan Orlean

Susan Orlean has been a staff writer at *The New Yorker* since 1992. She is the author of nine books: *Red Sox and Bluefish: And Other Things That Make New England New England* (1987); *The Orchid Thief: A True Story of Beauty and Obsession* (1998), which was adapted into the movie *Adaptation; Saturday Night* (1999); *The Bullfighter Checks Her Makeup: My Encounters with Extraordinary People* (2001); *My Kind of Place: Travel Stories from a Woman Who's Been Everywhere* (2004); *Throw Me a Bone: 50 Healthy, Canine Taste-Tested Recipes for Snacks, Meals, and Treats* (co-authored with Sally Sampson, 2011); *Animalish* (2011); *Rin Tin Tin: The Life and the Legend* (2011); and a children's book, *Lazy Little Loafers* (2006).

CB: Did you know you always wanted to be a nonfiction writer?

SO: I did. I've always loved reading, but I was always very attracted to the idea of being out in the world. I liked answering questions that I had about the world and things I was interested in. I liked exploring.

CB: So many of your subjects are what are considered "ordinary"—from a 10-year-old boy in "The American Man at Age Ten," to real estate agents, to the people we meet in your book *Saturday Night.* How do you know who will make a good subject for nonfiction?

SO: It's very much an intuitive thing. I don't think there's a formula, and I sometimes feel I wish I really knew. I think there's a way in which I have to really be surprised by something, and in the very initial stages of learning a little bit about a story, if it doesn't feel repeatedly surprising then I usually know there's not going to be enough there to keep me interested. Because it's really driven for me on matters of true curiosity.

CB: Can you share writing tips for capturing real people on the page and bringing them alive in a way that's memorable?

SO: I tend to go with a very natural approach. If I were actually trying to describe someone to someone else, your mind very naturally sorts out the impressions that you have, and you end up gravitating towards those details that are really salient and vivid. So I try to almost imagine that I'm simply telling the story out loud about someone. And I'm almost curious to see what things come to mind in describing them, what points seem to capture them most quickly and most vividly. And it can be very different for each story.

CB: You spend so much time researching your subjects—2 years in Florida working on *The Orchid Thief* and 10 years on *Rin Tin Tin,* 5 years on *Saturday Night.* Can you talk about the researching, interviewing, and writing process? Do you do one first and then the other? Do you write as you're doing research? What's that process like for you?

SO: I treat them as two. It's almost as if I have two entirely separate jobs, jobs that in some ways don't seem very similar, in fact. I do all my research before I write a word, so I'm doing the research, I'm out in the world, I'm talking to people, I'm exploring, I'm poking around, I'm gathering without any agenda to see where it leads me.

And the writing part of it is exactly the opposite, where I'm sequestered and I have a very specific agenda, which is "How do I distill what I've learned into a coherent, compelling story?" I don't feel like I can start writing until I have finished all the reporting because I wouldn't know what any individual thing means until I see the whole story as a completed experience; it doesn't feel to me at all obvious where I'm going to begin until I'm completely done learning everything I need to learn. And that can be very frustrating because I can go for long stretches where I think I have no idea where this story is going to begin, absolutely none, I just feel like it's a moment where you're kind of flailing about, and then when I sit down to write that's when things begin to funnel into a more coherent shape.

I also end up reporting a lot of material that ends up not being used because I follow threads and dangling bits and pieces to see where they'll lead me. And until I have the story laid out thematically, I don't know if any of those are going to be useful or not, but I feel that my way of learning is to just follow all of those blind alleys and see where they go, and I feel like they all end up influencing what I write about even if they aren't literally on the page.

Then I sit down to write, and it's a very entirely different experience.

CB: Annie Dillard once wrote that "there's nothing you can't do with [nonfiction]. … You get to make up your own form every time." Does that feel true to you? How do you know when you have a short-form piece or a long-form piece?

SO: That's a good question. Part of it is just practical: the magazine wants to know how long I think it will require to tell the story, so I kind of enter it with a rough idea of, "This is a piece that's 3,000 words, 8,000 words." It just seems that's going to be the amount of space I need to tell the story.

I happen to think a lot of subjects are very elastic and could go many different ways and many different shapes and forms. It's usually just a sense of how many layers the story has.

CB: So, for instance, when you were thinking about Rin Tin Tin, did you know that it was going to be a book from the get-go?

SO: I always knew it was going to be a book, and that was because the span of time was so great that I just immediately knew that it would be too difficult. Also, it seemed to be a waste to try to squeeze it into something shorter than a book. And I wanted the leisureliness of being able to fill in all the background. But I've never done a story before where immediately to tell the full story was going to require me to trace almost 100 years, and it just instantly struck me. I never thought of it as an article. I always thought of it as a book.

CB: Were there times when you were in despair when you were writing a long form like that over the course of 10 years?

SO: Oh, God. All the time. All the time. Books are very hard. You do so much reporting before you begin to even write the first word, so I almost think it's very natural that you spend a lot of that time wondering if it really is a book, why you are doing the book, is anyone going to care that you did the book? It just feels so wide open and so speculative without really any idea of where you're going.

Also because Rin Tin Tin was so big and amorphous, and because it took me so long, it was naturally a little bit more daunting, just because of the time, the pure fact of so much time and so much material, that at times I felt that this is just too much to wrestle into a book.

CB: Henry James once said that what to leave out is just as important as what to leave in. How do you make those decisions when you're writing when you have all that material?

SO: I think it's one of the most important lessons to learn both in a kind of line-by-line way—to be a tough editor—but also more conceptually. You would never stand in front of an audience and tell them a story that lasted 5 hours and expect them to remain interested: you would stand in front of them, and you would tell them the most compelling, exciting, engaging parts of that story. It doesn't mean that the 5 hours that you know isn't valuable: it's your job to know all of it and show the very best of it. As a reader, you want to come away feeling that the writer knows even more than they told you, that their knowledge and confidence is very deep, and that what they've shared with you is just the very best of it.

And I think you have to develop a reader's ear as a writer: you have to be able to hear it as if you were reading if for the fist time and see where it lags and see where it's dull. And sometimes it can be painful—there's something you just love and it doesn't really fit, and you just have to suck it up and take it out.

CB: What's one of the challenges of writing nonfiction?

SO: I think that's a challenge of writing in general: finding good stories, doing really good reporting, and making a good argument to a reader that the story is worth their time.

CB: And do you have a tip for an aspiring nonfiction writer about finding a good story or making a good argument?

SO: Finding a good story is just a lot of elbow grease. There's no magic to it. You just have to really look and listen, and read and poke around, and explore and work hard to find good stories and develop a kind of gut feeling for what will work as a conversation with the reader.

I think that you can never be lazy—that every sentence has to sell your story to the reader and be full of momentum and infused with the excitement that you hopefully felt when you were reporting it. That's not always possible if it's an assignment and you're doing it to make a living, but you've got to find something in the story that's going to push you and excite you because that's got to come out in the writing.

CB: Your pieces are a combination of profiles, travel writing, first person, history, do you think in terms of genre when you write, and crossing genre?

SO: I don't. Because I think genre is just a label, so when people ask me, "Do I like to call it creative nonfiction or literary journalism?" Well, I don't care. I don't care at all, and maybe it's because I know my work doesn't fit that comfortably in any one category, so by definition I resist them. But I don't think about genre, I really don't.

CB: How do you write about real people without offending them?

SO: My students ask me that, too, and my simple answer is, "Don't be offensive." You often have to say things that a person isn't going to like seeing on the page, and there's nothing you can do to prepare for that because sometimes people will be offended by something you never in a million years imagined would offend them. So you can't think about it too much.

But I think the main approach, which sounds sort of simplistic, is, if you really truly are nonjudgmental and look at your subjects with empathy, that's the only thing you can hope to do. And the fact is that it will be evident to the reader. It may not be evident to the subject, and you have to brace yourself for that because no one likes reading about themselves—in a weird way, everyone loves it and hates it at the same time—and you have to really brace yourself. And the only defense you can ever fall on is that you did it with the best of intentions. There's no way around that. And there will be people who will always surprise you and come at you later very upset, and it's a pretty unpleasant experience, but it's part of the job unfortunately.

I absolutely hate it. It sounds funny, but you have to be pure of heart. If you did something and you know in your heart that you were honest, there's nothing else you can do.

CB: What's the joy of writing nonfiction for you? Is it the research? The writing? Getting it right on the page?

SO: It is all of those things. I can't believe that I get to meet interesting people, do things that I dream about, and then [have] the job of sitting and just cobbling pretty sentences together and feel that there's some music on the page.

But then the third part of the real job is that I feel in some small way that I've introduced some people to things they've never thought about and ways of thinking about those things that they never thought they would experience. The idea that somebody could be moved to think or imagine something that they've never thought about before is marvelous: it's maybe the most ineffable and fabulous part of this job. And because it's nonfiction, because it's maybe making people think about people they never thought they could care about or parts of the world they never dreamed they'd learn about, there's a special pleasure because maybe they walk in the world in a different way now. And I'm not trying to make myself sound grand, but we're all affected by everything we read, and if you read a story about a person who seemed like a stranger and suddenly you feel some connection, it makes your world different. So the idea that I've perhaps done that at times is incredibly gratifying.

Laura Fraser

Laura Fraser is a San Francisco–based journalist, writing mentor, and memoirist whose latest book, *All Over the Map* (2010), is a travel memoir and sequel to her *New York Times* bestseller *An Italian Affair* (2001). A frequent contributor to magazines, her articles have been featured in *The New York Times; O, the Oprah Magazine; Gourmet; Afar; Tricycle Buddhist Review; Vogue; Mother Jones; More; Health; The Daily Beast; Salon.com;* and numerous other magazines and anthologies. She has won several awards for her work, including the International Association of Culinary Professionals (IACP) award for essay writing. Her first book was *Losing It: False Hopes and Fat Profits in the Diet Industry* (1998).

CB: How do you write about real people, like the professor in *An Italian Affair* or your friends in *All Over the Map*, without offending, betraying, or hurting them?

LF: I think the most important thing when writing about other people is to be fair and have compassion for them. In *An Italian Affair,* I have some lines where I basically say, "This is my story, my husband would certainly have a different story, but this is the way I see it." And even with him, I try to be fair. The other thing is that you have to look at your motivation for writing. If you're writing for revenge, first of all it's not going to be that interesting to read, and that's when you really are likely to end up being unfair to people.

My training is in journalism. I spent many years as a journalist before I wrote a memoir, and so as a journalist the question is always: How do I present this person's point of view as accurately as possible? And I think the same is true about memoir; you may have some feelings, but at the same time you need to have compassion and understanding for where that other person is coming from.

CB: How do you bring real people to the page? Do you think about physical description first or other traits?

LF: That's hard. One of the things that has helped me bring people to the page most is dialogue. I'm very attuned to language and to how people speak and whether they say things with humor. So I think one of the ways my characters come to life is by how they sound.

I think physical description is also important, and to describe more than the obvious—tall, thin, short, fat—but to catch the signature element about a person. That was very easy in *An Italian Affair* with the professor because he was such a character: he had a big beak-like nose, and curly hair, and always wore bracelets and a scarf, and just right there you get the idea of that particular kind of a Frenchman who comes from a hippy past.

Clothes can often be pretty revealing about character, and I don't mean just saying that it was a Prada bag, but you can tell from how someone dresses how sort of exuberant they are as a personality. You can also, of course, reveal character through action—how do people respond to events, what do they do, do they stay or do they go. I guess those are the main things.

CB: You come across as open and accessible, a real warm and intimate narrator in your work. How do you write about yourself with such candor? Do you worry that you're revealing too much?

LF: Thank you. I think the answer to making yourself a believable character is to remember that you're a character in this book and to be able to kind of distance yourself from the character. Remember that you're not telling people everything about your life; you're telling a story from your life, and the role that you played in that story, so you don't have to tell everything. You just have to be honest about whatever it is you're writing about.

I think that if you start writing with a critic on your shoulder who's going to say, "Well, what's your mother going to think about that?" or "What's your husband going to think?" you'll never get anywhere. So I always think it's best to write freely and then later consider what the consequences will be.

The other thing is, when you're writing, you have the opportunity to be your best self, so if you say that I seem very honest and accessible and intimate and warm in my writing, it's really my best self. I'm a much better person in writing than I am in person. That's the luxury I suppose of memoir.

I don't mean to say that you want to present yourself in an idealized fashion. I don't mean that at all. On the page, I have an opportunity to think before I describe the situation or to really consider other people's points of view and to bring out my best self in terms of compassion because I really do think that compassion is the key to writing a good memoir—compassion for yourself, compassion for other people, compassion for the whole situation. Because ultimately, what are you trying to teach the reader if it's not some type of compassion or some type of truth that you come to realize through hard experience?

CB: Your writing has appeared in *Best American Food Writing* a couple of times. Do you have secrets for writing about food?

LF: The problem with most food writers is that they describe things as "delicious." And that doesn't tell us a single thing about whatever it is they're writing about. So you have to really dive deep with your sensory experience when you're writing about food and go beyond "good" and "delicious."

The other thing is you need to realize food is a window into emotion, culture, history, and relationships. You can tell so much about a person by the way they eat. So it's really looking at the bigger picture about food. What does food say about us? You need to be able to use some metaphor and take your experience beyond the laundry list of ingredients and did you or did you not enjoy the food?

CB: You've also published a lot of travel essays. Do you have tips for writing about travel and exotic places without sounding like a guidebook?

LF: Travel writers generally speaking commit two types of sins. The first is not having a unity of tone. They may begin a story on a personal level, "I had always wanted to go to Egypt because my grandfather lived there one summer," or something like that, and they shift to, "Alexandria is home to the world's oldest library." Suddenly it sounds like it's a very different tone.

The other sin of travel writing is having no story. And people confuse a place with a story. But if you just say, "I want to write an article about the Seychelles" or "I want to write an article about

Lima," you have to say what is going on in the Seychelles or Lima or what's going on in your life that somehow going to the Seychelles or going to Lima fulfills a quest. There has to be a motivation for going to the place you're going. There has to be some way in which the place reveals something to you as a traveler or to your audience as sort of a surprising bit of culture or history that they didn't know about before.

So you have to have a story and a voice, and the voice has to have a unity of tone. And what happens in a travel story has to be more than you went there.

CB: You write both magazine articles and books. How do you know when you have enough material for either a book or an article, and do you think about form when you're writing?

LF: I suppose you just have to think, "How long is my reader going to be interested in this topic?" And generally speaking, it's a magazine article. I think it's hard to find a topic that lends itself to a whole book; you really have to have undergone some kind of transformation or had some kind of extraordinary experience.

I'd love to churn out a memoir a year, but my life isn't that interesting, and so I need to go farther afield in terms of what I write about. And that brings me to another topic, which is that navel gazing is only going to get you so far. Even in the memoir, you have to do research and dive into your subject in a way that's deeper than someone else would go—whether that's emotionally, [or] finding out something about history, [or] finding out something about a topic that pertains to your life. You really have to do a lot of research to write a memoir. People think that you can just hole up in your room and remember your experiences and that's good enough. And it just isn't.

CB: What research did you do for your two memoirs?

LF: I mostly did research just to get more information about the places that I visited so I could convey more to the reader. I did research about dishes and food. I did some research about the history of the places I was in.

And research with memoir takes a lot of different forms. The most extreme is David Carr's memoir, *The Night of the Gun*, where he deliberately goes out as a journalist to find out whether the memories that he had of the period in his life when he was addicted correspond with the memories that other people had. And it was really in some ways a meta memoir and a comment on our memories, which are never really true; they're always subjective. Another example, Victoria Costello, who wrote *The Complete Idiot's Guide to Memoir*, wrote about mental illness in her family, and she did a lot of research on the science of hereditability of mental illness, which is interesting. Obviously it pertained to her life, but she dug a lot deeper than "My grandfather laid down on the train tracks and committed suicide." It was what kinds of mental illness get passed through the generations, how you can tell, what can you do to prevent it, that kind of thing.

CB: Can you talk about some of the challenges of writing nonfiction that you've come up against?

LF: I think the hardest thing about writing nonfiction is coming up with the ideas. Often your ideas will build on each other, but then sometimes you'll just get tired of a certain area. One of my problems as a writer is that I'm a total generalist. I don't have any specific area that I write about. My first book was about the diet industry, and I became a real sort of expert about weight and women and weight and body issues. And I just could have kept on with that being my realm of expertise and probably had a much more successful career. But honestly, after finishing my first book, called *Losing It*, I never wanted to talk about weight or diets again. It was an exhausting amount of research, and I said what I had to say, and I just wasn't interested saying the same thing over and over and revising it with new research for the next 20 years.

So if you have a short attention span like I do, it's sometimes hard to just keep the ideas flowing. You have to go outside your experience. A writer I really admire for the stories he uncovers is Dave Eggers. I just read *Zeitoun*, and it's a fantastic book: an Arab-American family in New Orleans after Hurricane Katrina, [and it] has nothing to do with Dave Eggers' life, and yet he heard the story and felt moved to go and research and write about it. And he did a wonderful job, and as a result I think wrote a very important book …. So he's not afraid to go outside of his experience and try to understand people who are not like him. I really admire that, and I think that's probably one of the keys to be able to find good stories.

CB: Do you ever get stuck or blocked?

LF: Absolutely. It's taken me a long time between books to come up with another book, and that's just how it goes. I don't get stuck in the sense that I can't write an essay or I can't write an article. What I just tend to do is if something's not working on the book front, I turn to essays and articles. I'm pretty much always writing. If I have to, I'll just write a blog just to keep writing.

I think it's very important to keep in the practice. I feel writing is like playing the piano: you have to do it. You have to practice all the time. There's a lot to be learned about the craft, and you have to be patient with yourself as you learn the craft: structure, character, and dialogue. And you have to revise and trim down your prose and understand that you only get one main point per paragraph. It's a craft, and it takes a long time to become skilled at the craft, like anything else, like playing the piano, like ice skating.

My whole theory about learning to write or even starting to write is that you can't ask your brain two things at once, meaning you can't be creative and edit what you're doing and structure what you're doing at the same time. So you have to give yourself the time and space to write freely and understand that it's not going to be perfect, and then you have to go back and put on your critical head and work it.

CB: What piece of advice do you have for aspiring nonfiction writers?

LF: My entire career I've supported myself 100 percent, and it's never been easy. I live very frugally, and that's okay. I have a great lifestyle and a great life, and the fact that I've done travel writing has given me the opportunity to do a lot of things, but you're not in it for the money. And I see a lot of people get really frustrated about the fact that increasingly you can't make money writing. And it does no good to be bitter about it. Nor does it do any good to try to write what you think is going to be commercial because that will suck your soul. I think you have to figure out a way financially to make it work. So if that means you have a half-time job doing something else, well, good for you, you're making it work for yourself. That doesn't mean you're selling out because you're spending half your time writing PR reports or something; it means you're supporting your writing.

Scott Russell Sanders

Scott Russell Sanders is the author of 20 books of fiction and nonfiction, including most recently *A Private History of Awe* and *A Conservationist Manifesto.* His *Earth Works: Selected Essays* appeared in spring 2012. Among his honors are the Lannan Literary Award, the John Burroughs Essay Award, the Mark Twain Award, the Cecil Woods Award for Nonfiction, and fellowships from the Guggenheim Foundation and the National Endowment for the Arts. In 2010, he was named the National Winner of the Eugene and Marilyn Glick Indiana Authors Award. He is a Distinguished Professor Emeritus of English at Indiana University, where he taught from 1971 to 2009. He and his wife, Ruth, a biochemist, have reared two children in their hometown of Bloomington in the hardwood hill country of Indiana's White River Valley.

CB: This is a question my students always ask me; How do you come up with ideas for essays?

SRS: The process runs the other way around: the subjects of my essays find me. They might arise from haunting memories, puzzling encounters, or troubling events in my private life. They might be provoked by public events, such as our nation's latest war or climate disruption or political shenanigans. They might be sparked by my reading or by a conversation. I don't deliberately search for subject matter, the way a journalist or a scholar might. Instead, I respond to questions that nag at me. I begin an essay with a willingness to be changed by what I write. I do not set out to deliver something I already know, but to inquire into the unknown, to dive into confusion in search of greater clarity.

CB: Do you think about structure when you write an essay? That is, how long it will be, how short, how you will weave your material together?

SRS: When I am writing an essay that has been solicited for a magazine or anthology, typically I will have been given an approximate word count. Similarly, when I am writing an essay for delivery as a formal address at a conference or university, I will have in mind a length appropriate to the occasion. Otherwise, I enter the essay with no preconceptions about length, tone, or structure. I discover the appropriate form as I proceed. This is one aspect of my practice of essay writing as a way of discovery.

CB: How long does it take you typically to write an essay?

SRS: How long it takes me to write an essay varies according to the complexity and scale of the piece, and also according to the number of other tasks I am handling at the same time. When I am teaching or traveling, I may only be able to work on an essay for a few hours in a given week, and such pieces may require months for completion. When I am able to spend every morning on the essay, it may take only two or three weeks. On rare occasions, I have written an essay in a few days, usually because I have been brooding on the material, consciously or unconsciously, for a long while before I begin composing.

CB: How much research do you do before launching an essay?

SRS: Again, it depends on the nature of the essay. Typically, I make notes toward an essay for weeks or even months before I start composing. Those notes might include memories, images, passages from my reading, results of interviews, facts of various sorts, background information, hunches, and notions about the subject. The note-making itself is a mode of discovery, as I search for significance and patterns in the material. Often I do not know what the essay is *about* until I have completed a first draft. Most of my essays do not require the sort of formal research that used to take place in libraries or archives and that now takes place largely on the web. Naturally, I check facts, but I don't produce the sort of work that a journalist or scholar would produce. I value such work, and

I learn from it, but my own writing tends to be personal and reflective rather than investigative.

CB: You're known for the lyrical quality and beauty of your prose and for the warmth, honesty, and openness of your voice. How do you bring yourself to the page in this way?

SRS: "Voice" on the page is something that evolved gradually for me, as it does for most writers. When I set out, I was writing fiction, using narrators or point-of-view characters who were invented, and who were often quite different from me in personality, language use, background, and values. When I began writing essays in the late 1970s, I found a voice that felt like the one I used in letters to friends—an honest reflection of my character and concerns. While the speaker's persona in an essay or memoir—the character he or she projects on the page—is constructed out of words, and is in that sense artificial, it will feel authentic only if it reflects the actual human being behind the words. I don't think that young writers should worry overmuch about discovering their voice: it will develop of its own accord, if they keep reading, keep trying out the styles and approaches of writers whom they admire, and keep exploring their vital subjects.

CB: What are the joys of writing nonfiction?

SRS: There is pleasure in dwelling amidst language, this marvelous medium. There is satisfaction in shaping a sentence, a paragraph, or an entire work that rings true, that holds together as a shapely basket or chair or house might hold together. There is excitement in discovering the meaning of a puzzling episode, uncovering connections between seemingly unrelated experiences, finding answers to questions, telling stories, preserving worthy moments, and conveying all of this to readers. Of course it is gratifying to have one's work published, and it is natural for any writer to aspire to publication. But the work itself must be rewarding, regardless of whether other people ever see it.

CB: What are the challenges?

SRS: The challenges for the writer are abundant, as they are for every sort of artist. While it is easy to string words together, it is difficult to do so in a way that is fresh, revelatory, and compelling. For the writer of nonfiction, the difficulty may be compounded by the refractory or even painful nature of the material. Even if one writes well, publishing is never easy. Only a small fraction of those who aspire to become writers will be able to publish their work regularly. And of those who do publish regularly, few will be able to earn a living by their writing alone, and so they must become teachers, editors, waiters, carpenters, clerks, or employees of some other kind. The writing must get done with the remnants of time and energy left over from one's job. If one has a family, the challenge of finding sufficient time and mental space is even greater. The list of challenges could be extended. One is likelier to persevere as a writer if one begins with a realistic understanding of what this pursuit entails.

CB: What advice would you give to the aspiring nonfiction writer?

SRS: First, read widely and read the best quality work you can find—not only essays but also poetry, fiction, history, philosophy, any kind of literature that interests you, on any subject that interests you. But, again, seek out the best because you train your ear for language primarily through reading. Secondly, keep a journal—not a diary but a notebook in which you record ideas, images, vivid passages from your reading, overheard bits of conversation, interesting words, dreams, anything that might later become material for your writing. The notebook is also a good place to practice framing sentences and paragraphs, articulating themes, sketching scenes. Third, treasure your questions because, in pursuing them, you are likely to do your best writing. Think of the essay not as a way of delivering knowledge you already possess, but as a way of discovering new knowledge, a way of coming to understand something for the first time, a way of revealing connections and meanings that had been hidden. If you make discoveries, the writing will be fresh, and the reader will be attracted by the resulting energy.

Jo Ann Beard

Jo Ann Beard is the author of *The Boys of My Youth* (1999), a collection of autobiographical essays, and *In Zanesville* (2011), a novel. Her work has appeared in *The New Yorker, Tin House, Best American Essays* (2007 and 1997), and *O, the Oprah Magazine*, as well as in other magazines and anthologies. She is the recipient of a Whiting Foundation award and has received nonfiction fellowships from the John Simon Guggenheim Foundation and the New York Foundation for the Arts. She teaches nonfiction writing at Sarah Lawrence College and lives in Rhinebeck, New York.

CB: Where do you find your subjects, like Cheri Tremble in "Undertaker Please Drive Slow" or Werner Hoelflich in "Werner"?

JAB: These were both people I ran across in my regular day-to-day life. Cheri Tremble's daughter Sarah was a friend of a friend, and Werner was someone I got to know at an art colony; he was there as a painter.

CB: Can you describe your research and writing process for "Undertaker" and "Werner"? How much time do you spend researching? How much writing? How do you combine the reporting and imaginative parts of your work?

JAB: In both cases, I spent a few days interviewing and then the next couple of years writing the story; longer in the case of Cheri.

CB: It's been said that you push the envelope of nonfiction writing, for instance when you imagine Cheri Tremble's memories before her assisted suicide with Dr. Kevorkian or when you get inside Werner's head and write from his point of view in the eponymous story. How do you distinguish between fiction and nonfiction? And do you think about genre when you're writing?

JAB: I only think about writing when I'm writing, not about how to describe what I'm writing. Both of the essays you mention combine fact with moments of imaginary fact—I'm using that phrase facetiously—but even the facts, such as they are, come from some subjective party. In the case of Cheri Tremble, her close friends and her daughter were my sources, and each of them had a slightly different, or different hued, response to what were the same questions. So, to be fair to the story and the subject of the story, the writer has to do some interpreting and some extrapolating in order to get as close as she can manage to what she perceives as a probable truth. Keeping in mind that I never met the subject of that essay. But anyway, that's what I tried to do—honor Cheri by telling her story and honor the story by telling it in as truthful way as I could given the limitations.

In the case of Werner, I was able to write his story as he described it. He read it when I was done, and in a roundabout and somehow generous way said that it didn't really get at the experience as he remembered it, but that it didn't have any errors in it, per se. Because Werner is an artist, and very articulate and thoughtful, and because the event had happened long ago and he had had a chance to process it, and to understand how it affected him, his experience with it could never be that of a reader getting it for the first time or, for that matter, a writer writing it for the first time. Think of the most traumatic, or pivotal, event in your life and imagine someone writing it down and then a bunch of people reading about it. There's no way they could ever understand what it meant to you, how it changed you on a molecular level. But still it might be an interesting story.

CB: Similarly, you've just published a novel, *In Zanesville*, that has many similar themes to *Boys of My Youth*—family discord, female friendship, alcoholism in the family. What's the process like for you when you write fiction vs. nonfiction?

JAB: Well, to me it felt pretty much the same, except that I could make things up if I needed to. Even in the most gray area of my nonfiction, I don't make things up—I pull them from my own memory and assign them here and there, where metaphorical texture is required. In the Cheri Tremble essay, there is a moment when she remembers falling through the ice and seeing the other skaters above her before she is pulled out. That came from a story someone told me long ago. So the incident didn't belong to Cheri and didn't belong to me, but it happened to be in my storeroom of riveting images. And it fit with the idea of having one's life pass before one's eyes—the image of the skaters moving above her—and fit with the feeling of numbness and separation I imagined that a dying person must experience. Of being in such dire circumstances while the world ticks along in its normalness. Et cetera.

With Werner an example might be the parakeet in the tree, the splot of blue in the gray concrete environment of upper Manhattan. It was an image that identified him as a painter right off the bat and also as a person who was slightly displaced, an Oregonian in New York City. But that very image, plucked out of my own memory and assigned to Werner, turned out to be something Werner identified as his own. He apparently had looked up into the scanty trees one time and seen a parakeet. Or so he remembered after he read the essay.

So, with fiction the process of collecting and using those images feels the same—you need a bird in a tree to make your point, you conjure a bird in a tree either from memory or from imagination. It's just that with fiction there's no defensiveness involved or lengthy explanations about how the subject turned out to remember the same blue parakeet that you happened to have seen in 1981 when you were visiting the city for the first time.

CB: Annie Dillard wrote in "To Fashion a Text" that "there's nothing you can't do with [nonfiction]. No subject matter is forbidden, no structure is proscribed. You get to make up your own form every time." How do you think about structure when you're writing? For instance, did you think about interweaving all the threads in "The Fourth State of Matter"—your collie dying, unfaithful husband calling, and the tragic murders/suicide at Iowa State?

JAB: I don't think about structure when I'm writing. I think about it when I'm teaching, but that's about all. To quote myself from a few paragraphs ago: I only think about writing when I'm writing.

CB: What advice do you have for aspiring nonfiction writers?

JAB: The written word carries weight. Be aware that you have power over people when you are writing about them and use it wisely. And if you're writing memoir, don't make yourself the hero of the story. See your own flaws as well as you see the flaws of others. Also: surprise us.

Dinty W. Moore

Dinty W. Moore is author of numerous books, including *The Mindful Writer: Noble Truths of the Writing Life; Crafting the Personal Essay: A Guide to Writing and Publishing Creative Nonfiction;* and the memoir *Between Panic & Desire,* winner of the Grub Street Nonfiction Book Prize. He worked briefly as a police reporter, a documentary filmmaker, a modern dancer, a zookeeper, and a Greenwich Village waiter before deciding he was lousy at all of those jobs and really wanted to write memoir and short stories. Moore has published essays and stories in *The Southern Review, The Georgia Review, Harpers, The New York Times Sunday Magazine, The Philadelphia Inquirer Magazine, Gettysburg Review, Utne Reader,* and *Crazyhorse,* among numerous other venues. He lives in Athens, Ohio, where he grows heirloom tomatoes and edible dandelions.

CB: In the introduction to your most recent book, *The Mindful Writer* (2012), you write about your work as a struggle, stating that despite absorbing Buddha's core principles, your "work … went on as it always had: ploddingly, unevenly, and with consistent difficulty." Could you talk about your writing process?

DM: The blank page is both scary and challenging, and creating something out of nothing, generating entirely new material, is for me painful, endlessly frustrating, and often results in self-loathing. Even after having written probably 100 essays and stories and published 6 or so books, I usually conclude somewhere in the "write something entirely new" stage that I simply don't have anything to say, don't really know how to write, and am not smart enough to solve the simplest narrative problems.

And then somehow I fill up many, many pages—through stubbornness, primarily—and it is time to revise. At that stage, I am happy as a 3-year-old in a sandbox. Revision is glorious. I love moving the words on the page, rearranging vast chunks of prose, flipping the ending and the opening, finding even better ways to say what I've said somewhat shabbily. My dream life would be to wake up to find that the shoemaker's elves had created a first draft while I slept, and all I needed to do was put in weeks and weeks of revision, trying to help the shape and beauty to show itself through the thicket.

CB: You've written that you've worked at many different jobs and failed at them. Did you always know you wanted to be a writer? And that you wanted to focus on nonfiction?

DM: I wanted to write from the earliest age, but coming from a lower-middle-class, blue-collar family—my dad was an auto mechanic—I just assumed being a reporter for my local newspaper was as far as I could go. I imagined that people who wrote books, especially "literary" books, were all were born on Cape Cod, went to Harvard or Yale, had sailboats, and were related to George Plimpton. I did work for my local paper and then stopped writing for about 10 years, until it hit me at age 30: "This is what you always wanted to do. Try to make it work."

CB: You seem to amble upon your subjects, whether you're writing about Buddhism, the internet, your past, or Disneyland. How do you know when you have a subject worth writing about?

DM: I usually *don't* know that I have a subject worth writing about; I'm usually wracked with doubt until three or five drafts into a piece. But I have learned this valuable lesson: it is not the subject matter, or what you have to say about it, that drives a successful piece of writing, but rather it is the questions you are asking. If the questions are interesting and layered enough, the work will find its way.

CB: You write that you once spent four years working on a book that "never saw the light of day," except as an eight-page essay. How much do you think about form when you're writing—whether very short forms, such as the work you publish in *Brevity*, essays, or books?

DM: I usually begin thinking "this is an essay" or "this might be a book chapter," but I'm never sure if that means a 4-page essay/chapter or a 24 page essay/chapter until I dig into multiple drafts. The overall form of the piece changes drastically along the way. I am the sort of reviser who rips the seams and pulls all of the fabric apart at various stages and then reassembles.

CB: You've recently written a book, *Crafting the Personal Essay*. Do you think the personal essay is having a resurgence?

DM: It certainly seems to be. I've seen many more personal essays in literary magazines over the past 4 years than I did 10 years ago, and of course, the blog, when done thoughtfully, is a bit of an essay medium. The difference between memoir and personal essay can be hard to pin down sometimes, but it has to do with the amount of thinking on the page that the author does in a particular piece, versus pure scene and detail.

CB: What are the joys for you in writing nonfiction?

DM: There are many, actually. I love learning new things. I love (once that difficult blank page is conquered) to revise and find meaning. And I love reader feedback, when someone says that something I wrote was helpful to them.

CB: What are the struggles?

DM: Self-doubt. It never goes away.

CB: What makes a submission stand out for your journal *Brevity*?

DM: The short answer is that I want a piece of writing to make me look at the subject in a different way or think about an experience in a way that I hadn't previously considered. In a very short piece—we limit our writers to 750 words—that means a sharp focus and immediate movement from the first line of the essay. Whatever the writer is tackling, ultimately the work is about the self. So in travel writing, for instance, it is not enough to say "I went there, and it was exotic." I want to see a personal connection, feel why a place got under a certain writer's skin. If the piece is about a childhood incident, I want to be inside of that memory, not outside watching the writer remember it.

CB: Creative nonfiction has been called the form of the twentieth century. Where do you see it going in the future?

DM: I honestly have no idea, but I do know that the way we encounter text is changing and will continue to change. The e-book is no longer a pipedream, it is a reality, and it will reshape everything. I do believe the paper-and-ink book will continue to exist, but it will be an increasingly small portion of the overall market. What does that mean for writers? Stay tuned.

CB: What advice do you have for aspiring nonfiction writers?

DM: Focus less on the point you want to make and more on the simple question, "Do I have a good story to tell?" Be a storyteller first and an advocate, or literary stylist, or provocateur, or what have you, second. Writers often provide too much information. I don't want to be lectured to or treated like a child who needs to learn the moral of a story. I want to be pulled into the writing by a magnetic force that won't let go until the final word.

Mary Roach

Mary Roach is the author of the *New York Times* bestselling books *Stiff: The Curious Lives of Human Cadavers* (2003); *Bonk: The Curious Coupling of Science and Sex* (2008); *Spook: Science Tackles the Afterlife* (2005); and *Packing for Mars: The Curious Science of Life in the Void* (2010). Roach has worked as a freelance copy editor, done PR at the San Francisco Zoo, and as a journalist, written magazine articles for *Outside, National Geographic, New Scientist, Wired, The New York Times Magazine,* and other publications. "I often write about science," states Roach on her website, "though I don't have a science degree and must fake my way through interviews with experts I can't understand." The bestselling author also states, "I have no hobbies. I mostly just work on my books and hang out with my family and friends."

CB: You say in your biography that you have no background in science, yet how did you become a science writer?

MR: Kind of randomly. I was writing for general interest magazines, and at one point an editor from *Discover,* a science magazine which is still around, called and said, "Are you interested in doing some science writing?" And I said, "Sure." So I started writing for *Discover,* and I just really enjoyed it. So really it wasn't a plan; I was offered an opportunity and I took and I just stuck with it, although I don't exclusively do real science writing. Really, at the level I'm writing, it's almost not science writing. It is and it isn't.

CB: So many of your books are specific takes on subjects—the study of sexual physiology in *Bonk* and the pioneering researchers behind these studies, the physiological effects of space exploration, attempts to prove the afterlife—how do you find these subjects, and how do you decide they're book worthy?

MR: Great question. For me, it's very personal. I know it when I come across it. For example, with the example of *Bonk*, for some reason, I was looking through a back issue of *Film Quarterly*, and there was a reference to the "colposcopic" films of Masters and Johnson, and I went, "What is that?" It sounded kind of weird, and as it turns out it, it was films that were made through a phallus, a camera mounted in an acrylic plastic penis that women would have sex with so that they could study the female sexual response from the inside. And at that moment, I absolutely recognized that this was a perfect topic for me because it's got that wonderful surreal quality—bringing something private into the lab. It's wonderfully awkward, risky, bizarre, comical sometimes, brave, courageous. It was one of those things that I instantly went: that's my next book. I know it.

But I can't force the process. I just have to stumble onto it. It's easy to reject stuff that presents itself to me, but I can't make the next book kind of materialize. I don't know far in advance what I'll be doing.

CB: Do you come across topics that you know are not book worthy? Do you go down a lot of dead ends and then explore something and reject it?

MR: I come across a lot that seems kind of promising, like sleep. There are lots of strange things that happen in the realm of sleep, but that [topic] doesn't work for me because it's an internal state. I would find that frustrating to be stuck inside people's heads to study sleep. So I don't go very far down a dead end typically.

More often it's a chapter. I think I'm going to do a chapter in a book on something, and then I get there and I realize it's not that interesting or it doesn't fit anymore. So frequently, there'll be five or six things that I started a folder on thinking I would do a chapter about it, and then it didn't fit the focus of the book, or it just wasn't very interesting, or something went wrong and it didn't make the cut. So there's always a bunch of those aborted chapters, not so often a whole book where I'll abandon ship on the book, although I get halfway through sometimes and I think about quitting. But it's too late!

CB: One of the things you said in *Bonk* is that you get obsessed by your research. Reading your books, I'm always so impressed because you just seem so undaunted by the research process. Could you describe your research process and the process of book writing? Do you do research first and then write?

MR: It's a process that over the years I've come to see is a pattern. Although initially it doesn't feel that way. I don't do a terribly thorough book proposal. I did on my first book, but even then I don't stick to the book proposal because when I'm at that early phase, I really don't know very much about a topic. So I'm writing a proposal from this position of almost complete ignorance.

So what happens is that when I start the actual book, I could go through a period of about 2 to 3 months of just random spasming, flailing, where I think I'm going to do this, and I call a bunch of different people, and I really think I know what this book is but I have no idea. And there'll be this phase where almost every other day I'm redoing my outline, and I'm thinking, "This is what the book's about; this is what I'm going to cover," and then sometimes the very next day, I'll go, "Nah, nah, nah. That's not new. This is what the book is about; this is how it's going to go."

There's a couple of months where I'm really redoing the outline a couple of times a week. And then at a certain point it gels, and I realize this is it. Everything falls into place, and then it becomes a calmer process of filling in the blanks and setting up the things I know I'm going to do. There's still change that happens, chapters that get swapped out, or things that I stumble onto that I want to include, but I think it's the first 5 months where there's a very fluid structure, and I know enough to not get too flipped out during that process. I have to just accept the chaos, and I know that when I've learned enough about the topic, and I've sent out enough feelers and put out enough tentacles, I can kind of have a sense of what the book needs to be.

Initially [the research] is a lot of sending emails to total strangers, saying, "I've got this very vague book idea. It's really quite larval. I don't know what I'm doing. I don't know anything about the topic really, but your work sounds interesting. So I'm writing to see what you are going to be up to in the next year or two and could I visit?" I'm very honest with people up front. So I spend a lot of time contacting people that ultimately I won't be using their work or even going to visit them, but I just need to get a feel of the lay of the land, who's out there, and what I might cover and where I might go. And that's not just labs but archives and specific library collections and things.

The other thing that's very important for me is building the narrative structure, so I'm looking for settings. It's almost more like what a television production person does; they're looking for scenes and characters. I want to have a bunch of scenes going on in the present for my books—that's what I've done to date—so I'm doing a lot of writing to people that I don't know and really being very clear. "I need a narrative structure. I need people. I need dialogue. I need things going on. Can you help me? Do you know anything in your lab or in someone else's lab?"

It's a kind of a fun and exciting part of the book but also frustrating and a little daunting because you don't really know what's out there and if there's even going to be enough material. You're just hunting all the time, turning over rocks, looking for something fresh, interesting, surprising that will be happening in the next two years that you can report on.

CB: One of the ways that the facts and science come alive so well in your books is through your profiles of people, such as researchers. Do you think about including these profiles while you're researching and writing the book?

MR: It's always a bit of a grab bag. It's impossible to know before you arrive what somebody will really be like. People are very different in email. Sometimes you get a sense of what their character is from an email, but a lot of times you don't. Sometimes it's incredibly exciting and rewarding, like Dr. Hsu in *Bonk*, the erectile dysfunction surgeon, such a wonderful eccentric but passionate character, and from his email I had absolutely no idea what he was like. So I have just learned to go and hope for the best.

And sometimes someone can be very, very dry. It's not necessarily a bad thing; sometimes the juxtaposition of the extreme knowledge they have and my extreme ignorance makes for sort of amusing situations, like the chapter in *Spook* where I'm confronting this guy, Gerry Nahum, who's got a PhD in consciousness theory and he's frustrated trying to explain stuff that is way over my head. But that ended up being one of my favorite chapters just because of the dynamic between him and myself.

CB: You're not afraid to appear ignorant on the page, and I think that's part of what makes you such an appealing narrator. You don't pretend to know more than you do, and you've said that often you deal with experts and kind of fake your way through interviews. Do you have advice for new writers who are daunted by the research process?

MR: I've always got a tape recorder with me. So I know I can go back and transcribe what I have, and if I need to, I can call the person back and say, "You know what? I realize that I don't really understand this part of the conversation, and I wondered if you could help me." I'm always just very honest. Like with Gerry Nahum, I would say, "Pretend that you're talking to a seventh grader. Pretend that you're talking to a random person on the bus." And he'd go, "Mary, I'm making this as simple as I can." And, of course, it's the most complex multisyllabic jargon I've ever heard.

But I would tell somebody starting out: the vast majority of people involved in research are so flattered and happy that someone's interested in what they're doing, and they're so excited to be talking to you and that you're interested in them and you're going to write about them, they're willing to make it work. They're very generous with their time. They're very patient. Some are better than others at explaining things in an understandable way, but I find it's really, really rare [that they don't help], if you just say, "I don't have a background in this, and I know this must be annoying and tedious for you, but could you kind of explain these basics to me?"

Honestly, my interviews are not really like interviews, they're more like tutorials. I'm really sitting down with someone and saying, "Okay. For the next couple of hours you're going to explain the whole field to me. I don't have any questions written down for you. I don't have an agenda or arc to my interview. I don't really know very much and am fascinated by what you do and let's start here. Explain this to me. Explain that to me." For what I do, it's almost like a one-on-one classroom situation more than an interview. I can't speak for all nonfiction writers.

The thing I'm most worried about before I get on a plane to go visit some researcher in the field or in the lab is I need something interesting going on, even if it's 2 minutes of something interesting, just anything besides sitting in your office and showing me a PowerPoint. I'm more invested in getting the narrative and the scene and the setting and having that. I can always call back. I can always fill in the holes [and] get it explained by that person or someone else.

CB: You've written 4 bestselling books in less then 10 years. Do you have any tips for writers on how to be so prolific?

MR: I think of myself as really slow. It takes me 2 to 2½ years. And that's all that I'm doing, that's the other thing. I guess my tip would be, "Don't have any other life." If there's any way—and I haven't figured this out—to get yourself off of social media and email, that is a tremendous distraction for me, but I can't. I guess recognize that as an enemy of productive writing. And I don't have a good answer for how to deal with it because when it comes to promoting your books, some social media is necessary. Twitter is an interesting place to be. I actually like Twitter, but you can waste so much time on it though.

CB: Do you have a writing routine?

MR: I tend to do more interviews, phone calls, emails in the morning because anybody on the East Coast is going to disappear by 2 P.M. West Coast time. That kind of dictates my routine to a certain extent. I'm usually doing a mix of some reporting and some writing. I can't write for more than 2 to 3 hours in a day; that's about it for me. I don't know how people can write for 8 hours. I can't do it. But there's so much to be done: setting things up, contacting people, doing research, looking for things, and now Google Books and Google Scholar have meant fewer trips to the library, which is good and bad. So there's a lot of things to be done that aren't writing, so

I'm always doing a mix, which I like. I get antsy if I'm just writing for more than a few hours.

CB: Are there any times that you were particularly stuck in the middle of a book and wanted to just give it up?

MR: Yup. *Packing for Mars.* I remember clearly being very upset. And my husband was there, and I was like, "I quit. I give up. I can't do it." It was a week that I'd worked very, very hard to set up. There was a chapter that has to do with a cadaver capsule crash test, and NASA was very, very uncomfortable with having me there. But it was finally set, and I get this email from [the publicist at NASA] saying this is not going to work. "No, you can't go." And the very same day, the PR person at the Japanese aerospace exploration agency pulled out. I was going to watch the isolation where they were choosing new astronauts. She wrote and said, "You know, I'm sorry. I know I said you could come, but now somebody says that you can't." And there goes two chapters and to me pretty important chapters at that point. I just thought, I quit. I mean I'm banging my head against the wall week after week. I was just so fed up, but I couldn't quit because I had gotten my advance. I had a deadline.

So, in both cases, I just went. I told the woman in Japan, "Well, I have a nonrefundable ticket, and I'm coming, and hopefully you can let me sit down and at least talk to whoever this person is, and maybe we can work out a way where we both feel comfortable with this." It was really two days where everything kind of fell apart and reassembled itself.

It got back on track, but that day I really seriously wanted to quit. And I think in every book—maybe not as extreme—there is a point where things aren't working the way you thought they were, and you kind of lose your confidence in your ability to pull it off, so probably every book I've gone through that.

CB: I was going to ask about structure. It sounds like you outline before you begin the book, so do you have the structure of the book in mind when you write and for each chapter?

MR: I like to start writing as soon as I have all the material for a chapter. I like to write it while it's fresh, and I might have to rejigger it because I don't quite know where it's going to go. But I don't like to put off all the writing to the end. I like to be doing a mix of reporting and writing rather than go out and gather everything and write all 80,000 words. So it's a mix; some chapters I know exactly where they're going to fit and how to introduce them and how to set up the next chapter, and others I know that I'm going to have to mess with the end and the beginning of them a little bit.

I'm not one of those writers who has a very detailed outline and sticks to it: it's never more than one page.

CB: What's the joy of nonfiction writing for you?

MR: For me the joy is equal parts in the writing and the research. I love the way nonfiction affords me access to these other universes that I would never be able to step into. I do a lot of traveling, not necessarily overseas, but to kind of unusual destinations and places that you'd never set foot in otherwise. And to me that's an amazing gift. I love it, and I always enjoy the time I spend with the people in my books. I'm very fond of them. They're fascinating. They're smart. They're funny. It's just a privilege to spend time with them and write them up. And I enjoy writing, too. Sometimes the writing can be a little frustrating—sometimes there are passages where I'm explaining something [or] juggling a lot of facts and trying to make it fit the narrative, and it's not fitting that well, but ultimately it's a task I enjoy very much.

CB: Who are you reading? Who are your models?

MR: Right now, I'm reading Bill Bryson's book *At Home*, which is a book that goes through every room of the house and houses in general. I remember when I heard about this book, I couldn't imagine how that could be interesting. It's so fascinating. The amount of detailed research he does for one page of his book floors me. I have no idea how he does it. And he has this incredible vocabulary and wit. I'm always blown away by his books. This one in particular. It's like every paragraph, you're like "Wow, that's so interesting."

CB: What is your one piece of advice for the novice nonfiction writer?

MR: I'm going to paraphrase somebody else's advice, and I don't know who said this. I think it was one of the Barthelmes, Donald Barthelme or Frederick Bartheleme. I don't know if they got it from somebody else, but it's really good advice. And the advice is: leave out the parts that people will skip. I wish I could take credit for that line. I think what happens with nonfiction is, say you went to an archive and you spent 3 or 4 days there, and you feel like you spent all this time getting this material, you better use it. But that can't be the barometer of what goes in the book. The barometer has to be: is this really interesting? Is this going to be something people enjoy reading, or are they are going to skip over this part? If they're going to skip over it, then why is this there? I think that your sentences and your paragraphs and your chapters all have to earn their keep. They've got to be either interesting, advancing the narrative, or funny; otherwise, get rid of them. You don't want any filler. NO FILLER.

Resources

Whether you are interested in finding how-to books on the craft of writing nonfiction, must-read memoirs and narrative nonfiction, or online literary magazines and helpful websites, this section is your go-to resource. Here you'll find full bibliographic information for the books mentioned throughout.

Essential Books on the Craft of Nonfiction Writing

Allen, Marilyn, and Colleen O'Shea. *The Complete Idiot's Guide to Book Proposals & Query Letters*. Indianapolis, IN: Alpha Books, 2011.

Barrington, Judith. *Writing the Memoir: From Truth to Art, Second Edition*. Portland, OR: The Eighth Mountain Press, 2002.

Beason, Larry, and Mark Lester. *A Commonsense Guide to Grammar and Usage with 2009 MLA Update, Fifth Edition*. New York, NY: Bedford/St. Martin's, 2010.

Clark, Roy Peter. *Writing Tools: 50 Essential Strategies for Every Writer*. New York, NY: Little, Brown and Company, 2006.

Costello, Victoria. *The Complete Idiot's Guide to Writing a Memoir*. Indianapolis, IN: Alpha Books, 2011.

Dillard, Annie. *The Writing Life*. New York, NY: HarperCollins, 1989.

Forché, Carolyn, and Philip Gerard, eds. *Writing Creative Nonfiction: Introduction and insights from the teachers of the Associated Writing Programs*. Cincinnati, OH: Story Press, 2001.

Gerard, Philip. *Creative Nonfiction: Researching and Crafting Stories of Real Life.* Cincinnati, OH: Story Press, 1996.

Gornick, Vivian. *The Situation and the Story: The Art of Personal Narrative.* New York, NY: Farrar, Straus, and Giroux, 2002.

Gutkind, Lee. *The Art of Creative Nonfiction: Writing and Selling the Literature of Reality.* New York, NY: John Wiley & Sons, Inc., 1997.

Hampl, Patricia. *I Could Tell You Stories: Sojourns in the Land of Memory.* New York, NY: W. W. Norton & Co., 1999.

Hart, Jack. *Story Craft: The Complete Guide to Writing Narrative Nonfiction.* Chicago, IL: The University of Chicago Press, 2011.

King, Stephen. *On Writing: A Memoir of the Craft.* New York, NY: Scribner, 2000.

Kramer, Mark, and Wendy Call, eds. *Telling True Stories: A Nonfiction Writer's Guide from the Neiman Foundation at Harvard University.* New York, NY: Plume, 2007.

Lamott, Anne. *Bird by Bird: Some Instructions on Writing and Life.* New York, NY: Anchor, 1994.

LaPlante, Alice. *The Making of a Story: A Norton Guide to Creative Writing.* New York, NY: W.W. Norton & Company, 2007.

Lara, Adair. *Naked, Drunk, and Writing: Shed Your Inhibitions and Craft a Compelling Memoir or Personal Essay.* Berkeley, CA: Ten Speed Press, 2010.

Mencher, Melvin. *Melvin Mencher's News Reporting and Writing.* New York, NY: McGraw-Hill, 2010.

Moore, Dinty W. *Crafting the Personal Essay: A Guide for Writing and Publishing Creative Nonfiction.* Cincinnati, OH: Writer's Digest Books, 2010.

———. *The Mindful Writer: Noble Truths of the Writing Life.* Boston, MA: Wisdom Publications, 2012.

Murray, Donald M. *The Craft of Revision, Fifth Anniversary Edition.* Boston, MA: Wadsworth: 2001, 2012.

———. *Shoptalk: Learning to Write with Writers.* Portsmouth, NH: Boynton/Cook Publishers, 1990.

Roorbach, Bill. *Writing Life Stories: How to Make Memories into Memoirs, Ideas into Essays, and Life into Literature.* Cincinnati, OH: Story Press, 1998.

Rubie, Peter and Gary Provost. *How to Tell a Story: The Secrets of Writing Captivating Tales.* Cincinnati, OH: Writer's Digest Books, 1998.

Stanek, Lou Willett, Ph.D. *Writing Your Life: Putting Your Past on Paper.* New York, NY: Avon Books, 1996.

Stewart, James. B. *Follow the Story: How to Write Successful Nonfiction.* New York, NY: Touchstone Book, 1998.

Strunk, William Jr., and E. B. White. *The Elements of Style.* New York, NY: Longman, 1999.

Ueland, Brenda. *If You Want to Write: A Book about Art, Independence and Spirit.* St. Paul, MN: Graywolf Press, 1987.

Wald, Catherine. *The Resilient Writer: Tales of Rejection and Triumph from 23 Top Authors.* New York, NY: Persea Books, 2005.

Zinsser, William. *On Writing Well, 30th Anniversary Edition: The Classic Guide to Writing Nonfiction.* New York, NY: HarperPerennial, 2006.

———, ed. *Inventing the Truth: The Art and Craft of Memoir.* Boston, MA: Houghton Mifflin, 1987.

———. *Writing About Your Life: A Journey into the Past.* New York, NY: Marlowe & Company, 2004.

Books on Launching a Nonfiction Freelance Writing Career

Brewer, Robert Lee, ed. *2012 Writer's Market: The Most Trusted Guide to Getting Published*. Cincinnati, OH: Writer's Digest Books, 2012.

Formichelli, Linda, and Diana Burrell. *The Renegade Writer: A Totally Unconventional Guide to Freelance Writing Success*. Oak Park, IL: Marion Street Press, Inc., 2005.

Glatzer, Jenna. *Make a Real Living as a Freelance Writer: How to Win Top Writing Assignments*. White River Junction, VT: Nomad Press, 2004.

James-Enger, Kelly. *Ready, Aim, Specialize! Create Your Own Writing Specialty and Make More Money!, Second Edition*. Oak Park, IL: Marion Street Press, Inc., 2008.

———. *Six-Figure Freelancing: The Writer's Guide to Making More Money*. New York, NY: Random House, 2005.

Locke, John. *How I Sold 1 Million eBooks in 5 Months*. Longboat Key, FL: Telemachus Press, 2011.

Ragland, Margit Feury. *Get a Freelance Life*. New York, NY: Three Rivers Press, 2005.

Essential Reading for Nonfiction Writers

The following books are mentioned throughout *The Complete Idiot's Guide to Writing Nonfiction*.

Beard, Jo Ann. *The Boys of My Youth*. Boston, MA: Little, Brown and Company, 1998.

Carr, David. *The Night of the Gun. A reporter investigates the darkest story of his life. His own*. New York, NY: Simon and Schuster, 2009.

Capote, Truman. *In Cold Blood*. New York, NY: Random House, 1965, 2002.

Colwin, Laurie. *Home Cooking: A Writer in the Kitchen.* New York, NY: HarperPerennial, 1988.

Conover, Ted. *Newjack: Guarding Sing Sing.* New York, NY: Vintage, 2000.

Eggers, Dave. *A Heartbreaking Work of Staggering Genius.* New York, NY: Vintage, 2000.

Ephron, Nora. *Crazy Salad: Some Things About Women.* New York, NY: Modern Library, 2000.

Fraser, Laura. *An Italian Affair.* New York, NY: Vintage, 2002.

———. *All Over the Map.* New York, NY: Broadway, 2011.

Gornick, Vivian. *Fierce Attachments: A Memoir.* New York, NY: Touchstone Book, 1987.

Grealy, Lucy. *Autobiography of a Face.* New York, NY: HarperPerennial, 1994.

Hampl, Patricia. *In Virgin Time: In Search of the Contemplative Life.* New York, NY: Ballantine Books, 1993.

Junger, Sebastian. *The Perfect Storm: A True Story of Men Against the Sea.* New York, NY: W.W. Norton & Company, 1997.

Kidder, Tracy. *Among Schoolchildren.* New York, NY: HarperPerennial, 1990.

Knapp, Caroline. *The Merry Recluse: A Life in Essays.* New York, NY: Counterpoint, 2004.

Krakauer, Jon. *Into Thin Air: A Personal Account of the Mt. Everest Disaster.* New York, NY: Villard, 1997.

LeBlanc, Adrian Nicole. *Random Family: Love, Drugs, Trouble, and Coming of Age in the Bronx.* New York, NY: Scribner, 2003.

Lopate, Phillip, ed. *The Art of the Personal Essay: An Anthology from the Classical Era to the Present.* New York, NY: Random House, 1995.

McBride, James. *The Color of Water: A Black Man's Tribute to His White Mother.* New York, NY: Riverhead Books, 1996.

McPhee, John. *Coming into the Country*. New York, NY: Farrar, Straus, and Giroux, 1991.

Moon, William Least Heat. *Blue Highways: A Journey into America*. Boston, MA: Little, Brown and Company, 1982.

Moore, Judith. *Fat Girl: A True Story*. New York, NY: Hudson Street Press, 2005.

Olsen, Victoria C. *From Life: Julia Margaret Cameron and Victorian Photography*. New York, NY: Palgrave Macmillan, 2003.

Orlean, Susan. *The Orchid Thief: A True Story of Beauty and Obsession*. New York, NY: Ballantine, 1998.

———. *Rin Tin Tin: The Life and the Legend*. New York, NY: Simon and Schuster, 2011.

Pollitt, Katha. *Learning to Drive: And Other Life Stories*. New York, NY: Random House, 2007.

Roach, Mary. *Bonk: The Curious Coupling of Science and Sex*. New York, NY: W.W. Norton & Company, 2008.

———. *Packing for Mars: The Curious Science of Life in the Void*. New York, NY: W.W. Norton & Company, 2010.

———. *Spook: Science Tackles the Afterlife*. New York, NY: W.W. Norton & Company, 2006.

———. *Stiff: The Curious Lives of Human Cadavers*. New York: W.W. Norton & Company, 2003.

Roach, Mary, and Tim Folger, eds. *Best American Science and Nature Writing 2011*. New York, NY: Mariner Books, 2011.

Root, Robert L. Jr., and Michael Steinberg. *The Fourth Genre: Contemporary Writers of/on Creative Nonfiction, Sixth Edition*. New York, NY: Pearson Education Inc., 2011.

Sanders, Scott Russell. *A Private History of Awe*. New York, NY: North Point Press, 2006.

Sedaris, David. *Naked*. Boston, MA: Little, Brown and Company, 1997.

Sims, Norman, and Mark Kramer, eds. *Literary Journalism: A New Collection of the Best American Nonfiction*. New York, NY: Ballantine Books, 1995.

Sharman, Russell Leigh, and Cheryl Harris Sharman. *Nightshift NYC*. Berkeley, CA: University of California Press, 2008.

Thoreau, Henry David. *Walden*. Los Angeles, CA: Empire Books, 2013.

Trollope, Anthony. *An Autobiography*. Berkeley, CA: University of California Press, 1947.

Yagoda, Ben. *Memoir: A History*. New York, NY: Riverhead Books, 2009.

Online Literary Magazines for Nonfiction Writers

Agni Online: bu.edu/agni

Alaska Quarterly Review: www.uaa.alaska.edu/aqr/index.cfm

Bellingham Review: bhreview.org

Blackbird: www.blackbird.vcu.edu/index.htm

Brevity: creativenonfiction.org/brevity

Creative Nonfiction: creativenonfiction.org

Fourth Genre: Explorations in Nonfiction: msupress.msu.edu/journals/fg

The Gettysburg Review: www.gettysburgreview.com

Granta: granta.com

The Iowa Review: iowareview.uiowa.edu

Memoir Journal: memoirjournal.net

Ploughshares: pshares.org

River Teeth: A Journal of Narrative Nonfiction: riverteethjournal.com

Shenandoah: shenandoahliterary.org

TriQuarterly Online: triquarterly.org

The Virginia Quarterly Review: vqronline.org

Online Resources/Listservs/Organizations

Absolute Write: absolutewrite.com

American Society of Journalists and Authors: asja.org

Freelance Success: freelancesuccess.com

Mediabistro: mediabistro.com

National Writers Union: nwu.org

NewPages.com: newpages.com/literary-magazines

Poynter: poynter.org

ShelfAwareness: www.shelf-awareness.com

Winters, Zoe. *Smart Self-Publishing: Becoming an Indie Author.* Kindle Edition, 2010

Writer'sCafe.org: The Online Writing Community: www.writerscafe.org/

Resources for Bloggers

Book Blogger Directory: bookbloggerdirectory.wordpress.com

blogger.com/

https://www.tumblr.com/

http://wordpress.com/

The Book Lady's Blog: www.thebookladysblog.com

www.typepad.com/micro/

Index

C

I

J

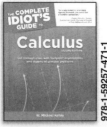
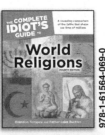